Further Acclaim for *Under the Tuscan Sun*

"Mayes [has] perfect vision. . . . I do not doubt that centuries from now, whoever lives in Bramasole will one day uncover bits of pottery used at Mayes' table. She has, by the sweat of her brow, and the strength of her vision, become a layer in the history of this place."
—*Los Angeles Times*

"Irresistible . . . a sensuous book for a sensuous countryside."
—*Minneapolis Star-Tribune*

"Armchair travel at its most enticing . . . Mayes' delightful recipes, evocative descriptions of the nearby village of Cortona, and thoughtful musings on the Italian spirit only add to the pleasure. Can we really blame ourselves for wanting to strap Mayes down in some ratty armchair while we go live in her farmhouse?"
—*Booklist*

"Can we bear yet another book about buying and remodeling a tumble-down house in some sunny foreign country? The answer, in the case of *Under the Tuscan Sun,* is a simple, unqualified yes. . . . Warmth and light nearly glow from these pages, a tribute to the sun, symbol of hope and renewal."
—*Cleveland Plain Dealer*

"Carefully written . . . an unusual memoir of one woman's challenge to herself and its successful transformation into a satisfying opportunity to improve the quality of her life."
—*Library Journal*

"A model for the open, curious mind and the questing soul . . . Those who want to find parts of themselves they didn't know existed, take risks, have an adventure . . . and discover another culture altogether, with its different rhythms, tastes, smells, and ways of being human—those readers will find in Mayes a kindly, eager, tough-spirited guide."
—*Houston Chronicle*

"Luscious . . . delightful . . . In the search for writers who thrill you just with their mastery of the language, include Frances Mayes."
—*San Jose Mercury News*

"A report from our dream Italy, still rural, still devoted to beauties that are not artificial. . . . Mayes has a profoundly sensual relation to everything she touches, from texture to food. . . . Her description of meals that we, alas, didn't get to eat evoke in me satisfaction without jealousy, like paintings."
—*Boston Globe*

UNDER
THE
TUSCAN
SUN

AT HOME IN ITALY

FRANCES
MAYES

Broadway Books
New York

ACKNOWLEDGMENTS

Many thanks to my agent, Peter Ginsberg, of Curtis Brown Ltd. and to Jay Schaefer, my editor at Chronicle Books. Special thanks to Kate Chynoweth, also of Chronicle Books. Jane Piorko of *The New York Times*, Elaine Greene of *House Beautiful*, and Rosellen Brown, guest editor of *Ploughshares*, published early versions of parts of this book: *mille grazie*. Friends and family members deserve at least a bottle of Chianti and a handful of Tuscan poppies: Todd Alden, Paul Bertolli, Anselmo Bettarelli, Josephine Carson, Ben Hernandez, Charlotte Painter, Donatella di Palme, Rupert Palmer, Lyndall Passerini, Tom Sterling, Alain Vidal, Marcia and Dick Wertime, and all the Wilcoxons. Homage to the memory of Clare Sterling for the gift of her verve and knowledge. To Ed Kleinschmidt and Ashley King, incalculable thanks.

First Broadway Books trade paperback edition published 1997.
First Broadway Books export edition published 1998.
Designed by Tolleson Design, SF, CA

The Library of Congress has catalogued the paperback edition as:

Mayes, Frances.
    Under the Tuscan sun : at home in Italy / by Frances Mayes.
    p. cm.
    Excerpts from this book appeared in the New York Times, Ploughshares, and House beautiful.
    ISBN 0-7679-0038-3 (pbk.)
    1. Tuscany (Italy)—Description and travel. 2. Tuscany (Italy)—Social life and customs. 3. Mayes, Frances. 4. Cookery, Italian.
I. Title.
DG734.23.M38   1997
945'.5—dc21
                                    97-20218
                                        CIP

Export edition ISBN 0-7679-0280-7

00 01 02 20 19 18 17 16 15 14 13 12 11

for ANN CORNELISEN

"WHAT ARE YOU GROWING HERE?" THE UPHOL-
sterer lugs an armchair up the walkway to the house but
his quick eyes are on the land.

"Olives and grapes," I answer.

"Of course, olives and grapes, but what else?"

"Herbs, flowers—we're not here in the spring to plant
much else."

He puts the chair down on the damp grass and scans
the carefully pruned olive trees on the terraces where we
now are uncovering and restoring the former vineyard.
"Grow potatoes," he advises. "They'll take care of themselves." He points to the third terrace. "There, full sun,
the right place for potatoes, red potatoes, yellow, potatoes
for *gnocchi di patate*."

And so, at the beginning of our fifth summer here, we
now dig the potatoes for our dinner. They come up so
easily; it's like finding Easter eggs. I'm surprised how
clean they are. Just a rinse and they shine.

The way we have potatoes is the way most everything
has come about, as we've transformed this abandoned
Tuscan house and land over the past four years. We watch

Francesco Falco, who has spent most of his seventy-five years attending to grapes, bury the tendril of an old vine so that it shoots out new growth. We do the same. The grapes thrive. As foreigners who have landed here by grace, we'll try anything. Much of the restoration we did ourselves; an accomplishment, as my grandfather would say, out of the fullness of our ignorance.

In 1990, our first summer here, I bought an oversized blank book with Florentine paper covers and blue leather binding. On the first page I wrote ITALY. The book looked as though it should have immortal poetry in it, but I began with lists of wildflowers, lists of projects, new words, sketches of tile in Pompeii. I described rooms, trees, bird calls. I added planting advice: "Plant sunflowers when the moon crosses Libra," although I had no clue myself as to when that might be. I wrote about the people we met and the food we cooked. The book became a chronicle of our first four years here. Today it is stuffed with menus, postcards of paintings, a drawing of a floor plan of an abbey, Italian poems, and diagrams of the garden. Because it is thick, I still have room in it for a few more summers. Now the blue book has become *Under the Tuscan Sun,* a natural outgrowth of my first pleasures here. Restoring, then improving, the house; transforming an overgrown jungle into its proper function as a farm for olives and grapes; exploring the layers and layers of Tuscany and Umbria; cooking in a foreign kitchen and discovering the many links between the food and the culture—these intense joys frame the deeper pleasure of learning to live another kind of life. To bury the grape tendril in such a way that it shoots out new growth I recognize easily as a metaphor for the way life must change from time to time if we are to go forward in our thinking.

During these early June days, we must clear the terraces of the wild grasses so that when the heat of July strikes and the land dries, we'll be protected from fire. Outside my window, three men with weed machines sound like giant bees. Domenico will be arriving tomorrow to disc the terraces, returning the chopped grasses to the soil. His tractor follows the looping turns established by oxen long ago. Cycles. Though the weed machines and the discer make shorter work, I still feel that I fall into this ancient ritual of summer. Italy is thousands of years deep and on the top layer I am standing on a small plot of land, delighted today with the wild orange lilies spotting the hillside. While I'm admiring them, an old man stops in the road and asks if I live here. He tells me he knows the land well. He pauses and looks along the stone wall, then in a quiet voice tells me his brother was shot here. Age seventeen, suspected of being a Partisan. He keeps nodding his head and I know the scene he looks at is not my rose garden, my hedge of sage and lavender. He has moved beyond me. He blows me a kiss. *"Bella casa, signora."* Yesterday I found a patch of blue cornflowers around an olive tree where his brother must have fallen. Where did they come from? A seed dropped by a thrush? Will they spread next year over the crest of the terrace? Old places exist on sine waves of time and space that bend in some logarithmic motion I'm beginning to ride.

I open the blue book. Writing about this place, our discoveries, wanderings, and daily life, also has been a pleasure. A Chinese poet many centuries ago noticed that to re-create something in words is like being alive twice. At the taproot, to seek change probably always is related to the desire to enlarge the psychic place one lives in. *Under the Tuscan Sun* maps such a place. My reader, I hope, is like a friend who comes to visit, learns to mound flour on the thick marble counter and work in the egg, a friend who wakes to the four calls of the cuckoo in the linden and walks down the terrace paths singing to the grapes; who picks jars of plums, drives with me to hill towns of round towers and spilling geraniums, who wants to see the olives the first day they are olives. A guest on holiday is intent on pleasure. Feel the breeze rushing around those hot marble statues? Like old peasants, we could sit by the fireplace, grilling slabs of bread and oil, pour a young Chianti. After rooms of Renaissance virgins and dusty back roads from Umbertide, I cook a pan of small eels fried with garlic and sage. Under the fig where two cats curl, we're cool. I've counted: the dove coos sixty times per minute. The Etruscan wall above the house dates from the eighth century B.C. We can talk. We have time.

Cortona, 1995

BRAMARE: (ARCHAIC) TO YEARN FOR

I AM ABOUT TO BUY A HOUSE IN A FOREIGN COUN-
try. A house with the beautiful name of Bramasole. It is
tall, square, and apricot-colored with faded green shutters, ancient tile roof, and an iron balcony on the second
level, where ladies might have sat with their fans to watch
some spectacle below. But below, overgrown briars, tangles of roses, and knee-high weeds run rampant. The
balcony faces southeast, looking into a deep valley, then
into the Tuscan Apennines. When it rains or when the
light changes, the facade of the house turns gold, sienna,
ocher; a previous scarlet paint job seeps through in rosy
spots like a box of crayons left to melt in the sun. In
places where the stucco has fallen away, rugged stone
shows what the exterior once was. The house rises above
a *strada bianca,* a road white with pebbles, on a terraced
slab of hillside covered with fruit and olive trees.
Bramasole: from *bramare,* to yearn for, and *sole,* sun:
something that yearns for the sun, and yes, I do.

The family wisdom runs strongly against this decision.
My mother has said "Ridiculous," with her certain and
forceful stress on the second syllable, "RiDICulous," and

my sisters, although excited, fear I am eighteen, about to run off with a sailor in the family car. I quietly have my own doubts. The upright seats in the *notaio's* outer office don't help. Through my thin white linen dress, spiky horsehairs pierce me ever time I shift, which is often in the hundred-degree waiting room. I look over to see what Ed is writing on the back of a receipt: Parmesan, salami, coffee, bread. How can he? Finally, the signora opens her door and her torrential Italian flows over us.

The *notaio* is nothing like a notary; she's the legal person who conducts real-estate transactions in Italy. Ours, Signora Mantucci, is a small, fierce Sicilian woman with thick tinted glasses that enlarge her green eyes. She talks faster than any human I have ever heard. She reads long laws aloud. I thought all Italian was mellifluous; she makes it sound like rocks crashing down a chute. Ed looks at her raptly; I know he's in thrall to the sound of her voice. The owner, Dr. Carta, suddenly thinks he has asked too little; he *must* have, since we have agreed to buy it. We think his price is exorbitant. We *know* his price is exorbitant. The Sicilian doesn't pause; she will not be interrupted by anyone except by Giuseppe from the bar downstairs, who suddenly swings open the dark doors, tray aloft, and seems surprised to see his *Americani* customers sitting there almost cross-eyed in confusion. He brings the signora her midmorning thimble of espresso, which she downs in a gulp, hardly pausing. The owner expects to claim that the house cost one amount while it really cost much more. "That is just the way it's done," he insists. "No one is fool enough to declare the real value." He proposes we bring one check to the *notaio's* office, then pass him ten smaller checks literally under the table.

Anselmo Martini, our agent, shrugs.

Ian, the English estate agent we hired to help with translation, shrugs also.

Dr. Carta concludes, "You Americans! You take things so seriously. And, *per favore,* date the checks at one-week intervals so the bank isn't alerted to large sums."

Was that the same bank I know, whose sloe-eyed teller languidly conducts a transaction every fifteen minutes, between smokes and telephone calls? The signora comes to an abrupt halt, scrambles the papers into a folder and stands up. We are to come back when the money and papers are ready.

*

A window in our hotel room opens onto an expansive view over the ancient roofs of Cortona, down to the dark expanse of the Val di Chiana. A hot and wild wind—the *scirocco*—is driving normal people a little crazy. For me, it seems to reflect my state of mind. I can't sleep. In the United States, I've bought and sold a few houses before—loaded up the car with my mother's Spode, the cat, and the ficus for the five- or five-thousand-mile drive to the next doorway where a new key would fit. You *have* to churn somewhat when the roof covering your head is at stake, since to sell is to walk away from a cluster of memories and to buy is to choose where the future will take place. And the place, never neutral of course, will cast its influence. Beyond that, legal complications and contingencies must be worked out. But here, absolutely everything conspires to keep me staring into the dark.

Italy always has had a magnetic north pull on my psyche. Houses have been on my mind for four summers of renting farmhouses all over Tuscany. In the first place Ed and I rented with friends, we started calculating on the first night, trying to figure out if our four pooled savings would buy the tumbled stone farm we could see from the terrace. Ed immediately fell for farm life and roamed over our neighbors' land looking at the work in progress. The Antolinis grew tobacco, a beautiful if hated crop. We could hear workers shout *"Vipera!"* to warn the others of a poisonous snake. At evening, a violet blue haze rose from the dark leaves. The well-ordered farm looked peaceful from the vantage point of our terrace. Our friends never came back, but for the next three vacations, the circuitous search for a summer home became a quest for us—whether we ever found a place or not, we were happening on places that made pure green olive oil, discovering sweet country Romanesque churches in villages, meandering the back roads of vineyards, and stopping to taste the softest Brunello and the blackest Vino Nobile. Looking for a house gives an intense focus. We visited weekly markets not just with the purchase of picnic peaches in mind; we looked carefully at all the produce's quality and variety, mentally forecasting birthday dinners, new holidays, and breakfasts for weekend guests. We spent hours sitting in piazzas or sipping lemonade in local bars, secretly getting a sense of the place's ambiance. I soaked many a heel blister in a hotel bidet, rubbed bottles of lotion on my feet, which had covered miles of stony streets. We hauled histories and guides and wildflower books and novels in and out of rented houses and hotels. Always we asked local people where they liked to eat and headed to restaurants our many guidebooks never mentioned. We both have an insatiable curiosity about each jagged castle ruin on the hillsides. My idea of heaven still is to drive the gravel farm roads of Umbria and Tuscany, very pleasantly lost.

Cortona was the first town we ever stayed in and we always came back to it during the summers we rented near Volterra, Florence, Montisi, Rignano, Vicchio, Quercegrossa, all those fascinating, quirky houses. One had a kitchen two people could not pass in, but there was a slice of a view of the Arno. Another kitchen had no hot water and no knives, but the house was built into medieval ramparts overlooking vineyards. One had several sets of china for forty, countless glasses and silverware, but the refrigerator iced over every day and by four the door swung open, revealing a new igloo. When the weather was damp, I got a tingling shock if I touched anything in the kitchen. On the property, Cimabue, legend says, discovered the young Giotto drawing a sheep in the dirt. One house had beds with back-crunching dips in the middles. Bats flew down the chimney and buzzed us, while worms in the beams sent down a steady sifting of sawdust onto the pillows. The fireplace was so big we could sit in it while grilling our veal chops and peppers.

We drove hundreds of dusty miles looking at houses that turned out to be in the flood plain of the Tiber or overlooking strip mines. The Siena agent blithely promised that the view would be wonderful again in twenty years; replanting stripped areas was a law. A glorious medieval village house was wildly expensive. The saw-toothed peasant we met in a bar tried to sell us his childhood home, a windowless stone chicken house joined to another house, with snarling dogs lunging at us from their ropes. We fell hard for a farm outside Montisi; the *contessa* who owned it led us on for days, then decided she needed a sign from God before she could sell it. We had to leave before the sign arrived.

As I think back over those places, they suddenly seem preposterously alien and Cortona does, too. Ed doesn't think so. He's in the piazza every afternoon, gazing at the young couple trying to wheel their new baby down the street. They're halted every few steps. Everyone circles the carriage. They're leaning into the baby's face, making noises, praising the baby. "In my next life," Ed tells me, "I want to come back as an Italian baby." He steeps in the piazza life: the sultry and buffed man pushing up his sleeve so his muscles show when he languidly props his chin in his hand; the pure flute notes of Vivaldi drifting from an upstairs window; the flower seller's fan of bright flowers against the stone shop; a man with no neck at all unloading lambs from his truck. He slings them like flour sacks over his shoulder and the lambs' eyeballs bulge out. Every few minutes, Ed looks up at the big clock that has kept time for so long over this piazza. Finally, he takes a stroll, memorizing the stones in the street.

Across the hotel courtyard a visiting Arab chants his prayers toward dawn, just when I finally can fall asleep. He sounds as though he is gargling with salt water. For hours, he rings the voice's changes over a small register, over and over. I want to lean out and shout, "Shut up!" Now and then I have to laugh. I look out, see him nodding in the window, a sweet smile on his face. He reminds me so much of tobacco auctioneers I heard in hot warehouses in the South as a child. I am seven thousand miles from home, plunking down my life savings on a whim. Is it a whim? It feels very close to falling in love and that's never really whimsical but comes from some deep source. Or does it?

＊

Each time we step out of the cool, high rooms of the hotel and into the sharp-edged sun, we walk around town and like it more and more. The outdoor tables at Bar Sport face the Piazza Signorelli. A few farmers sell produce on the steps of the nineteenth-century *teatro* every morning. As we drink espresso, we watch them holding up rusty hand scales to weigh the tomatoes. The rest of the piazza is lined with perfectly intact medieval or Renaissance *palazzi*. Easily, someone might step out any second and break into *La Traviata*. Every day we visit each keystoned medieval gate in the Etruscan walls, explore the Fiat-wide stone streets lined with Renaissance and older houses and the even narrower *vicoli,* mysterious pedestrian passageways, often steeply stepped. The bricked-up fourteenth-century "doors of the dead" are still visible. These ghosts of doors beside the main entrance were designed, some say, to take out the plague victims—bad luck for them to exit by the main entrance. I notice in the regular doors, people often leave their keys in the lock.

Guidebooks describe Cortona as "somber" and "austere." They misjudge. The hilltop position, the walls and upright, massive stone buildings give a distinctly vertical feel to the architecture. Walking across the piazza, I feel the abrupt, angular shadows fall with Euclidean purity. I want to stand up straight—the upright posture of the buildings seems to carry over to the inhabitants. They walk slowly, with very fine, I want to say, *carriage*. I keep saying, "Isn't she beautiful?" "Isn't he gorgeous?" "Look at *that* face—pure Raphael." By late afternoon, we're sitting again with our espressi, this time facing the other piazza. A woman of about sixty with her daughter and the teenage granddaughter pass by us, strolling, their arms linked, sun on their vibrant faces. We don't know why light has such a luminous quality. Perhaps the sunflower crops radiate gold from the surrounding fields. The three women look peaceful, proud, impressively pleased. There should be a gold coin with their faces on it.

Meanwhile, as we sip, the dollar is falling fast. We rouse ourselves from the piazza every morning to run around to all the banks, checking their posted exchange rates. When you're cashing traveler's checks for a last-minute spree at the leather market, the rate doesn't matter that much, but this is a house with five acres and every lira counts. A slight drop at those multiples makes the stomach drop also. Every hundred lire it falls, we calculate how much more expensive the house becomes. Irrationally, I also calculate how many pairs of shoes that could buy. Shoes, before, have been my major purchase in Italy, a secret sin. Sometimes I'd go home with nine new pairs: red snakeskin flats, sandals, navy suede boots, and several pairs of black pumps of varying heels.

Typically, the banks vary in how much commission they bite when they receive a large transfer from overseas. We want a break. It looks like a significant chunk of interest they'll collect, since clearing a check in Italy can take weeks.

Finally, we have a lesson in the way things work. Dr.

Carta, anxious to close, calls his bank—the bank his father and his father-in-law use—in Arezzo, a half hour away. Then he calls us. "Go there," he says. "They won't take a commission for receiving the money at all, and they'll give you whatever the posted rate is when it arrives."

His savvy doesn't surprise me, though he has seemed spectacularly uninterested in money the entire time we have negotiated—just named his high price and stuck to it. He bought the property from the five old sisters of a landowning family in Perugia the year before, thinking, he said, to make it a summer place for his family. However, he and his wife inherited property on the coast and decided to use that instead. Was that the case, or had he scooped up a bargain from ladies in their nineties and now is making a bundle, possibly buying coast property with our money? Not that I begrudge him. He's smart.

Dr. Carta, perhaps fearing we might back out, calls and asks to meet us at the house. He roars up in his Alfa 164, Armani from stem to stern. "There is something more," he says, as though continuing a conversation. "If you follow me, I will show you something." A few hundred feet down the road, he leads us up a stone path through fragrant yellow broom. Odd, the stone path continues up the hill, curving along a ridge. Soon we come to a two-hundred-degree view of the valley, with the cypress-lined road below us and a mellow landscape dotted with tended vineyards and olive groves. In the distance lies a blue daub, which is Lake Trasimeno; off to the right, we see the red-roofed silhouette of Cortona cleanly outlined against the sky. Dr. Carta turns to us triumphantly. The flat paving stones widen here. "The

Romans—this road was built by the Romans—it goes straight into Cortona." The sun is broiling. He goes on and on about the large church at the top of the hill. He points out where the rest of the road might have run, right through Bramasole's property.

Back at the house he turns on an outside faucet and splashes his face. "You'll enjoy the finest water, truly your own abundant *acqua minerale,* excellent for the liver. *Eccellente!*" He manages to be at once enthusiastic and a little bored, friendly and slightly condescending. I am afraid we have spoken too bluntly about money. Or maybe he has interpreted our law-abiding American expectations about the transaction as incredibly naive. He lets the faucet run, cupping his hand under the water, somehow leaning over for a drink without dislodging the well-cut linen coat tossed over his shoulders. "Enough water for a swimming pool," he insists, "which would be perfect out on the point where you can see the lake, overlooking right where Hannibal defeated the Romans."

We're dazzled by the remains of a Roman road over the hill covered with wildflowers. We will follow the stone road into town for a coffee late in the afternoons. He shows us the old cistern. Water is precious in Tuscany and was collected drop by drop. By shining a flashlight into the opening, we've already noticed that the underground cistern has a stone archway, obviously some kind of passageway. Up the hill in the Medici fortress, we saw the same arch in the cistern there and the caretaker told us that a secret underground escape route goes downhill to the valley, then to Lake Trasimeno. Italians take such remains casually. That one is allowed to own such ancient things seems impossible to me.

❋

When I first saw Bramasole, I immediately wanted to hang my summer clothes in an *armadio* and arrange my books under one of those windows looking out over the valley. We'd spent four days with Signor Martini, who had a dark little office on Via Sacco e Vanzetti down in the lower town. Above his desk hung a photo of him as a soldier, I assumed for Mussolini. He listened to us as though we spoke perfect Italian. When we finished describing what we thought we wanted, he rose, put on his Borsolino, and said one word, *"Andiamo,"* let's go. Although he'd recently had a foot operation, he drove us over nonexistent roads and pushed through jungles of thorns to show us places only he knew about. Some were farmhouses with roofs collapsed onto the floor, miles from town and costing the earth. One had a tower built by the Crusaders, but the *contessa* who owned it cried and doubled the price on the spot when she saw that we really were interested. Another was attached to other farmhouses where chickens were truly free range—they ran in and out of the houses. The yard was full of rusted farm equipment and hogs. Several felt airless or sat hard by the road. One would have required putting in a road—it was hidden in blackberry brambles and we could only peer in one window because a coiled black snake refused to budge from the threshold.

We took Signor Martini flowers, thanked him and said good-bye. He seemed genuinely sorry to see us go.

The next morning we ran into him in the piazza after coffee. He said, "I just saw a doctor from Arezzo. He might be interested in selling a house. *Una bella villa,*" he added emphatically. The house was within walking distance of Cortona.

"How much?" we asked, although we knew by then he cringes at being asked that direct question.

"Let's just go take a look," was all he said. Out of Cortona, he took the road that climbs and winds to the other side of the hill. He turned onto the *strada bianca* and, after a couple of kilometers, pulled into a long, sloping driveway. I caught a glimpse of a shrine, then looked up at the three-story house with a curly iron fanlight above the front door and two tall, exotic palm trees on either side. On that fresh morning, the facade seemed radiant, glazed with layers of lemon, rouge, and terracotta. We both became silent as we got out of the car. After all the turns into unknown roads, the house seemed just to have been waiting all along.

"Perfect, we'll take it," I joked as we stepped through the weeds. Just as he had at other houses, Signor Martini made no sales pitch; he simply looked with us. We walked up to the house under a rusted pergola leaning under the weight of climbing roses. The double front door squawked like something alive when we pushed it open. The house's walls, thick as my arm is long, radiated coolness. The glass in the windows wavered. I scuffed through silty dust and saw below it smooth brick floors in perfect condition. In each room, Ed opened the inside window and pushed open the shutters to one glorious view after another of cypresses, rippling green hills, distant villas, a valley. There were even two bathrooms that functioned. They were not beautiful, but *bathrooms,* after all the houses we'd seen with no floors, much less plumbing. No one had lived there in thirty years and the grounds seemed like an enchanted garden, overgrown and tumbling with blackberries and vines. I could see Signor Martini regarding the grounds with a country-man's practiced eye. Ivy twisted into the trees and ran over fallen terrace walls. *"Molto lavoro,"* much work, was all he said.

During several years of looking, sometimes casually, sometimes to the point of exhaustion, I never heard a house say *yes* so completely. However, we were leaving the next day, and when we learned the price, we sadly said no and went home.

During the next months, I mentioned Bramasole now and then. I stuck a photo on my mirror and often wandered the grounds or rooms in my mind. The house is a metaphor for the self, of course, but it also is totally real. And a *foreign* house exaggerates all the associations houses carry. Because I had ended a long marriage that was not supposed to end and was establishing a new relationship, this house quest felt tied to whatever new identity I would manage to forge. When the flying fur from the divorce settled, I had found myself with a grown daughter, a full-time university job (after years of part-time teaching), a modest securities portfolio, and an entire future to invent. Although divorce was harder than a death, still I felt oddly returned to myself after many years in a close family. I had the urge to examine my life in another culture and move beyond what I knew. I wanted something of a *physical* dimension that would occupy the mental volume the years of my former life had. Ed shares my passion for Italy completely and also shares the boon of three-month summer breaks from university teaching. There we would have long days for exploring and for our writing and research projects. When he is at the wheel, he'll *always* take the turn down the intriguing little road. The language, history, art, places in Italy are endless—two lifetimes wouldn't be enough. And, ah, the foreign self. The new life might shape itself to the contours of the house, which already is at home in the landscape, and to the rhythms around it.

In the spring, I called a California woman who was starting a real-estate development business in Tuscany. I asked her to check on Bramasole; perhaps if it had not sold, the price had come down. A week later, she called from a bar after meeting with the owner. "Yes, it's still for sale, but with that particular brand of Italian logic, the price has been raised. The dollar," she reminded me, "has fallen. And that house needs a lot of work."

Now we've returned. By this time, with equally peculiar logic, I've become fixed on buying Bramasole. After all, the only thing wrong is the expense. We both love the setting, the town, the house and land. If only one little thing is wrong, I tell myself, go ahead.

Still, this costs a *sacco di soldi*. It will be an enormous hassle to recover the house and land from neglect. Leaks, mold, tumbling stone terraces, crumbling plaster, one funky bathroom, another with an adorable metal hip bathtub and a cracked toilet.

Why does the prospect seem fun, when I found remodeling my kitchen in San Francisco a deep shock to my equilibrium? At home, we can't even hang a picture without knocking out a fistful of plaster. When we plunge the stopped-up sink, forgetting once again that the disposal doesn't like artichoke petals, sludge seems to rise from San Francisco Bay.

On the other hand, a dignified house near a Roman road, an Etruscan (Etruscan!) wall looming at the top of the hillside, a Medici fortress in sight, a view toward Monte Amiata, a passageway underground, one hundred and seventeen olive trees, twenty plums, and still un-counted apricot, almond, apple, and pear trees. Several figs seem to thrive near the well. Beside the front steps there's a large hazelnut. Then, proximity to one of the most superb towns I've ever seen. Wouldn't we be crazy not to buy this lovely house called Bramasole?

What if one of us is hit by a potato chip truck and can't work? I run through a litany of diseases we could get. An aunt died of a heart attack at forty-two, my grandmother went blind, all the ugly illnesses . . . What if an earthquake shakes down the universities where we teach? The Humanities Building is on a list of state struc-tures most likely to fall in a moderately severe quake. What if the stock market spirals down?

I leap out of bed at three A.M. and step in the shower, letting my whole face take the cold water. Coming back to bed in the dark, feeling my way, I jam my toe on the iron bed frame. Pain jags all the way up my backbone. "Ed, wake up. I think I've broken my toe. How can you sleep?"

He sits up. "I was just dreaming of cutting herbs in the garden. Sage and lemon balm. Sage is *salvia* in Italian." He has never wavered from his belief that this is a brilliant idea, that this is heaven on earth. He clicks on the bedside lamp. He's smiling.

My half-on toenail is hanging half off, ugly purple spreading underneath. I can't bear to leave it or to pull it off. "I want to go home," I say.

He puts a Band-Aid around my toe. "You mean Bramasole, don't you?" he asks.

*

This sack of money in question has been wired from California but has not arrived. How can that be, I ask at the bank, money is wired, it arrives instantaneously. More shrugs. Perhaps the main bank in Florence is holding it. Days pass. I call Steve, my broker in California, from a bar. I'm shouting over the noise of a soccer match on the TV. "You'll have to check from that end;" he shouts back, "it's long gone from here and did you know the government there has changed forty-seven times since World War II? This money was well invested in tax-free bonds and the best growth funds. Those Australian bonds of yours earned seventeen percent. Oh well, *la dolce vita.*"

The mosquitoes (*zanzare* they're called, just like they sound) invade the hotel with the desert wind. I spin in the sheets until my skin burns. I get up in the middle of the night and lean out the shuttered window, imagining all the sleeping guests, blisters on their feet from the stony streets, their guidebooks still in their hands. We could still back out. Just throw our bags in the rented Fiat and say *arrivederci.* Go hang out on the Amalfi coast for a month and head home, tanned and relaxed. Buy lots of sandals. I can hear my grandfather when I was twenty: "Be realistic. Come down out of the clouds." He was furious that I was studying poetry and Latin etymology, something utterly useless. Now, what am I thinking of? Buying an abandoned house in a place where I hardly can speak the language. He probably has worn out his shroud turning over in his grave. We don't have a mountain of reserves to bale us out in case that mysterious something goes wrong.

*

What is this thrall for houses? I come from a long line of women who open their handbags and take out swatches of upholstery material, colored squares of bathroom tile, seven shades of yellow paint samples, and strips of flowered wallpaper. We love the concept of four walls. "What is her house like?" my sister asks, and we both know she means what is *she* like. I pick up the free real-estate guide outside the grocery store when I go somewhere for the weekend, even if it's close to home. One June, two friends and I rented a house on Majorca; another summer I stayed in a little *casa* in San Miguel de Allende in which I developed a serious love for fountained courtyards and bedrooms with bougainvillea cascading down the balcony, the austere Sierra Madre. One summer in Santa Fe, I started looking at adobes there, imagining I would become a Southwesterner, cook with chilies, wear squash blossom turquoise jewelry—a different life, the chance to be extant in another version. At the end of a month I left and never have wanted to return.

I love the islands off the Georgia coast, where I spent summers when I was growing up. Why not a weathered gray house there, made of wood that looks as though it washed up on the beach? Cotton rugs, peach iced tea, a watermelon cooling in the creek, sleeping with waves churning and rolling outside the window. A place where my sisters, friends, and their families could visit easily. But I keep remembering that anytime I've stepped in my own footprints again, I haven't felt renewed. Though I'm susceptible to the pull to the known, I'm just slightly more susceptible to surprise. Italy seems endlessly alluring to me—why not, at this point, consider the opening of *The Divine Comedy:* What must one do in order to grow? Better to remember my father, the son of my very literal-minded, penny-pinching grandfather. "The family motto," he'd say, "is 'Packing and Unpacking.' " And also, "If you can't go first class, don't go at all."

Lying awake, I feel the familiar sense of The Answer arriving. Like answers on the bottom of the black fortune-telling eight ball that I loved when I was ten, often I can feel an idea or the solution to a dilemma floating up through murky liquid, then it is as if I see the suddenly clear white writing. I like the charged zone of waiting, a mental and physical sensation of the bends as something mysterious zigzags to the surface of consciousness.

What if you did *not* feel uncertainty, the white writing says. Are you exempt from doubt? Why not rename it excitement? I lean over the wide sill just as the first gilded mauve light of sunrise begins. The Arab is still sleeping. The undulant landscape looks serene in every direction. Honey-colored farmhouses, gently placed in hollows, rise like thick loaves of bread set out to cool. I know some Jurassic upheaval violently tossed up the hills, but they appear rounded as though by a big hand. As the sun brightens, the land spreads out a soft spectrum: the green of a dollar bill gone through the wash, old cream, blue sky like a blind person's eye. The Renaissance painters had it just right. I never thought of Perugino, Giotto, Signorelli, et al., as realists, but their background views are still here, as most tourists discover, with dark cypress trees brushed in to emphasize each composition the eye falls on. Now I see why the red boot on a gold and blond angel in the Cortona museum has such a glow, why the Madonna's cobalt dress looks intense and deep. Against this landscape and light, everything takes on a primary outline. Even a red towel drying on a line below becomes totally saturated with its own redness.

Think: What if the sky doesn't fall? What if it's glorious? What if the house is transformed in three years? There will be by then hand-printed labels for the house's olive oil, thin linen curtains pulled across the shutters for siesta, jars of plum jam on the shelves, a long table for feasts under the linden trees, baskets piled by the door for picking tomatoes, arugula, wild fennel, roses, and rosemary. And who are we in that strange new life?

*

Finally the money arrives, the account is open. However, they have no checks. This enormous bank, the seat of dozens of branches in the gold center of Italy, has no checks to give us. "Maybe next week," Signora Raguzzi explains. "Right now, nothing." We sputter. Two days later, she calls. "I have ten checks for you." What is the big deal with checks? I get boxes of them at home. Signora Raguzzi parcels them out to us. Signora Raguzzi in tight skirt, tight T-shirt, has lips that are perpetually wet and pouting. Her skin glistens. She is astonishingly gorgeous. She wears a magnificent square gold necklace and bracelets on both wrists that jangle as she stamps our account number on each check.

"What great jewelry. I love those bracelets," I say.

"All we have here is gold," she replies glumly. She is

bored with Arezzo's tombs and piazzas. California sounds good to her. She brightens every time she sees us. "Ah, California," she says as a greeting. The bank begins to seem surreal. We're in the back room. A man wheels in a cart stacked with gold ingots—actual small bricks of gold. No one seems to be on guard. Another man loads two into dingy manila folders. He's plainly dressed, like a workman. He walks out into the street, taking the ingots somewhere. So much for Brinks delivery—but what a clever plainclothes disguise. We turn back to the checks. There will be no insignia of boats or palm trees or pony express riders, there will be no name, address, driver's license, Social Security number. Only these pale green checks that look as though they were printed in the twenties. We're enormously pleased. That's close to citizenship—a bank account.

Finally we are gathered in the *notaio's* office for the final reckoning. It's quick. Everyone talks at once and no one listens. The baroque legal terms leave us way behind. A jackhammer outside drills into my brain cells. There's something about two oxen and two days. Ian, who's translating, stops to explain this archaic spiral of language as an eighteenth-century legal description of the amount of land, measured by how long it would take two oxen to plow it. We have, it seems, two plowing days worth of property.

I write checks, my fingers cramping over all the times I write *milione*. I think of all the nice dependable bonds and utility stocks and blue chips from the years of my marriage magically turning into a terraced hillside and a big empty house. The glass house in California where I lived for a decade, surrounded by kumquat, lemon, mock orange, and guava, its bright pool and covered patio with wicker and flowered cushions—all seem to recede, as though seen through the long focus in binoculars. *Million* is such a big word in English it's hard to treat it casually. Ed carefully monitors the zeros, not wanting me to un-wittingly write *miliardo,* billion, instead. He pays Signor Martini in cash. He never has mentioned a fee; we have found out the normal percentage from the owner. Signor Martini seems pleased, as though we've given him a gift. For me this is a confusing but delightful way to conduct business. Handshakes all around. Is that a little cat smile on the mouth of the owner's wife? We're expecting a parchment deed, lettered in ancient script, but no, the *notaio* is going on vacation and she'll try to get to the paperwork before she leaves. *"Normale,"* Signor Martini says. I've noticed all along that someone's word is still taken for that. Endless contracts and stipulations and con-tingencies simply have not come up. We walk out into the brutally hot afternoon with nothing but two heavy iron keys longer than my hand, one to a rusted iron gate, the other to the front door. They look nothing like the keys to anything I've ever owned. There is no hope for spare copies.

Giuseppe waves from the door of the bar and we tell him we have bought a house. "Where is it?" he wants to know.

"Bramasole," Ed begins, about to say where it is.

"Ah, Bramasole, *una bella villa!"* He has picked cher-ries there as a boy. Although it is only afternoon, he pulls us in and pours a *grappa* for us. "Mama!" he shouts. His mother and her sister come in from the back and every-one toasts us. They're all talking at once, speaking of us as the *stranieri,* foreigners. The *grappa* is blindingly strong. We drink ours as fast as Signora Mantucci nips her espresso and wander out in the sun. The car is as hot as a pizza oven. We sit there with the doors open, suddenly laughing and laughing.

＊

We'd arranged for two women to clean and for a bed to be delivered while we signed the final papers. In town we picked up a bottle of cold *prosecco,* then stopped at the *rosticceria* for marinated zucchini, olives, roast chicken, and potatoes.

We arrive at the house dazed by the events and the *grappa.* Anna and Lucia have washed the windows and exorcised layers of dust, as well as many spiders' webs. The second-floor bedroom that opens onto a brick terrace gleams. They've made the bed with the new blue sheets and left the terrace door open to the sound of cuckoos and wild canaries in the linden trees. We pick the last of the pink roses on the front terrace and fill two old Chianti bottles with them. The shuttered room with its whitewashed walls, just-waxed floors, pristine bed with new sheets, and sweet roses on the windowsill, all lit with a dangling forty-watt bulb, seems as pure as a Franciscan cell. As soon as I walk in, I think it is the most perfect room in the world.

We shower and dress in fresh clothes. In the quiet twilight, we sit on the stone wall of the terrace and toast each other and the house with tumblers of the spicy *prosecco,* which seems like a liquid form of the air. We toast the cypress trees along the road and the white horse in the neighbor's field, the villa in the distance that was built for the visit of a pope. The olive pits we toss over the wall, hoping they will spring from the ground next year. Dinner is delicious. As the darkness comes, a barn owl flies over so close that we hear the whir of wings and, when it settles in the black locust, a strange cry that we take for a greeting. The Big Dipper hangs over the house, about to pour on the roof. The constellations pop out, clear as a star chart. When it finally is dark, we see that the Milky Way sweeps right over the house. I forget the stars, living in the ambient light of a city. Here they are, all along, spangling and dense, falling and pulsating. We stare up until our necks ache. The Milky Way looks like a flung bolt of lace unfurling. Ed, because he likes to whisper, leans to my ear. "Still want to go home," he asks, "or can this be home?"

A HOUSE AND THE LAND IT TAKES
TWO OXEN TWO DAYS TO PLOW

I ADMIRE THE BEAUTY OF SCORPIONS. THEY LOOK like black-ink hieroglyphs of themselves. I'm fascinated, too, that they can navigate by the stars, though how they ever glimpse constellations from their usual homes in dusty corners of vacant houses, I don't know. One scurries around in the bidet every morning. Several get sucked into the new vacuum cleaner by mistake, though usually they are luckier: I trap them in a jar and take them outside. I suspect every cup and shoe. When I fluff a bed pillow, an albino one lands on my bare shoulder. We upset armies of spiders as we empty the closet under the stairs of its bottle collection. Impressive, the long threads for legs and the fly-sized bodies; I can even see their eyes. Other than these inhabitants, the inheritance from the former occupants consists of dusty wine bottles—thousands and thousands in the shed and in the stalls. We fill local recycling bins over and over, waterfalls of glass raining from boxes we've loaded and reloaded. The stalls and *limonaia* (a garage-sized room on the side of the house once used for storing pots of lemons over the winter) are piled with rusted pans, newspapers from 1958, wire, paint cans, debris. Whole ecosystems of spiders and scorpions are destroyed, though hours later they seem to have regenerated. I look for old photos or antique spoons but see nothing of interest except some handmade iron tools and a "priest," a swan-shaped wooden form with a hook for a hanging pan of hot coals, which was pushed under bedcovers in winter to warm the clammy sheets. One cunningly made tool, an elegant little sculpture, is a hand-sized crescent with a worn chestnut handle. Any Tuscan would recognize it in a second: a tool for trimming grapes.

When we first saw the house, it was filled with fanciful iron beds with painted medallions of Mary and shepherds holding lambs, wormy chests of drawers with marble tops, cribs, foxed mirrors, cradles, boxes, and lugubrious bleeding-heart religious pictures of the Crucifixion. The owner removed everything—down to the switchplate covers and lightbulbs—except a thirties kitchen cupboard and an ugly red bed that we cannot figure out how to get down the narrow back stairs from the third floor. Finally we take the bed apart and throw it piece by piece from the window. Then we stuff the mattress through the window and my stomach flips as I watch it seem to fall in slow motion to the ground.

The Cortonese, out for afternoon strolls, pause in the road and look up at all the mad activity, the car trunk full of bottles, mattress flying, me screaming as a scorpion falls down my shirt when I sweep the stone walls of the stall, Ed wielding a grim-reaper scythe through the weeds. Sometimes they stop and call up, "How much did you pay for the house?"

I'm taken aback and charmed by the bluntness. "Probably too much," I answer. One person remembered that long ago an artist from Naples lived there; for most, it has stood empty as far back as they can remember.

Every day we haul and scrub. We are becoming as parched as the hills around us. We have bought cleaning supplies, a new stove and fridge. With sawhorses and two planks we set up a kitchen counter. Although we must bring hot water from the bathroom in a plastic laundry pan, we have a surprisingly manageable kitchen. As one who has used Williams-Sonoma as a toy store for years, I begin to get back to an elementary sense of the kitchen. Three wooden spoons, two for the salad, one for stirring. A sauté pan, bread knife, cutting knife, cheese grater, pasta pot, baking dish, and stove-top espresso pot. We brought over some old picnic silverware and bought a few glasses and plates. Those first pastas are divine. After long work, we eat everything in sight then tumble like field hands into bed. Our favorite is spaghetti with an easy sauce made from diced *pancetta,* unsmoked bacon, quickly browned, then stirred into cream and chopped wild arugula (called *ruchetta* locally), easily available in our driveway and along the stone walls. We grate *parmigiano* on top and eat huge mounds. Besides the best salad of all, those amazing tomatoes sliced thickly and served with chopped basil and mozzarella, we learn to make Tuscan white beans with sage and olive oil. I shell and simmer the beans in the morning, then let them come to room temperature before dousing them with the oil. We consume an astonishing number of black olives.

Three ingredients is about all we manage most nights, but that seems to be enough for something splendid. The idea of cooking here inspires me—with such superb ingredients, everything seems easy. An abandoned slab of marble from a dresser top serves as a pastry table when I decide to make my own crust for a plum tart. As I roll it out with one of the handblown Chianti bottles I rescued from the debris, I think with amazement of my kitchen in San Francisco: the black and white tile floor, mirrored wall between cabinets and counter, long counters in gleaming white, the restaurant stove big enough to take off from the San Francisco airport, sunlight pouring in the skylight, and, always, Vivaldi or Robert Johnson or Villa Lobos to cook to. Here, the determined spider in the fireplace keeps me company as she knits her new web. The stove and fridge look starkly new against the flaking whitewash and under the bulb hanging from what looks like a live wire.

Late in the afternoons I take long soaks in the hip bath filled with bubbles, washing spiderwebs out of my hair, grit from my nails, necklaces of dirt from around my neck. I have not had a necklace of dirt since I used to play Kick the Can on long summer evenings as a child. Ed emerges reborn from the shower, tan in his white cotton shirt and khaki shorts.

The empty house, now scrubbed, feels spacious and pure. Most of the scorpions migrate elsewhere. Because of the thick stone walls, we feel cool even on the hottest days. A primitive farm table, left in the *limonaia,* becomes our dining table on the front terrace. We sit outside talking late about the restoration, savoring the Gorgonzola with a pear pulled off the tree, and the wine from Lake Trasimeno, just a valley away. Renovation seems simple, really. A central water heater, with a new bath and existing baths routed to it, new kitchen—but simple, soul of simplicity. How long will the permits take? Do we really need central heat? Should the kitchen stay where it is, or wouldn't it really be better where the ox stall currently is? That way, the present kitchen could be the living room, with a big fireplace in it. In the dark we can see the shadowy vestiges of a formal garden: a long, overgrown boxwood hedge with five huge, ragged topiary balls rising out of it. Should we rebuild the garden with these strange remnants? Cut them out of the hedge? Take out the ancient hedge altogether and plant something informal, such as lavender? I close my eyes and try to have a vision of the garden in three years, but the overgrown jungle is too indelibly imprinted in my brain. By the end of dinner, I could sleep standing up, like a horse.

The house must be in some good alignment, according to the Chinese theories of Feng Shui. Something is giving us an extraordinary feeling of well-being. Ed has the energy of three people. A lifelong insomniac, I sleep like one newly dead every night and dream deeply harmonious dreams of swimming along with the current in a clear green river, playing and at home in the water. On the first night, I dreamed that the real name of the house was not Bramasole but Cento Angeli, One Hundred Angels, and that I would discover them one by one. Is it bad luck to change the name of a house, as it is to rename a boat? As a trepid foreigner, I wouldn't. But for me, the house now has a secret name as well as its own name.

*

The bottles are gone. The house is clean. The tile floors shine with a waxy patina. We hang a few hooks on the backs of doors, just to get our clothes out of suitcases. With milk crates and a few squares of marble left in the stall, we fashion a couple of bedside tables to go with our two chairs from the garden center.

We feel prepared to face the reality of restoration. We walk into town for coffee and telephone Piero Rizzatti, the *geometra*. The translations "draftsman" or "surveyor" don't quite explain what a *geometra* is, a professional without an equivalent in the United States—a liaison among owner, builders, and town planning officials. Ian has assured us that he is the best in the area, meaning also that he has the best connections and can get the permits quickly.

The next day Ian drives out with Signor Rizzatti and his tape measurer and notepad. We begin our cold-eyed tour through the empty house.

The bottom floor is basically five rooms in a row— farmer's kitchen, main kitchen, living room, horse stall, another stall—with a hall and stairs after the first two rooms. The house is bisected by its great stairwell with stone steps and handwrought iron railing. A strange floor plan: The house is designed like a dollhouse, one room deep with all the rooms about the same size. That seems to me like giving all your children the same name. On the upper two floors, there are two bedrooms on either side of the stairs; you must go through the first room to get to the other. Privacy, until recently, wasn't much of an issue for Italian families. Even Michelangelo, I recall, slept four abed with his masons when he worked on a project. In the great Florentine *palazzi,* you must go through one immense room to get to the next; corridors must have seemed a waste of space.

The west end of the house—one room on each floor—is walled off for the *contadini,* the farm family who worked the olive and grape terraces. A narrow stone stairway runs up the back of that apartment and there's no entrance from the main house, except through that kitchen's front door. With their door, the two doors going into the stalls, and the big front door, there are four French doors across the front of the house. I envision them with new shutters, all flung open to the terrace, lavender, roses, and pots of lemons between them, with lovely scents wafting into the house and a natural movement of inside/outside living. Signor Rizzatti turns the handle of the farm kitchen door and it comes off in his hand.

At the back of the apartment, a crude room with a toilet cemented to the floor—one step above a privy—is tacked onto the third floor of the house. The farmers, with no running water upstairs, must have used a bucket-flush method. The two real bathrooms also are built off the back of the house, each one at a stair landing. This ugly solution is still common for stone houses constructed before indoor plumbing. Often I see these loos jutting out, sometimes supported by flimsy wooden poles angling into the walls. The small bath, which I take to be the house's first, has a low ceiling, stone checkerboard floor, and the charming hip bath. The large bathroom must have been added in the fifties, not long before the house was abandoned. Someone had a dizzy fling with tile—floor-to-ceiling pink, blue, and white in a butterfly design. The floor is blue but not the same blue. The shower simply drains into the floor, that is to say, water spreads all over the bathroom. Someone attached the showerhead so high on the wall that the spray creates a breeze and the angled shower curtain we hung wraps around our legs.

We walk out onto the L-shaped terrace off the second-floor bedroom, leaning on the railing for the stupendous view of the valley from one direction and of fruit and olive trees from the others. We're imagining, of course, future breakfasts here with the overhanging apricot tree in bloom and the hillside covered with wild irises we see the scraggly remains of everywhere. I can see my daughter and her boyfriend, slathered in tanning oil, reading novels on chaise longues, a pitcher of iced tea between them. The terrace floor is just like the floors in the house, only the tile is beautifully weathered and mossy. Signor Rizzatti, however, regards the tiles with a frown. When we go downstairs, he points to the ceiling of the *limonaia,* just underneath the terrace, which also is caked with moss and is even crumbling in some spots. Leaks. This looks expensive. The scrawls on his notepad cover two pages.

We think the weird layout suits us. We don't need eight bedrooms anyway. Each of the four can have an adjoining study/sitting room/dressing room, although we decide to turn the room next to ours into a bathroom. Two bathrooms seem enough but we'd love the luxury of a private bath next to the bedroom. If we can chop out the farmer's crude toilet attached to that room, we'll have a closet off the bath, the only one in the house. With his metal tape, the *geometra* indicates the ghost of a door leading into the farmer's former bedroom from the bedroom we'll have. Reopening it, we think, will be a quick job.

On the bottom floor, the line of rooms is not that

convenient. When we first saw the house, I'd said airily, "We can knock these walls out and have two big rooms down here." Now our *geometra* tells us we may open the walls only about six feet because of earthquake precautions. Staying here has given me an inner sense of the construction. I see how the first floor walls bow near the floor, accommodating the large stones in the foundation. The house was built in a way not unlike the stone terraces, without mortar, stones stacked and wedged. From the depths of the doorways and windowsills, I see that the walls thin as they go up. The yard-thick walls on the first floor are maybe half that on the third. What holds the house together as it goes up? Can inserting a few modern I beams of steel in those openings do the job of stones I couldn't even reach around?

When the great dome of the *duomo* was conceived in Florence, no one knew the technique for constructing so large a half sphere. Someone proposed building it over an immense mound of dirt piled in the cathedral. Money would be hidden throughout the pile and, on completion of the dome, the peasants would be invited to dig for coins and cart away the dirt. Fortunately, Brunelleschi figured out how to engineer his dome. I hope someone built this house on solid principles also but still I begin to have misgivings about taking out the fortress-thick walls on the first floor.

The *geometra* is full of opinions. He thinks the apartment's back staircase should come out. We love it, a secret escape. He thinks we should replaster the cracked and crumbling stucco facade, paint it ocher. No way. I like the colors that change as the light does and the intense glow of golds when it rains, as though the sun seeps into the walls. He thinks our first priority should be the roof. "But the roof doesn't leak—why bother it, when there are so many other pressing things?" We explain to him that we won't be able to do everything at once. The house cost the earth. The project will have to be spread out. We will do much of the work ourselves. Americans, I try to explain, sometimes are "do it yourself" people. As I say this I see a flash of panic cross Ed's face. "Do it yourself" doesn't translate. The *geometra* shakes his head as though all is hopeless if he has to explain things as basic as these.

He speaks to us kindly, as if through precise enunciation we will understand him. "Listen, the roof must be consolidated. They will preserve the tiles, number them, place them again in the same order, but you will have insulation; the roof will be strengthened."

At this point, it's either the roof or central heating, not both. We debate the importance of each. After all, we'll be here mostly in the summer. But we don't want to freeze at Christmas when we come over to pick the olives. If we're ever going to put heat in, it needs to go in at the same time as the water system and plumbing. The roof can be done anytime—or never. Right now, water is held in a cistern in the farmer's bedroom. When you shower or flush, a pump comes on and well water gurgles into the cistern. Individual hotwater heaters (miraculously, they work) hang above each shower. We'll need a central water heater, a large cistern connected to it so that the noisy pump isn't continuously working.

We decide on the heating. The *geometra,* feeling sure that we will come to our senses, says he will apply for a roof permit as well.

At some low point in the house's life, someone madly painted the chestnut beams in every room with a hideous vinegar varnish. This unimaginable technique once was popular in the South of Italy. You paint over real beams with a sticky goo, then comb through it to simulate wood! Sandblasting, therefore, is a top priority. An ugly job but fast, and we'll do the sealing and waxing ourselves. I once refinished a sailor's sea chest and found it fun. We'll need door and window repairs. All the window casements and interior shutters are covered with the same faux wood concoction. This genius of the beams and windows is probably responsible for the fireplace, which is covered with ceramic tiles that resemble bricks. What a strange mind, to cover the real thing with an imitation of something real. All this must go, along with the blue tiles covering the wide windowsill, the butterflies in the bathroom. Both the main kitchen and the farmers' kitchen sport ugly cement sinks. His list is now three pages long. The farmers' kitchen has floors made of crushed marble tiles, super ugly. There are a lot of ancient-looking wires coiled near the ceilings on white porcelain knobs. Sometimes sparks come flying out when I switch on a light.

The *geometra* sits on the terrace wall, mopping his face with an enormous monogrammed linen handkerchief. He looks at us with pity.

✳

Rule one in a restoration project: Be there. We will be seven thousand miles away when some of the big work is done. We brace ourselves for bids for the work.

Nando Lucignoli, sent to us by Signor Martini, drives

up in his Lancia and stands at the bottom of the driveway, looking not at the house but at the view of the valley. I think he must be a deep admirer of landscape but see that he is talking on a cellular phone, waving his cigarette and gesturing to the air. He tosses the phone onto the front seat.

"*Bella posizione.*" He waves his Gauloises again as he shakes hands, almost bowing to me. His father is a stonemason and he has become a contractor, an extraordinarily good-looking one. Like many Italian men, his cologne or aftershave surrounds him with a lemony, sunny aura only slightly dispelled by the cigarette smoke. Before he says anything more, I'm sure he's the contractor for us. We take him on a tour of the house. "*Niente, niente,*" he repeats, nothing. "We'll run the heating pipes in channels on the back of the house, a week; the bathroom—three days, signora. One month, everything. You'll have a perfect house; just lock the door, leave me the key and when you come back, everything will be taken care of." He assures us he can find old bricks to match the rest of the house for the new kitchen in the stall. The wiring? He has a friend. The terrace bricks? He shrugs, oh, some mortar. Opening the walls? His father is expert in that. His slicked-back black hair, wanting to revert to curls, falls over his forehead. He looks like Caravaggio's Bacchus—only he has moss-green eyes and a slight slouch, probably from leaning into the speed of his Lancia. He thinks my ideas are wonderful, I should have been an architect, I have excellent taste. We sit out on the stone wall and have a glass of wine. Ed goes inside to make coffee for himself. Nando draws diagrams of the water lines on the back of an envelope. My Italian is charming, he says. He understands everything I try to say. He says he will drop off his estimate tomorrow. I am sure it will be reasonable, that through the winter Nando and his father and a few trusted workers will transform Bramasole. "Enjoy yourself—leave it to me," he says as his tires spin on the driveway. As I wave good-bye, I notice that Ed has stayed on the terrace. He's noncommittal about Nando, saying only that he smelled like a *profumeria,* it's affected to smoke Gauloises, and that he didn't think the central heating could be installed that way at all.

Ian brings up Benito Cantoni, a yellow-eyed, solidly built short man who bears a strange resemblance to Mussolini. He's around sixty so he must have been a namesake. I remember that Mussolini actually was named for the Mexican Benito Juárez, who fought French oppression. Odd to think of that revolutionary name travelling through the dictator and into this quiet man whose wide, blank face and bald head shine like a polished nut. When he speaks, which is little, he uses the local Val di Chiana dialect. He cannot understand a word either of us says and we certainly can't understand him. Even Ian has trouble. Benito worked on the restoration of the chapel at Le Celle, a nearby monastery, a solid recommendation. We're even more impressed when Ian drives us out to look at a house he's restoring near Castiglione del Lago, a farmhouse with a tower supposedly built by the Knights Templar. The work looks careful. His two masons, unlike Benito, have big smiles.

Back at Bramasole, Benito walks through, not even taking a note. He radiates a calm confidence. When we ask Ian to request an estimate, Benito balks. It is impossible to know the problems he might run into. How much do we want to spend? (What a question!) He is not sure about the floor tiles, of what he will uncover when he takes the bricks off the upstairs terrace. A small beam, he notices, needs replacing on the third floor.

Estimates are foreign to builders around here. They're used to working by the day, with someone always at home to know how long they were there. This projecting is just not the way they do business, although they will sometimes say "Under three days" or *"Quindici giorni."* *Quindici giorni*—fifteen days—we learned is simply a convenient term meaning the speaker has no idea but imagines that the time is not entirely open ended. *"Quindici minuti,"* we'd learned by missing a train, means a few minutes, not the fifteen it indicates, even when spoken by the train conductor about a departure. I think most Italians have a longer sense of time than we do. What's the hurry? Once up, a building will stand a long, long time, perhaps a thousand years. Two weeks, two months, big deal.

Removing the walls? He doesn't advise it. He makes gestures, indicating the house collapsing around us. Somehow, Benito will come up with a number and will give it to Ian this week. As he leaves he flashes a smile at last. His square yellow teeth look strong enough to bite through brick. Ian endorses him and discounts Nando as "the playboy of the western world." Ed looks pleased.

Our *geometra* recommends the third contractor, Primo Bianchi, who arrives in an Ape, one of those miniature three-wheel trucks. He, too, is miniature, scarcely five feet tall, stout and dressed in overalls with a red kerchief around his neck. He rolls out and salutes us formally with an old word, *"Salve, signori."* He looks like one of Santa's workers, with gold-rimmed glasses, flyaway white hair, tall boots. *"Permesso?"* he asks before we go through the door. At each door he pauses and repeats, *"Permesso?"* as though he might surprise someone undressing. He holds his cap in his hand in a way I recognize from my father's mill workers in the South; he's used to being the "peasant" speaking to the *"padrone."* He has, however, a confident sense of himself, a pride I often notice in waiters, mechanics, delivery people here. He tries the window latches and swings the doors. Pokes the tip of his knife in beams to check for rot, wiggles loose bricks.

He comes to a spot in the floor, kneels and rubs two bricks that are a slightly lighter color. *"Io,"* he says, beaming, pointing to his chest, *"molti anni fa."* He replaced them many years ago. He then tells us he was the one who installed the main bath and that he used to come every December and help haul the big lemon pots that lined the terrace into the *limonaia* for the winter. The house's owner was his father's age, a widower then, whose five daughters had grown and moved away. When he died, the daughters left the house vacant. They refused to part with it but no one cared for the place for thirty years. Ah, the five sisters of Perugia I imagine in their narrow iron beds in five bedrooms, all waking at once and throwing open the shutters. I don't believe in ghosts, but from the beginning I sensed their heavy black braids twisted with ribbons, their white nightgowns embroidered with their initials, their mother with silver brushes lining them up before the mirror each night for one hundred strokes.

On the upstairs terrace, he shook his head. The bricks

must come up, then an underlayer of tarpaper and insulation installed. We had a feeling he knew what he was talking about. The central heating? "Keep the fire going, dress warmly, signora, the cost is formidable." The two walls? Yes, it could be done. Decisions are irrational. We both knew Primo Bianchi was the right man for the restoration.

*

If the gun is on the mantel in chapter one, there must be a bang by the end of the story.

The former owner had not just affirmed the bounty of water, he had waxed lyrical. It was a subject of great pride. When he showed us around the property's borders, he'd opened a garden faucet full blast, turning his hands in the cold well water. "This was a watering spot for the Etruscans! This water is known to be the purest—the whole Medici water system," he said, gesturing to the walls of the fifteenth-century fortress at the top of the hill, "runs through this land." His English was perfect. Without doubt, he knew about water. He described the watercourses of the mountains around us, the rich supply that flowed through our side of Monte Sant'Egidio.

Of course, we had the property inspected before we bought it. An impartial *geometra* from Umbertide, miles away over the hills, gave us detailed evaluations. The water, he agreed, was plentiful.

While I am taking a shower after six weeks of ownership, the water slows, then trickles, then drips, then stops. Soap in hand, I stand there without comprehension for several moments, then decide the pump must have been turned off accidentally, or, more likely, the power has gone off. But the overhead light is on. I step out and rub off the soap with a towel.

Signor Martini drives out from his office bringing a long string marked with meters and a weight on the end. We lift the stone off the well and he lowers the weight. *"Poco acqua,"* he announces loudly as the weight hits bottom. Little water. He hauls it up, black roots hanging off, and only a few inches of string are wet. The well is a measly twenty meters deep, with a pump that must have ushered in the Industrial Revolution. So much for the expertise of the impartial *geometra* from Umbertide. That Tuscany is in the third year of a serious drought doesn't help either.

"Un nuovo pozzo," he announces, still louder. Meanwhile, he says, we will buy water from a friend of his who will bring it in a truck. Fortunately, he has a "friend" for every situation.

"Lake water?" I ask, imagining little toads and slimy green weed from Trasimeno. He assures us it's pure water, even has fluoride in it. His friend simply will pump umpteen liters into the well and it will be adequate for the rest of the summer. In fall, a new *pozzo,* deep, with fine water—enough for a swimming pool.

The swimming pool had become a leitmotif while we were looking for houses. Since we are from California, everyone who showed us a house assumed that naturally we would want a pool first thing. I remembered that years ago, while visiting in the East, I was asked by the pale-faced son of a friend if I taught my classes in my bathing suit. I liked his vision. After owning a pool, I think the best way to enjoy the water is to have a friend who has a pool. Dealing with overnight neon green transformations of water is not in my vacation plans. There is trouble enough here.

And so we buy a truckload of water, feeling half foolish and half relieved. We only have two weeks left at Bramasole and paying Martini's friend certainly is cheaper than going to a hotel—and not nearly as humiliating. Why the water doesn't just seep into the dried-out water table, I don't know. We shower fast, drink nothing but bottled water, eat out frequently, and enrich the dry cleaners. All day we hear the rhythmic pounding of well-drilling equipment rising from the valley below us. Others, it seems, don't have deep wells either. I wonder if anyone else in Italy ever has had a load of water dumped into the ground. I keep confusing *pozzo,* well, with *pazzo,* crazy, which is what we must be.

By the time we start to get a grasp on what the place needs—besides water—and who we are here, it's time to go. In California, students are buying their texts, consulting their class schedules. We arrange for permit applications. The estimates are all astronomical—we'll have to do more of the work ourselves than I imagined. I remember getting a shock when I changed the switchplate on an electrical outlet in my study at home. Ed once put his foot through the ceiling when he climbed into the attic to check for a roof leak. We call Primo Bianchi and tell him we'd like for him to do the main work and will be in touch when the permits come through. Bramasole, fortunately, is in a "green zone" and a "*belle arti* zone," where nothing new can be built and houses are protected from alterations that would change their architectural integrity. Because permits require both local and national approval, the process takes months—even a year. We hope Rizzatti is as well-connected as we have heard he is. Bramasole must stand empty for another winter. Leaving a dry well leaves a dry taste as well.

When we see the former owner in the piazza just before we leave, he is congenial, his new Armani tossed over his shoulders. "How is everything at Bramasole?" he asks.

"Couldn't be better," I reply. "We love everything about it."

❋

As I closed the house, I counted. Seventeen windows, each with heavy outside shutters and elaborate inside windows with swinging wooden panels, and seven doors to lock. When I pulled in the shutters, each room was suddenly dark, except for combs of sunlight cast on the floor. The doors have iron bars to hook in place, all except the *portone,* the big front door, which closes with the iron key and, I suppose, makes the elaborate locking of the other doors and windows moot, since a determined thief easily could batter his way in, despite the solid *thumft, thumft* of the lock turning twice. But the house has stood here empty through thirty winters; what's one more? Any thief who pushed into the dark house would find a lone bed, some linens, stove, fridge, and pots and pans.

Odd, to pack a bag and drive away, just leave the house standing there in the early morning light, one of my favorite times, as though we'd never been there at all.

We head toward Nice, across Tuscany toward the Ligurian coast. The toasted hills, fields of drooping sunflowers, and the exit signs with the magical names flash by: Montevarchi, Firenze, Montecatini, Pisa, Lucca, Pietrasanta, Carrara with its river milky with marble dust. Houses are totally anthropomorphic for me. They're so *themselves*. Bramasole looked returned to itself as we left, upright and contained, facing the sun.

I keep hearing myself singing, "The cheese stands alone" as we whiz in and out of tunnels. "What *is* that you're singing?" Ed is passing cars at 140 kilometers an hour; I'm afraid he has taken rather naturally to the blood sport of Italian driving.

"Didn't you play The Farmer in the Dell in first grade?"

"I was into Capture the Flag. Girls played those singing games."

"I always liked it at the end when we boomed out, 'The cheese stands alone,' emphasizing every syllable. It's sad to leave, knowing the house will just stand there all winter and we'll be busy and won't even think about it."

"Are you crazy—we'll be thinking every day about where we want things, what we'll plant—and how much we're going to be robbed."

At Menton, we check into a hotel and spend the late afternoon swimming in the Mediterranean. Italy is now that far off arm of land in the hazy twilight. Somewhere, light years away, Bramasole is now in shadow; the afternoon sun has dipped below the crest of the hill above us. Further light years away, it's morning in California; light is spilling into the dining room where Sister the cat is warming her fur on the table under the windows. We walk the long promenade into town and have bowls of *soupe au pistou* and grilled fish. Early the next day we drive to Nice and fly away. As we speed down the runway, I glimpse a fringe of waving palms against the bright sky; then we lift off and are gone for nine months.

SISTER WATER, BROTHER FIRE

JUNE. WE'RE TOLD THAT WINTER WAS FIERCE AND spring was unusually profligate with bloom. Poppies have lingered and the fragrance of spiky yellow broom still fills the air. The house looks as if more sun soaked in during these months I've been gone. The finish that faux painters all over creation are trying to perfect, the seasons have managed admirably. Otherwise, all is the same, giving me the illusion that the months away were only a few days. A moment ago I was hacking weeds and now I'm at it again, though frequently I stop. I am watching for the man with the flowers.

A sprig of oleander, a handful of Queen Anne's and fennel bound with a stem, a full bouquet of dog roses, dandelion puffs, buttercups, and lavender bells—every day I look to see what he has propped up in the shrine at the bottom of my driveway. When I first saw the flowers, I thought the donor was a woman. I would see her soon in her neat navy print dress with a market bag hung over the handlebars of a battered bicycle.

A bent woman in a red shawl does come early some mornings. She kisses her fingertips, then touches them to the ceramic Mary. I have seen a young man stop his car, jump out for a moment, then roar off. Neither of these brings flowers. Then one day I saw a man walking down the road from Cortona. He was slow and dignified. I heard the crunch of his steps on the road stop for a moment. Later, I found a fresh clump of purple sweet peas in the shrine, and yesterday's wild asters thrown down into the pile of other wilting and dead bundles.

Now I wait for him. He examines what wildflowers the roadside and fields offer, leans to pick what he fancies. He varies his selection, bringing new blooms as they spring up. I'm up on a high terrace, hacking ivy off stone walls and chopping off dry limbs of neglected trees. The profusion of flowers stops me every few minutes. I don't know enough of the English names, much less the Italian. One plant, shaped like a little tabletop Christmas tree, is spiked all over with white flowers. I think we have wild red gladioluses. Lusty red poppies literally carpet the hillsides, their vibrancy cooled by clusters of blue irises, now withering to an ashy gray. The grass brushes my knees. When I stop just to look, the pilgrim is approaching. He pauses in the road and stares up at me. I wave but he does not wave back, just blanky stares as though I, a foreigner, am a creature unaware of being looked at, a zoo animal.

The shrine is the first thing you see when you come to the house. Cut into a curved stone wall, it's an ordinary one in these parts, a porcelain Mary on a blue background, in the Della Robbia style, centered in an arched niche. I see other shrines around the countryside, dusty and forgotten. This one is, for some reason, active.

He's an old man, this wayfarer with his coat draped over his shoulders and his slow contemplative walk down

the road. Once I passed him in the town park and he
gravely said, *"Buon giorno,"* but only after I spoke first.
He had taken off his cap for a moment and I saw a fringe
of white hair around his bald crown, which is bright as a
lightbulb. His eyes are cloudy and remote, a stony blue. I
also have seen him in town. He is not gregarious, does
not join friends for coffee at bars, does not stop his stroll
through the main street to greet anyone. I begin to get
the idea that he is possibly an angel, since his coat always
hangs around his shoulders, and since he seems to be
invisible to everyone but me. I remember the dream I had
the first night I spent here: I would discover one hundred
angels one by one. This angel, though, has a body. He
wipes his forehead with his handkerchief. Perhaps he was
born in this house, or he loved someone here. Or the
pointed cypresses that line this road, each one commemorating a local boy who died in World War I (so many
from such a small town), remind him of friends. His
mother was a great beauty and stepped into carriages on
this spot, or his father was tight as a whip and forbade
him to enter the house ever again. He thanks Jesus daily
for saving his daughter from the perils of surgeons in
Parma. Or perhaps this is just the far point of his daily
walk, a pleasant habit, a tribute to the Walk God. Whatever, I hesitate to wipe the road dust from Mary's face, or
shine the blue to gloss with a cloth, even to disturb the
mound of stiff bouquets piled on the ground, still intact.
There's a life in old places and we're always passing
through. He makes me feel wide circles surrounding this
house. I will be learning for years what I can touch and
what I can't, and how I can touch. I imagine the five
sisters of Perugia who held this family property, letting

the closed stone rooms grow coats of fluffy white mold, letting vines strangle the trees, letting plums and pears thud to the ground summer after summer. They would not let go. As girls here, did they wake at the same moment in the mornings, push open the shutters of five bedrooms, and draw the same breath of new green air? Some such memory held the house to them.

Finally they let go and I, who simply happened by, now hold eighteenth-century maps showing where the property ends. At a triangular point below that, I discover cantilevered steps jutting out of a stone wall that was put together as neatly as a crossword puzzle. The sculptural integrity of limestone stairs extending into the air was only some farmer's ingenious method of stepping up to the next terrace. Lacy blue and gray lichen over the years erased the evidence of a foot, but when I run my hand over the step, I feel a slight dip in the center.

From this high terrace I look down on the house. In places where the plaster is broken, the stone called *pietra serena,* square and solid, shows. In front, the two palm trees rising on either side of the front door make the house look as though it should be in Costa Rica or Tangier. I like palms, their dry rattle in the wind and their touch of the exotic. Over the double front door, with its fanlight, I see the stone and wrought-iron balcony, just large enough to step out on and admire the spilling geraniums and jasmine I will plant.

From this terrace, I can't see or hear the workers' chaos going on below. I see our olive trees, some stunted or dead from the famous freeze of 1985, others flourishing, flashing silver and green. I count three figs with their large improbable leaves, visualizing yellow lilies beneath them. I can rest here marveling over the hummocky hills, cypress-lined road, cerulean skies with big baroque clouds that look as if cherubs could peer from behind them, distant stone houses barely brushed in, neat (will ours ever look like that?) terraces of olive and grape.

That I have acquired a shrine amazed me. What amazes me more is that I have taken on the ritual of the man with the flowers. I lay the clippers down in the grass. He approaches slowly, the bouquet almost behind him. When he is at the shrine I never watch. Later, I will walk down the terrace, down the driveway to see what he left. The brilliant yellow broom called *ginestra* and red poppies? Lavender and wheat? I always touch his blade of weed tying that ties them together.

*

Ed is two levels up, chopping rampaging ivy out of a black locust tree. At every ominous crack or snap I expect to see him careening down the terraces. I pull at tough runners in a stone wall. Ivy kills. We have miles of the stuff. It causes stone walls to fall. Some of the trunks are as big as my ankle. I think of the ivy I have in pretty jardinières on my mantle in San Francisco, imagine that in my absence they will bolt, strangle the furniture, cover the windows. As I move along this wall, my footing becomes more canted because the terrace starts to angle down. The cool scents of crushed lemon balm and *nepitella,* tiny wild mint, rise from around my feet. I lean into the wall, cut a runner of ivy, then rip it out. Dirt flies in my face and little stones crumble out, hitting my shoes. I disturb not at all a long snake taking a siesta. Its head is (how far?) in the wall, tail dangling out about two feet. Which way would he exit—back out or go farther in and U-turn? I skip ten feet on either side and begin to snip again. And then the wall disappears and I almost disappear into a hole.

I call Ed to come down. "Look—is this a well? But how could there be a well *in* the wall?" He scrambles down to the terrace just above me and leans over to look. Where he is, both ivy and blackberries are unnaturally dense.

"It looks like an opening up here." He turns on the weed machine then, but when blackberries keep choking the filaments, he resorts to the grim-reaper scythe. Slowly, he uncovers a chute lined with stones. The immense back stone curves down like a playground slide and disappears underground, opening in the wall I'm trimming. We look at the terrace above him—nothing. But two terraces up, in a line from here, we see another unnaturally large blackberry clump.

Perhaps we just have water and wells on the brain. A few days before, when we arrived for the summer, we were greeted by trucks and cars along the road and a pile of dirt in the driveway. The new well, drilled by a friend of Signor Martini, was almost finished. Giuseppe, the plumber who was installing the pump, somehow had driven his venerable *cinque cento* over a low stone edge of the driveway. He introduced himself to us politely, then turned to kick and curse the car. *"Madonna serpente! Porca Madonna!"* The Madonna is a snake? A pig? He raced the engine but the three wheels remaining on the ground couldn't get enough traction to spin his axle off the stone. Ed tried to rock the car and dislodge it. Giuseppe kicked his car again. The three well drillers laughed at him, then helped Ed literally lift the toy-sized car off and over to level ground. Giuseppe hoisted the new pump out of the car and headed for the well, still muttering about the Madonna. We watched them lower it the three hundred feet down. This must be the deepest well in Christendom. They had hit water quickly but Signor Martini told them to keep going, that we never wanted to run out of water again. We found Signor Martini in the house, overseeing Giuseppe's assistant. Without our even thinking of it, they have moved the water heater from the older bathroom to the kitchen so we'll have hot water in our improvised kitchen this summer. I'm touched that he has had the house cleaned and has planted marigolds and petunias around the palm trees—a touch of civilization in the overgrown yard.

He looks tanned already and his foot is healed. "How is your business?" I ask. "Sell many houses to unsuspecting foreigners?"

"Non c'è male," not bad. He beckons for us to follow. At the old well, he pulls a weight out of his pocket and plunks it down the opening. Immediately we hear it hit water. He laughs. *"Pieno, tutto pieno."* Over the winter the old well has completely filled.

I read in a local history book that Torreone, the area of Cortona where Bramasole sits, is a watershed; on one side of us, water runs to the Val di Chiana. On the other, water runs down to the valley of the Tiber. We already are intrigued by the underground cistern near the driveway. Shining a light down the round opening, we've contemplated the stone arch tall enough to stand under and a deep pool our longest stick can't measure. I remember a Nancy Drew I liked at nine, *The Mystery in the*

Old Well, though I don't recall the story. Medici escape routes seem more dramatic. Looking down into the cistern taps my first memory of historical Italy—Mrs. Bailey, my sixth-grade teacher, drawing the soaring arches of a Roman aqueduct on the board, explaining how ingenious the ancient Romans were with water. The Acqua Marcia was sixty-two miles long—that's two thirds of the way from Fitzgerald, Georgia, to Macon, she pointed out—and some of the arches still exist from the year 140. I remember trying to grasp the year 140, meanwhile overlapping the arches onto the Ben Hill County highway north.

The cistern opening seems to disappear into a tunnel. Though there is footing on either side of the pool, neither of us is brave enough to lower ourselves the fifteen dank feet underground to investigate. We stare into the dark, wondering how large the scorpions and vipers are, just out of sight. Above the cistern a *bocca,* a mouth, opens in the stone wall, as though water should pour into the cistern.

As we strip the ivy's thick roots and webs off the stone walls, we realize that the chute we're uncovering must be connected to the opening above the cistern. Over the next few days we discover four stone chutes running downhill from terrace to terrace and ending at a large square mouth that goes underground for about twenty-five feet, then reappears on the lowest terrace above the cistern, just as we suspected. The backs of all the chutes have the big single stone curved for the water to flow down. When the channels are cleaned out, water will cascade into the cistern after rains. I start to wonder if, with a small recirculating pump connected to the cistern, perhaps some of the water can fall all the time. After the experience of the dry well, the trickle and splash of falling water would be music indeed. Fortunately, we didn't stumble into these chutes last year as we blithely meandered the terraces admiring wildflowers and identifying fruit trees.

On the third-level terrace wall, a rusted pipe crumbles off as we hack at thorny blackberries. At the base, we discover a flat stone. As we shovel off dirt and pour on water, it grows. Something gigantic is buried here. Slowly, we uncover the roughly carved stone sink that once was used in the kitchen, before the "improved" concrete sink was installed. I'm afraid it's broken but we scrub mud away, wedge it out of its hole with a pick, and find intact the single stone, four feet long, about eighteen inches wide and eight inches thick, with a shallow indented basin for washing and with drainage ridges chipped out on either side. The corner drain is clogged with roots. We've been sorry our house didn't have this original and very characteristic object. Many old houses have similar sinks in place, draining directly out the kitchen wall and off a scallop-shaped stone shelf into the yard. I would like to wash my glasses in this prototype sink. We'll put it against the house outside under the trees, a place to keep ice and wine for parties and to wash up after gardening. It has been used to scrub enough crusty pots in its day; from now on: an honored place to fill a glass, a place for a pitcher of roses on the stone. It will be returning to good use after many years buried in dirt.

After a few more minutes of chopping, I'm about twelve feet down from the stone sink when two rusted hooks appear under the leaves. Beneath them, again we see a glimpse of flat stone. Ed shovels off a mound of dirt. In the middle, he hits a latch, around which is twisted a rusty coil of wire. We make out a circular opening. He has to angle the shovel in the crack to pry up the long-covered stone lid.

It is late afternoon, just after a thunderstorm, when the light turns that luminous gold I wish I could bottle and keep. Off comes the lid and the light that falls down strikes clear water in a wide natural cleft of white stone. We can see another undulation of the stone, too, where the water becomes aqua. We lie on our stomachs on the ground, taking turns sticking our heads and the flashlight down the hole. Fig roots seeking moisture slither down the rock wall. On the bottom, we see a big can on its side and easily read the magnified green words *Olio d'Oliva*. Not exactly like finding a Roman torso or amphora with dancing satyrs. A rusty pipe leans against the back of the white stone and we notice that it emerges just below the two hooks—someone stopped it up with a wine cork. It now seems obvious that the hooks once secured a hand pump and that this is a lost natural spring, hidden for years. How long? But wait. Just beneath the stone covering lies a remnant of another opening. What appears to be a corner of two layers of carved travertine lintel angles for a couple of feet, then disappears into rock. If the top were dug away, would this be an open pool? I read about a man nearby who went in his backyard on Christmas Eve to pick lettuce for dinner and caved into an Etruscan tomb with elaborate sarcophagi. Is this simply a fortuitous opening in rock that supplied water for farming? Why the carving? Why was the carving recovered with a plainer stone? This must have been covered when the second well nearby was dug. Now we have a third well; we're the latest layer of water seekers, our technology—the high-whining drills able to pierce any rock—long removed from that of the discoverer of this secret opening in the earth.

We call Signor Martini to come see this miraculous finding. Hands in pockets, he doesn't even lean over. *"Boh,"* he says (*boh* is an all purpose word, sort of "Well," "Oh," "Who knows?" or dismissal), then he waves a hand over it. *"Acqua."* He regards our fascination with abandoned houses and such things as ancient wells as further evidence that we are like children and must be humored in our whimsies. We show him the stone sink and explain that we will dig it out, clean it, and have it put up again. He simply shakes his head.

Giuseppe, who has come along, gets more excited. He should have been a Shakespearean actor. He punctuates every sentence with three or four gestures—his body totally participates in every word he speaks. He practically stands on his head looking down the hole. *"Molto acqua."* He points in both directions. We thought the well opened only in one, but because he is dangling upside down, he sees that the natural declivity of the rock extends in the opposite direction also. "O.K., yes!" These are his only English words, always uttered with arms wide apart, embracing an idea. He wants to install a new hand pump for garden use. We already have seen bright green pumps in the hardware store out in the Val di Chiana farm country. We buy one the next day, uncork the pipe, and place the pump right on the old hooks. Giuseppe teaches us to prime the pump by pouring water into it while pumping the handle rhythmically. Here's a motion long lost to my gene pool, but the creaky-smooth movement feels natural. After a few dry gulps, icy fresh water spills out into the bucket. We do have the presence of mind not to drink untested water. Instead, we open a bottle of wine on the terrace. Giuseppe wants to know about Miami and Las Vegas. We're looking out over the jungle growth on the hills. Giuseppe thinks the palm trees are what we really need to tend to. How will we ever trim them? They're taller than any ladder. After two glasses, Giuseppe shimmies up to the top of the taller one. He has the biggest grin I've ever seen. The tree leans and he slides down fast, too fast, lands in a heap on the ground. Ed quickly opens another bottle.

❋

As it turns out, the former owner was right about the water. If the water setup doesn't exactly rival the gardens of the Villa d'Este, it is ingenious enough to keep us digging and exploring for many days. The elaborate underground system makes us understand precisely how precious water is in the country. When it flows, you figure out ways to save it; when it is plentiful, as now, you must respect it. St. Francis of Assisi must have known this. In his poem "The Canticle of the Creatures," he wrote, "Be praised, O Lord, for Sister Water, the which is so useful, humble, precious and chaste." We convert instantly to short showers, to turning off the water quickly when washing dishes and brushing our teeth.

Interesting that this oldest well has channels on either side of it to divert runoff so that any extra water flows into the cistern. As we clean around the cistern, we find two stone tubs for washing clothes and more hooks in the stone wall above it, where another pump must have hung. Do not waste a drop. And there, not five feet away from the natural well, the old one that went dry last summer— now replenished fully by the winter rains. The hand pump for potted plants, Ed decides, the old well for the grass, and for the house, our fine new *pozzo,* a hundred meters deep, drilled through solid rock.

"Wonderful water," the *pozzoaiolo,* the well driller, assures us as we pay him a fortune, "down to inferno but cold as ice." We count out the cash. He does not want a check; why would anyone use a check unless they didn't actually have the money? *"Acqua, acqua,"* he says, gesturing over the entire property. "Enough water for a swimming pool."

✻

We noticed, vaguely, when we bought the house that a stone wall perpendicular to the front had tumbled down in a few places. Weeds, sumac, and fig sprouted along the fallen rocks. The first time we saw the house the section of the yard above that wall was topped with forty feet of rose-covered pergola lined with lilacs. When we returned to negotiate for the purchase, the pergola was gone, torn down in a zeal to clean up the place. The roses and lilacs were leveled. When I lifted my eyes from that debacle to the house, I saw that the faded green shutters were repainted a glossy dark brown. Stunned, we hardly noticed the heaps of stones. Later, we realized that a 120-foot-long wall of immense stone would have to be rebuilt. We forgot about the romantic pergola with its climbing roses.

During those few weeks here last summer after buying

the house, Ed started to take down parts of the wall adjacent to the tumbled sections. He thought stone building sounded gratifying—finding just the right stone to slide into place, tapping it in with a mallet, scoring stone surfaces, hitting them precisely to direct the split. The ancient craft is appealing; so is the good hard labor. An alarming pile of stones grew daily, as did his muscles. He became a little obsessed. He bought thick leather gloves. Big rocks went in one line, small ones in another, and flat ones in another. Like all the terrace walls on the property, this was drywall, with a depth of more than a yard: nicely fitted and stacked stones in front, neat as a jigsaw, with smaller ones behind. The structure leaned backward, to counteract the natural downward heave of the hillside. Unlike the lovely stone fences of New England, which cleared the fields of stone, these actually are structural; only with braced terraces is a hillside like ours an olive farm or vineyard. On one terrace where the stones fell, a large almond tree also toppled.

When we had to leave, about thirty feet of the wall lay in orderly piles. Ed was enthusiastic about stonework, though slightly daunted by the excavation and the surprising depth of stonework behind the facade of the wall. But instead of the miles to go, we noticed the huge heaps of stones he'd stacked.

Over the winter we read *Building with Stone* by Charles McRaven. Ideas such as sealing out moisture and foundations and frost lines started to crop up. The height of the remaining wall was not the actual height the rebuilt wall would have to be to support the broad terrace leading up to the house. Besides being 120 feet long, the wall must be fifteen feet high, buttressed from behind. As we read about packed fill, thrust, balance, and all the ways the earth shifts when it freezes, we began to think we had the Great Wall of China on our hands.

We were absolutely right. We've just had several experienced *muratori,* masons, out to view the remains. This job is a monster. Restoration work inside seems dwarfed beside this project. Still, Ed envisions himself apprenticed to a rugged man in a cap, a stone artist. *Santa Madonna, molto lavoro,* much work, each *muratore* exclaims in turn. *Molto. Troppo,* too much. We learn that Cortona recently adopted codes for walls such as this one because we're in an earthquake zone. Reinforced concrete will be required. We are not prepared to mix concrete. We have five acres of blackberry and sumac jungle to deal with, trees that need pruning. Not to mention the house. The wall estimates are astronomical. Few even want to tackle the job.

This is how in Tuscany we build the Great Wall of Poland.

Signor Martini sends a couple of his friends by. I forewarn him that we are interested in getting the work done immediately and that we want a price for *fratélli,* brothers, not for *stranieri,* foreigners. We are recovering from the new well and still awaiting permits so the major house work can begin. His first friend says sixty days of labor. For his price we could buy a small steamer and motor around Greece. The second friend, Alfiero, gives a surprisingly reasonable estimate, plus has the terrific idea that another wall should run along the row of linden trees on an adjacent terrace. When you don't speak a language well, many of your cues for judging people are missing. We both think he is fey—an odd quality for a mason—

but Martini says he is *bravo*. We want the work done while we are in residence, so we sign a contract. Our *geometra* doesn't know him and cautions us that if he's available he probably is not good. This kind of reasoning doesn't sink in with us.

The schedule calls for work to begin the following Monday. Monday, Tuesday, and Wednesday pass. Then a load of sand arrives. Finally, at the end of the week, Alfiero appears with a boy of fourteen and, to our surprise, three big Polish men. They set to work and by sundown, amazingly, the long wall is down. We watch all day. The Poles lift one-hundred-pound stones as though they were watermelons. Alfiero speaks not a word of Polish and they speak about five words of Italian. Fortunately, the language of manual labor is easy to act out. *"Via, via,"* Alfiero waves at the stones and they have at them. The next day they excavate dirt. Alfiero exits, to go to other jobs, I suppose. The boy, Alessandro, purely pouts. Alfiero is his stepfather and evidently is trying to teach the boy about work. He looks like a little Medici prince, petulant and bored as he stands around listlessly kicking stones with the toe of his tennis shoe. The Poles ignore him. From seven until twelve they don't stop. At noon they drive off in their Polski Fiat, returning at three for five more solid hours of labor.

The Italians, who have been "guest workers" at many times and in many countries, are thrown by the phenomenon happening in their own country. During this second summer at Bramasole, the newspapers are tolerant to indignant about Albanians literally washing up on the shores of southern Italy. Living in San Francisco, a city where immigrants arrive daily, we cannot get excited

about their problem. Americans in cities have realized
that migrations are on the increase; that the whole demo-
graphic tapestry is being rewoven on a vast scale in the
late twentieth century. Europe is having a harder time
coming to grips with this fact. We have our own poor,
they tell us incredulously. Yes, we say, we do, too. Italy is
amazingly homogeneous; it is rare to see a black or Asian
face in Tuscany. Recently, Eastern Europeans, finding
the German work force at last full of people like themselves, began arriving in this prosperous part of northern
Italy. Now we understood Alfiero's estimate for the
work. Instead of paying the normal Italian twenty-five
thousand to thirty thousand lire per hour, he is able to
pay nine thousand. He assures us they are legal workers
and are covered by his insurance. The Poles are pleased
with the hourly wage; at home, before the factory went
kaput, they barely earned that much in a day.

Ed grew up in a Polish-American Catholic community in Minnesota. His parents were born of Polish immigrants and grew up speaking Polish on farms on the
Wisconsin-Minnesota border. Of course, Ed knows no
Polish. His parents wanted the children to be All American. The three words he tried out with the Poles they
couldn't understand. But these men he can't understand
seem very familiar. He's used to names like Orzechowski,
Cichosz, and Borzyskowski. Passing in the yard, we nod
and smile. The way we finally make contact with them
comes through poetry. One afternoon I come across a
poem by Czeslaw Milosz, long exiled in America but
quintessentially a Polish poet. I knew he'd made a trium-
phant journey back to Poland a few years ago. When
Stanislao crossed the front terrace with the wheelbarrow,

I asked, "Czeslaw Milosz?" He lit up and shouted to the two others. After that, for a couple of days, when I passed one or the other of them, he would say, "Czeslaw Milosz," as though it were a greeting, and I would answer, *"Sì,* Czeslaw Milosz." I even knew I was pronouncing the name correctly because I'd once practiced his name when I had to introduce the poet at a reading. For several days before that, I'd referred to him to myself as "Coleslaw" and had anxiety that I would stand up before the audience and introduce him that way.

Alfiero becomes a problem. He lights like a butterfly on one project after another, starting something, doing a sloppy job, then taking off. Some days he just doesn't show up at all. When reasonable questioning doesn't work, I revert to the old Southern habit of throwing a fit, which I find I still can do impressively. For a while, Alfiero straightens up and pays attention, then like the whimsical child that he is, he loses his focus. He has a charm. He throws himself into playful descriptions of frog races, fast Moto Guzzis, and quantities of wine. Patting his belly, he speaks in the local dialect and neither of us understands much of what he says. When it's time to throw a fit, I call Martini, who does understand. He nods, secretly amused, Alfiero looks abashed, the Poles let no expression cross their faces, and Ed is mortified. I say that I am *malcontenta.* I use waving gestures and shake my head and stamp my foot and point. He has used rows of tiny stones under rows of big stones, there are vertical lines in the construction, he has neglected to put a foundation in this entire section, the cement is mostly sand. Martini begins to shout, and Alfiero shouts back at him, since he dares not shout at me. I hear the curse *"Porca*

Madonna" again, a serious thing to say, and *"Porca miseria,"* pig misery, one of my favorite curses of all times. After a scene, I expect sulking but, no, he turns up sunny and forgetful the next day.

"Buttare! Via!" Take it down, take it away. Signor Martini starts to kick at Alfiero's work. "Where did your mother send you to school? Where did you learn to make cement like sand castles?" Then they both turn and shout at the Poles. Now and then Martini rushes in the house and calls Alfiero's mother, his old friend, and we hear him shouting at her, then subsiding into soothing sounds.

They must think, privately, that we are brilliant to know so much about wall building. What neither Signor Martini nor Alfiero realizes is that the Poles let us know when something is not right. *"Signora,"* Krzysztof (we call him Cristoforo, as he wishes) says, motioning to me, *"Italia cemento."* He crumbles too-dry cement between his fingers. *"Polonia cemento."* He kicks a rock-hard section of the retaining wall. This has become a nationalistic issue. "Alfiero. *Poco cemento.*" He puts his fingers to his lips. I thank him. Alfiero is using too little cement in his mixture. Don't tell. They begin to roll their eyes as a signal, or, after Alfiero departs, which usually is early in the day, to show us problems. Everything Alfiero touches seems bad, but we have a contract, they work for him, and we are stuck with him. However, without him, we would not have met the Poles.

Near the top of the wall, they uncover a ground-level stump. Alfiero maintains it is *non importa*. We see Riccardo shake his head quickly, so Ed says authoritatively that it will have to be dug out. Alfiero relents but wants to pour on *gasolio* to kill it. We point to the pristine new well not twenty feet away. The Poles began to dig and two hours later are still digging. Beneath the exposed stump, a mammoth three-legged root has wrapped itself around a stone as big as an automobile tire. Hundreds of inveigling roots shoot out in all directions. Here is the reason much of the wall had fallen in the first place. When they finally wrench it out, they insist on evening the legs and top, the stone still entwined. They load it in a wheelbarrow and take it up to the lime tree bower, where it will remain, the ugliest table in Tuscany.

They sing while they heave stone and their voices begin to sound like the way the work of the world should sound. Sometimes Cristoforo sings in a falsetto, a strangely moving song, especially coming from his big brown body. They never skimp on a minute's work, even though their boss is gone all the time. On days when their supplies are gone because Alfiero forgets to reorder, he capriciously tells them not to work. We hire them to help clear the terraces of weeds. Finally we have them sanding all the inside shutters. They seem to know how to do everything and work about twice as fast as anyone I've ever seen. At the end of the day, they strip and rinse off with the hose, dress in clean clothes, then we have a beer.

Don Fabbio, a local priest, lets them live in a back room of the church. For about five dollars apiece, he feeds all three of them three meals a day. They work six days a week—the priest does not allow them to work on Sunday—exchanging all the lire they make into dollars and stashing it away to take home for their wives and children. Riccardo is twenty-seven, Cristoforo thirty, and Stanislao forty. During the weeks they work, our Italian deteriorates. Stanislao has worked in Spain, so our communication begins to be an unholy mixture of four languages. We pick up Polish words: *jutro,* tomorrow; *stopa,* foot; *brudny,* dirty; *jezioro,* lake. Also something that sounds like *grubbia,* which was their name for Signor Martini's sloping stomach. They learned "beautiful" and "idiot" and quite a few Italian words, mostly infinitives.

Despite Alfiero, the wall is strong and beautiful. A curving flight of stairs, with flat tops on either side for pots of flowers, connects the first two terraces. The well and cistern have stone walls around them. From below, the wall looks immense. It's hard to get used to, since we liked the tumbled look, too. Like the other walls, soon it will have tiny plants growing in the cracks. Because the stone is old, it already looks natural in the landscape, if a bit tall. Now comes the pleasure of planning the walkway from the driveway around the well to the stone steps, the flowers and herbs for the border, and the flowerings and shadows of small trees along the wall. First we plant a white hibiscus, which pleases us by blooming immediately.

On a Sunday morning the Poles arrive after church, dressed in pressed shirts and trousers. We've seen them only in shorts. They've bought identical sandals at the local supermarket. Ed and I are clipping weeds when they arrive. We're dirty, wearing shorts, sweaty—reversed roles. Stanislao has a Soviet Union camera that looks to be from the thirties. We have Coca-Cola and they take several pictures. Anytime we serve them Coke, they always say, "Ah, America!" Before changing for work, they take us down to the wall and dig the dirt away from

a few feet of the foundation. In large letters, they've written POLONIA in the concrete.

✳

Bramasole's staircase ascends three floors with a handmade wrought-iron railing, whose symmetrical curves
add a little rhythm to climbing. The fanlight, the bedroom terrace railing, only slightly rusted, and the railing
around the balcony above the front door all employed
some blacksmith for a long winter. The gate at the bottom of the driveway once was a stately entrance but like
most things here, has been left to time far too long. The
bottom bulges where lost tourists banged into it while
turning around, after realizing they were on the wrong
road to the Medici fortress. The lock has long since
rusted and the hinges on one side have given way at the
top, letting the gate drag.

Giuseppe has brought a friend, a maestro of iron, to
see if our front gate can be salvaged. Giuseppe thinks not.
We need something more suitable for the *bella villa*. The
man who unfolds from Giuseppe's *cinque cento* could have
stepped from behind a time shield of the Middle Ages.
He is as tall and gaunt as Abraham Lincoln; he wears
black overalls and his unusually black hair has no gleam.
Hard to account for his strangeness; somehow he looks as
though he's made out of something else. He uses few
words but smiles shyly. I like him at once. Silently, he
fingers the gate all over. Everything he has to say runs
through his hands. It's easy to sense that he has given his
life to this craft out of love. Yes, he nods, the gate can be
repaired. The question is time. Giuseppe is disappointed.
He envisions something grander. He draws shapes in the

air with his arms, an arching top with arrows. A new one, more elaborate, with lights and an electronic device so we can be buzzed in the house and merely press a button for the gate to swing open. He has brought us this artist and we want him to *repair*?

We go to the shop to see the possibilities. En route, Giuseppe careens to the roadside and we leap out to see other gates this maestro has made. Some with swordlike designs, some with complex interlinking circles and wheat sheaves. One is topped with the initials of the owner, one, oddly, with a crown. We like the curved tops, the hoops and rings more than the more formidable arrow-topped ones, which seem like remnants of the time when the Guelfs and Ghibellines were looting and burning each other. All are obviously made to last forever. He rubs each one, saying nothing, letting the quality of his work speak for itself. I begin to imagine a small stylized sun at the center of ours, with twisted rays.

Ferro battuto, wrought iron, is an ancient craft in Tuscany. Every town has intricate locks on medieval doors, curly lanterns, holders for standards, garden gates, even fanciful iron animals and serpents shaped into rings for tying horses to the wall. Like other artisan traditions, this one is fast disappearing and it's easy to see why. The key word in blacksmith is black. His shop is charred, soot covers him, the antiquated equipment, and the forges that seem to have changed very little since Hephaestus lit the fire in Aphrodite's stove. Even the air seems hung with a fine veil of soot. All his neighbors have gates made by him. It must be satisfying to see one's work all around like that. His own house has a square patterned balcony, a flirtation, no doubt, with *moderne,* redeemed by attached

baskets for flowers. The shop faces the house and between them are hens, ten or so cages of rabbits, a vegetable garden, and a plum tree with a handmade wooden
ladder leaning up into the laden branches. After supper,
he must climb up a few rungs and pick his dessert. My
impression that he stepped out of time strengthens.
Where *is* Aphrodite, surely somewhere near this forge?

"Time. Time is the only thing," he says. "I am *solo*. I
have a son but . . ."

I can't imagine, at the end of the twentieth century,
someone choosing this dark forge with traffic whizzing
by, this collection of bands for wine barrels, andirons,
fences, and gates. But I hope his son does step into it, or
someone does. He brings over a rod that ends with a
squared head of a wolf. He just holds it out to me, without a word. It reminds me of torch holders in Siena and
Gubbio. We ask for an estimate to repair the *cancello,* also
for an estimate for a new gate, rather simple but with a
running form similar to the iron stair railing in the house,
maybe a sun shape at the top closing, to go with the
house's name. For once, we don't start asking for the date
of completion, the one thing we've learned to insist on to
counter the enviable Latin sense of endless time.

Do we really need a handmade gate? We keep saying,
Let's keep it simple, this is not our real home. But somehow I know we'll want one he makes, even if it takes
months. Before we leave, he forgets us. He's picking up
pieces of iron, holding them in both hands for the heft or
balance. He wanders among the anvils and hot grates.
The gate will be in good hands. Already I can imagine its
clank as I close it behind me.

*

The well and the wall feel like significant accomplishments. The house, however, still is untouched. Until the main jobs are finished, there is little to do. No point in painting, when the walls will have to be opened for the heating pipes. The Poles have stripped the windows and have begun scrubbing down the whitewash in preparation for painting. Ed and I work on the terraces or travel around selecting bathroom tile, fixtures, hardware, paint; we look, too, for the old thin bricks for the new kitchen's floor. One day we buy two armchairs at a local furniture store. By the time they're delivered, we realize they're awkward and the dark paisley fabric rather weird, but we find them sumptuously comfortable, after sitting upright in the garden chairs for weeks. On rainy nights we pull them face-to-face with a cloth-covered crate between them, our dining table with a candle, jam jar with wild-flowers, and a feast of pasta with eggplant, tomatoes, and basil. On cool nights we build a twig fire for a few minutes, just to take the damp chill off the room.

Unlike last summer, this July is rainy. Impressive storms hit frequently. In the daytime, I'm thrilled because of my childhood in the South, where they really know how to put on the sound and light. San Francisco rarely has thunderstorms and I miss them. "This heat has to break," my mother would say, and it would, with immense cracks and bolts followed by sheet lightning when the whole sky flashes on a million kilowatts. Often the storms seem to arrive at night. I'm sitting up in bed, drawing kitchen and bathroom plans on graph paper; Ed is reading something I never expected to see him reading.

Instead of the Roman poets, tonight it's *Plastering Skills*. Beside him is *The Home Water Supply*. Rain starts to clatter in the palm trees. I go to the window and lean out, then quickly step back. Bolts spear into the ground— jagged like cartoon drawings of lightning—four, five, six at once, surrounding the house. Thunderheads swarm over the hills and the quiet rolling suddenly changes its tune and starts to explode so close it feels like my own backbone snapping. The house shakes; this is serious. The lights go out. We fasten the windows inside and still the wind whips rain through cracks we didn't know were there. Spooky wind sucks in and out of the chimney. Wild night. Rain lashes the house and the two silly palms give and give in the wind. I smell ozone. I am certain the house has been struck. This storm has selected our house. It won't move on; we're the center and may be washed downhill to Lake Trasimeno. "Which would you prefer," I ask, "landslide or direct hit by lightning?" We get under the covers like ten-year-olds, shouting "Stop!" and "No!" each time the sky lights up. Thunder enters the walls and rearranges the stones.

When the big storm starts passing to the north, the black sky is left washed clean for stars. Ed opens the window and the breeze sends in pine scent from blown-down limbs and scattered needles. The electricity still is out. As we sit propped up on pillows, waiting for our hearts to slow down, we hear something at the window. A small owl has landed on the sill. Its head swivels back and forth. Perhaps its perch was blown down or it is disoriented by the storm. When the moon breaks through the clouds, we can see the owl staring inside at us. We don't move. I'm praying, Please don't come in the room. I am deathly afraid of birds, a holdover phobia from childhood, and yet I am entranced by the small owl. Owls seem always to be more than themselves, totemic in America, symbolic at least, and here, mythological as well. I think of Minerva's owl. But really it's just a small creature that belongs to this hill. We have seen its larger forebears several times at evening. Neither of us speaks. Since it stays, we finally fall asleep and wake in the morning to see that it has flown. At the window, only the quarter of six light—raked gold angling across the valley, suffusing the air briefly before the sun clears the hills and lifts into the absolved, clear day.

THE WILD ORCHARD

THE WATERMELON HOUR—A FAVORITE PAUSE IN the afternoon. Watermelon is arguably the best taste in the world, and I must admit that the Tuscan melons rival in flavor those Sugar Babies we picked hot out of the fields in South Georgia when I was a child. I never mastered the art of the thump. Whether the melon is ripe or not, the thump sounds the same to me. Each one I cut, however, seems to be at its pinnacle—toothy crispness, audacious sweetness. When we're sharing melon with the workers, I notice that they eat the white of the melon. When they finish, their rind is a limp green strip. Sitting on the stone wall, sun on my face, big slice of watermelon—I'm seven again, totally engrossed in shooting seeds between my fingers and spooning out circles from the dripping quarter moon of fruit.

Suddenly, I notice the five pine trees edging the driveway are full of activity. It sounds as though squirrels are pulling Velcro apart, or biting into *panini,* those hard Italian rolls. A man leaps from his car, quickly picks up three cones, and speeds off. Then Signor Martini arrives. I expect he's bringing news of someone who can plow the terraces. He picks up a cone and shakes it against the wall. Out come black nubs. He cracks one with a rock and holds up a husk-covered oval. *"Pinolo,"* he announces. Then he points to the dusky beads scattered all over the driveway. *"Torta della nonna,"* he states, in case I missed the significance. Better still, I think, pesto to make with all the proliferating basil that resulted from sticking six plants in the ground. I love pine nuts on salads. Pine nuts! And I've been stepping on them.

Of course I knew that *pinoli* come from pine trees. I've even inspected trees in my yard at home to see if, somewhere hidden in the cone, I would find pine nuts. I never thought of the trees lining the driveway as the bearers; thus far they simply have been trees that need no immediate attention. They're those painterly-looking pines, sometimes stunted by coastal winds, that line many Mediterranean beach towns, the kind Dante wandered among at Ravenna when he was in exile there. These along the driveway are feathery and tall. Imagine that plain *pino domestico* (I see in my tree book) will yield those buttery nuts, so delicious when toasted. One of the *nonnas* who make all those heavy *pinolo* studded tarts must have lived here. She must have made delectable ravioli with ground *noccioli,* hazelnut, stuffing, and macaroons and other *torte,* too, because there also are twenty almonds and a shady hazelnut tree that droops with its crop of nuts. The *nocciolo* grows with a chartreuse ruff around the nut, as though each one is ready to be worn in a lapel. The almonds are encased in tender green velvet. Even the tree that collapsed over the terrace and must be dying has sent out a plentiful crop.

Perhaps Signor Martini should be back at the office,

prepared to show more foreign clients houses without roofs or water, but he joins me picking up the *pinoli*. Like most Italians I've met, he seems to have time to give. I love his quality of becoming involved in the moment. The sooty covering quickly blackens our hands. "How do you know so many things—were you born in the country?" I ask. "Is this the one day the cones fall?" He has told me previously that the hazelnuts are ripe on August 22, feast day of the foreign St. Filbert.

He tells me he grew up in Teverina, on down the road from Bramasole's *località,* and lived there until the war. I would love to know if he turned partisan or if he stuck to Mussolini until the end, but I merely ask if the war came near Cortona. He points up to the Medici fortress above the house. "The Germans occupied the fort as a radio communication center. Some of the officers quartered in the farmhouses came back after the war and bought those places." He laughs. "Never understood why the peasants weren't helpful." We've piled twenty or so cones on the wall.

I don't ask if this house was occupied by Nazis. "What about the partisans?"

"Everywhere," he says, gesturing. "Even thirteen-year-old boys—killed while picking strawberries or tending sheep. Shot. Mines everywhere." He does not continue. Abruptly, he says his mother died at ninety-three a few years ago. "No more *torta della nonna.*" He is in a wry mood today. After I squash several *pinoli* flat with a stone, he shows me how to hit so that the shell releases the nut whole. I tell him my father is dead, my mother confined since a major stroke. He says he is now alone. I don't dare ask about wife, children. I have known him two summers and this is the first personal information we have exchanged. We gather the cones into a paper bag and when he leaves he says, *"Ciao."* Regardless what I've learned in language classes, among adults in rural Tuscany *ciao* is not tossed about. *Arrivederla* or, more familiarly, *arrivederci* are the usual good-byes. A little shift has occurred.

After half an hour of banging pine nuts, I have about four tablespoons. My hands are sticky and black. No wonder the two-ounce cellophane bags at home are so expensive. I have in mind that I will make one of those ubiquitous *torta della nonnas,* which seem sometimes to be the beginning and end of Italian desserts. The French and American variety of desserts is simply not of interest in the local cuisine. I'm convinced you have to have been raised on most Italian sweets to appreciate them; generally, their cakes and pastries are too dry for my palate. *Torta della nonna,* fruit tarts, perhaps a *tiramisu* (a dessert I loathe)—that's it, except in expensive restaurants. Most pastry shops and many bars serve this grandmother's torte. Though they can be pleasing, sometimes they taste as though *intonaco,* plaster, is one of the ingredients. No wonder Italians order fruit for dessert. Even gelato, which used to be divine all over Italy, is not dependably good anymore. Though many advertise that the gelato is their own, they neglect to say it's sometimes made with envelopes of powdered mix. When you find the real peach or strawberry gelato, it's unforgettable. Fortunately, fruit submerged in bowls of cool water seems perfect at the end of a summer dinner, especially with the local *pecorino,* Gorgonzola, or a wedge of *parmigiano.*

Translating grams into cups as best I can, I copy a

recipe from a cookbook. Hundreds of versions of *torta della nonna* exist. I like the kind with polenta in the cake and a thin layer of filling in the middle. I don't mind the extra hour to pound open the pine nuts that at home I would have pulled from the freezer. First, I make a thick custard with two egg yolks, $1/3$ cup flour, 2 cups milk, and $1/2$ cup sugar. This makes too much, for my purposes, so I pour two servings into bowls to eat later. While the custard cools, I make the dough: $1-1/2$ cups polenta, $1-1/2$ cups flour, $1/3$ cup sugar, $1-1/2$ teaspoons baking powder, 4 oz. butter cut into the dry ingredients, one whole egg plus one yolk stirred in. I halve the dough and spread one part in a pie pan, cover with custard, then roll out the other half of the dough and cover the custard, crimping the edges of the dough together. I sprinkle a handful of toasted pine nuts on top and bake at 350° for twenty-five minutes. Soon the kitchen fills with a promising aroma. When it smells done, I place the golden *torta* on the kitchen windowsill and dial Signor Martini's number. "My *torta della nonna* is ready," I tell him.

When he arrives I brew a pot of espresso, then cut him a large piece. With the first forkful, he gets a dreamy look in his eyes.

"*Perfetto*" is his verdict.

※

Besides the nuts, the original *nonna* planned more of an Eden here. What's left: three kinds of plums (the plump Santa Rosa type are called locally *coscia di monaca*, nun's thigh), figs, apples, apricots, one cherry (half dead), apples, and several kinds of pears. Those ripening now are small green-going-to-russet, with a crisp sweetness. Her

gnarly apples—I'd love to know what varieties they are—
may not be salvageable, but they're now putting forth
dwarfish fruit that looks like the before pictures in ads for
insect sprays. Many of the trees must be volunteers;
they're too young to have been alive when someone lived
here, and often they're in odd places. Since four plums
are directly below a line of ten on a terrace, they obviously sprang from fallen fruit.

I'm sure she gathered wild fennel, dried the yellow
flowers, and tossed the still-green bunches onto the fire
when she grilled meat. We uncover grapes buried in the
brush along the edges of the terraces. Some aggressive
ones still send out long tangles of stems. Tiny bunches are
forming. Along the terraces like a strange graveyard, the
ancient grape stones are still in place—knee-high stones
shaped like headstones, with a hole for an iron rod. The
rod extends beyond the edge of the terrace, thereby giving the grower more space. Ed strings wire from rod to
rod and lifts the grapes up to train them along the wire.
We're amazed to realize that the whole place used to be a
vineyard.

At the huge *enoteca* in Siena, a government-sponsored
tasting room where wines from all over Italy are displayed
and poured, the waiter told us that most Italian vineyards
are less than five acres, about our size. Many small growers join local cooperatives in producing various kinds of
wine, including *vino da tavola,* table wine. As we hoe
weeds around the vines, naturally, we begin to think of a
year 2000 Bramasole Gamay or Chianti. The uncovered
grapes explain the heaps of bottles we inherited. They
may yield the rough-and-ready red served in pitchers in
all the local restaurants. Or perhaps the flinty Grechetto, a

lemon white wine of this area. Ah, yes, this land was waiting for us. Or we for it.

Nonna's most essential, elemental ingredient surely was olive oil. Her woodstove was fired with the prunings; she dipped her bread in a plate of oil for toast, she doused her soups and pasta sauces with her lovely green oil. Cloth sacks of olives hung in the chimney to smoke over the winter. Even her soap was made from oil and the ashes from her fireplace. Her husband or his employee spent weeks tending the olive terraces. The old lore was to prune so that a bird could fly through the main branches without brushing its wings against the leaves. He had to know exactly when to pick. The trees can't be wet or the olives will mildew before you can get them to the mill. To prepare olives to eat, all the bitter glucoside must be leached out by curing them in salt or soaking them in lye or brine. Besides the practical, a host of enduring superstitions determine the best moment to pick or plant; the moon has bad days and good. Vergil, a long time ago, observed farmers' beliefs: Choose the seventeenth day after the full moon to plant, avoid the fifth. He also advises scything at night, when dew softens the stubble. I'm afraid Ed might veer off a terrace if he tried that.

Of our olives, some are paradigms—ancient, twisted, gnarled. Many are clusters of young shoots that sprang up in a circle around damaged trunks. In this benign crescent of hillside, it's hard to imagine the temperature dropping to minus six degrees, as it did in 1985, but gaps between trees reveal huge dead stumps. The olives will have to be revived from their long neglect. Each tree needs to be cleared of encroaching sumac, broom, and weeds, then pruned and fertilized. The terraces must be plowed and cleaned. This is major work but it will have to wait. Since olives are almost immortal, another year won't hurt.

"An olive leaf he brings, pacific sign," Milton wrote in *Paradise Lost*. The dove that flew back to the ark with the branch in its beak made a good choice. The olive tree does impart a sense of peace. It must be, simply, the way they participate in time. These trees are here and will be. They were here. Whether we are or someone else is or no one, each morning they'll be twirling their leaves and inching up toward the sun.

A few summers ago, a friend and I hiked in Majorca above Soller. We climbed across and through miles of dramatic, enormous olives on broad terraces. Up high, we came upon stone huts where the grove tenders sheltered themselves. Although we got lost and encountered a pacing bull in a meadow, we felt this immense peace all day, walking among those trees that looked and may have been a thousand years old. Walking these few curving acres here give me the same feeling. Unnatural as it is, terracing has a natural feel to it. Some of the earliest methods of writing, called boustrophedon, run from right to left, then from left to right. If we were trained that way, it probably is a more efficient way to read. The etymology of the word reveals Greek roots meaning "to turn like an ox plowing." And that writing is like the rising terraces: The U-turn space required by an ox with plow suddenly loops up a level and you're going in the other direction.

*

The five *tiglio* trees, old world lindens or limes, bear no fruit. They provide shade along the broad terrace beside the house when the sun will not allow us on the front terrace. We have lunch under the *tigli* almost every day. Their blossoms are like pearly earrings dangling from the leaves, and when they open—all it seems on the same day—fragrance envelopes the whole hillside. At the height of bloom, we sit on the upstairs patio, just adjacent to the trees, trying to identify the fragrance. I think it smells like the perfume counter in the dime store; Ed thinks it smells like the oil his uncle Syl used to slick back his hair. Either way, it attracts every bee in town. Even at night, when we take our coffee up to the patio, they are working the flowers over. Their collective buzz sounds like a major swarm approaching. It's both lulling and alarming. Ed stays in the doorway at first because he's allergic to bee sting, but they aren't interested in us. They have their honey sacs to fill, their legs to dust with pollen.

Allergic or not, Ed longs for beehives. He tries to get me interested in being the beekeeper. He takes the fact that I never have been stung by a bee to mean that they won't sting me. I point out that I once was stung by a whole nest of wasps but somehow that doesn't count. He imagines a row of hives at the end of the lime trees. "You'll be fascinated when you look in the hive," he says. "When it's hot, dozens of workers stationed at the door whir their wings to cool the queen." I've noticed that he has collected lots of local honeys. Frequently there's a pot of hot water on the stove with a jar of waxy, stiff honey softening in it. The acacia is pale and lemony; the dark chestnut is so thick a spoon will stand up straight in it. He has a jar of *timo,* thyme honey, and, of course, the *tiglio.* The wildest is *macchia,* from the salty coastal shrubs of Tuscany. "The queen bee's life is totally overrated. All she does is lay eggs, lay eggs. She takes *one* nuptial flight. That one stuns her with enough fertile power to be trapped in the hive forever. The workers—the sexually undeveloped females—have the best life. They have fields of flowers to roll in. Imagine turning over and over inside a rose." I can tell he's carried away with the idea. I'm getting interested myself.

"What do they eat inside the hive all winter?"

"Beebread."

"Beebread? Are you serious?"

"It's a mixture of pollen and honey. And the worker excretes gold wax from her stomach for the comb. Those neat hexagons!"

I try to imagine the size of a worker bee's intestinal system, how many times she must fly from the hive to the *tiglio* to make even a tablespoon of honey. A thousand times? A jar must represent a million flights of bees carrying a heavy cargo of honeydew, their legs sticky with pollen. In *The Georgics,* which is sort of an ancient farmer's almanac, Vergil writes that bees lift small stones to ballast themselves as they fly through boisterous east winds. He is wise on the subject of bees but not entirely to be trusted; he thought they would generate spontaneously from the decayed carcass of a cow. I like the image of a bee clutching a small stone, like a football player holding the ball to his chest as he barrels down the field. "Yes, I can see four hives painted green. I like the beekeeper's gear, that medieval-looking veil, lifting the dark combs—we could roll our own candles from the wax." Now I'm drawn into this idea.

But he stands up and leans out into the dizzying fragrance. Practicality has left him. "The wasps are anarchistic, whereas the bees . . ."

I gather up the coffee cups. "Maybe we should wait until the house is done."

✳

Figs reveal water. On the terraces they grow near the stone chutes we discovered. The natural well has webby roots crawling down into it from the fig above. I'm mixed on figs. The fleshy quality feels spooky. In Italian, *il fico*, fig, has a slangy turn into *la fica*, meaning vulva. Possibly because of the famous fig leaf exodus from Eden, it seems like the most ancient of fruits. Oddest, too—the fig flower is inside the fruit. To pull one open is to look into a complex, primitive, infinitely sophisticated life cycle tableau. Fig pollination takes place through an interaction with a particular kind of wasp about one eighth of an inch long. The female bores into the developing flower inside the fig. Once in, she delves with her oviposter, a curved needle nose, into the female flower's ovary, depositing her own eggs. If her oviposter can't reach the ovary (some of the flowers have long styles), she still fertilizes the fig flower with the pollen she collected from her travels. Either way, one half of this symbiotic system is served—the wasp larvae develop if she has left her eggs or the pollinated fig flower produces seed. If reincarnation is true, let me not come back as a fig wasp. If the female can't find a suitable nest for her eggs, she usually dies of exhaustion inside the fig. If she can, the wasps hatch inside the fig and all the males are born without wings. Their sole, brief function is sex. They get up and fertilize the females, then help them tunnel out of the fruit. Then they die. The females fly out, carrying enough sperm from the tryst to fertilize all their eggs. Is this appetizing, to know that however luscious figs taste, each one is actually a little graveyard of wingless male wasps? Or maybe the sensuality of the fruit comes from some flavor they dissolve into after short, sweet lives.

❋

The women in my family always have made bread and butter pickles and muscadine jellies and watermelon rind pickles and peach preserves and plum butters. I feel drawn to the scalding kettle, with a flat of rapidly softening raspberries leaking juice on the counter, to the syrupy clove-scented bowls of sweet peaches about to be poured into an astringent vinegar bath, to ring-finger-sized cucumbers. In California, I've cried over rubber sealing rings that turned to gum, over jams that wouldn't jam, over a cauldron of guavas that made two dozen jars of gray jelly instead of the clear exotic topaz I expected. I don't have the gene my mother had for laying-by rows of crimson and emerald jars of fruit preserves and the little pickled things called *sottaceto* (under vinegar) here. When I look at the product of a sweating afternoon, all I can think is "Botulism?"

This long-lost owner who placed the fruit trees on a terrace so they sweetly dangle over a grassy walk, she, I'm sure, had a shelf under the stairs for her confitures, and no qualms about breaking open her spicy plums on a January morning. Here, I think, I'll master the art my mother should have passed to me as easily as she passed her taste for hand-painted china and expensive shoes.

From the Saturday market I lug a box of prime

peaches downhill to the car. They are so beautiful all I really want to do is pile them in a basket and look at the delicious colors. In the one cookbook I have here so far, I find Elizabeth David's recipe for peach marmalade. Nothing could be simpler: The halved peaches simply are cooked with a little sugar and water, cooled, then cooked again the next day, until the preserves set when ladled onto a saucer. Elizabeth David notes, "This method makes a rather extravagant but very delicious preserve. Unfortunately it tends to form a skin of mold within a very short time, but this does not affect the rest of the jam, some of which I have kept for well over a year, even in a damp house." I'm a little bothered by this mold note, and she's vague about sterilizing jars and never mentions listening for the *whoosh* of the seal I heard as Mother's green tomato pickles cooled. I remember my mother tapping the tops to make sure the lid had sucked down. It sounds as though Elizabeth David just dishes it up into the jars then forgets it, scraping off mold with impunity before spreading some on her toast. Still, she says "rather extravagant but very delicious," and if Elizabeth David says that, I believe her. Since I have all these peaches, I decide to make seven pounds and just eat the rest. We'll use the preserves this summer before an unappetizing mold can form in this damp house. I'll give some to new friends, who will wonder why I'm not painting shutters instead of stirring fruit.

I drop the peaches into boiling water for a moment, watching the rosy colors intensify, then spoon them out and slide the skins off as easily as taking off a silk slip. This recipe is simple, not even a few drops of lemon juice or a grating of nutmeg or a clove or two. I remember my mother putting in a kernel from inside the peach pit, an almond-scented secret nut. Soon the kitchen fills with a fly-attracting sweetness. The next day, I boil the jars for good measure, while the fruit cooks down again, then spoon it in. I have five lovely jars of jam, peachy but not too sweet.

The *forno* in Cortona bakes a crusty bread in their wood oven, a perfect toast. Breakfast is one of my favorite times because the mornings are so fresh, with no hint of the heat to come. I get up early and take my toast and coffee out on the terrace for an hour with a book and the green-black rows of cypresses against the soft sky, the hills pleated with olive terraces that haven't changed since the seasons were depicted in medieval psalters. Sometimes the valley below is like a bowl filled up with fog. I can see hard green figs on two trees and pears on a tree just below me. A fine crop coming in. I forget my book. Pear cobbler, pear chutney, pear ice, green figs (would the wasps already be in green figs?) with pork, fig fritters, fig and *nocciolo* tart. May summer last a hundred years.

WHIR OF THE SUN

THE HOUSE, ONLY TWO KILOMETERS FROM TOWN, feels like a deep country place. We can't see any neighbors, although we hear the man way above us calling *vieni qua,* come here, to his dog. The summer sun hits like a religious conviction. I can tell time by where the sun strikes the house, as though it were a gigantic sundial. At five-thirty, the first rays smack the patio door, routing us out of bed and giving us the pleasure of dawn. At nine, a slab of sunlight falls into my study from the side window, my favorite window in the house for its framed view over the cypresses, the groves in the valley, and out into the Apennines. I want to paint a watercolor of it but my watercolors are awful, fit only to be stored on a closet shelf. By ten, the sun swings high over the front of the house and stays there until four, when a cut of shadow across the lawn signals that the sun is heading toward the other side of the mountain. If we walk to town that way in late afternoon, we see a prolonged, grandiose sunset over the Val di Chiana, lingering until it finally just dissolves, leaving enough streaked gold and saffron behind to light a way home until nine-thirty, when indigo dark sets in.

On moonless nights it is as black as inside an egg. Ed has gone back to Minnesota for his parents' fiftieth wedding anniversary. A shutter bangs; otherwise, the silence reverberates so strongly that I think I can hear my own blood circulating. I expect to lie awake, to imagine a drug-crazed intruder with an Uzi creeping up the stairs in the dark. Instead, in the wide bed with flowered sheets, I spread my books, cards, and notepaper around me and indulge in the rare act of writing letters to friends. A second indulgence goes straight back to high-school days—consuming a plate of brownies and a Coke while copying paragraphs and verses I like into my notebook. If only Sister, my black long-haired cat, were here. She is truly a good companion for solitude. It's far too hot for her to sleep against my feet, as she likes to do; she would have to stay on a pillow at the foot of the bed. I sleep like one newly born and in the morning have coffee on the patio, walk to town for groceries, work on the land, come in for water, and it is only ten o'clock. Hours go by without the need to speak.

After a few days, my life takes on its own rhythm. I wake up and read for an hour at three A.M.; I eat small snacks—a ripe tomato eaten like an apple—at eleven and three rather than lunch at one. At six I'm up, but by siesta time, the heat of the day, I'm ready for two hours in bed. Slumber sounds heavier than sleep, and with the hum of a small fan, it's slumber I fall into. At last, I have time to take a coverlet outside at night and lie on my back with the flashlight and the star chart. With the Big Dipper easily fixed right over the house, I finally locate Pollux in

Gemini and Procyon in Canis Minor. I forget the stars and here they are, so alive all along, pulsing and falling.

A French woman and her English husband walk up the driveway and introduce themselves as neighbors. They've heard Americans bought the place and are curious to meet those mad enough to take on this ordeal of restoration. They invite me to lunch the next day. Since both are writers and are restoring their small farmhouse, we fall into instant camaraderie. Should they have the staircase here or there, what to do with this tiny room, would a bedroom in the animal stall downstairs be too dark? The *comune* won't allow you to cut windows, even in almost airless farmhouses; exteriors must remain intact on historical property. They invite me to dinner the next night and introduce me to two other foreign writers, French and Asian-American. By the time Ed returns in a week, we're invited to the house of these writers.

The table is set under a shady grape arbor. Cold salads, cold wine, fruit, a grand cheese soufflé somehow steamed on top of the stove. Heat shimmers around the olive trees in the distance. On the stone patio, we're cool. We're introduced to the other guests: novelists, journalists, translators, a nonfiction writer—all older expatriates who've settled in these hills and restored properties. To live wholly in another country fascinates me. I'm curious how the trip or assignment to Italy turned into a lifetime for each of them and I ask Fenella, the international journalist, on my right, about this. "You can't imagine what Rome was in the fifties. Magic. I simply fell in love—like you fall in love with a person—and schemed to find a way to stay there. It wasn't easy. I got on as a stringer for Reuters. Look at the old movies and you'll see there were almost no cars. This was not long after the war and Italy was devastated, but the *life*! It was unbelievably cheap, too. Of course we didn't have much money but we lived in enormous apartments in grand *palazzi* for nothing. Every time I went back to America, I just couldn't wait to get back. It wasn't a rejection—or maybe it was. Anyway, I've never wanted to be anywhere else."

"We feel the same way," I say, and then realize that's not really the truth. I succumb totally to the "magic" of this place, but I know the appeal to me is partly the balance it restores to my life in America. I'm not about to leave there, even if I could. I try to amend what I've said. "My job at home is hard but I really love it—I'm pushed by it. And San Francisco is not home at the blood root, but it's a lucky, very beautiful place to live, earthquakes and all. Spending time here lets me escape the craziness and violence and downright surreal aspects of America, and my own overscheduled life. Three weeks after arrival, I realize I've let down some guard that is so instinctive to me, living in an American city, that I don't realize I have it." She looks at me with sympathy. At this point, the violence in America is hard for anyone to comprehend. "Literally, my pulse slows," I continue. "Even so, I sense that I can best develop my thinking there—it's my culture, my rough edge, my past." I'm not sure I've explained myself well. She raises her glass to me.

"*Esatto,* my daughter feels the same. You didn't come along in time to know Rome back then. It's terrible now. But then it was irresistible." I suddenly realize they're in double exile, from the United States and from Rome.

Max joins in. He had to go to Rome last week and the

traffic was horrendous, then the gypsies accosted him, as if he were a tourist, pressing their cardboard against him in an effort to distract him while they tried to pick his pocket. "Long ago, I learned to put the evil eye on them," he tells Ed and me. "They scatter then." They all agree, Italy is not what it used to be. What is? All my adult life I've heard how Silicon Valley used to be all orchards, how Atlanta used to be genteel, how publishing used to be run by gentlemen, how houses used to cost what a car costs now. All true, but what can you do but live now? Our friends who've recently bought a place in Rome are wild about the city. We love it. Maybe living with Bay Bridge traffic and San Francisco prices prepares us for anything.

One guest is a writer I have long admired. She moved here about twenty years ago, after living for years in the postwar wild south of Italy and then in Rome. I knew she lived here and even had been given her telephone number by a mutual acquaintance in Georgia, where she now spends a part of every year. Cold calls always have been hard for me to make and I am a little awed by the woman who wrote, in luminous, austere prose, about the dark, raucous, convoluted lives of women down in ravaged Basilicata.

Elizabeth is across the table and down from me. I see her cover her glass with her hand as Max starts to pour wine. "You know I never drink wine at lunch." Ah, the austerity. She wears a blue cotton shirt with some vaguely religious-looking medallion around her neck. She has a dead-level blue gaze, fair skin, and a voice I think has a touch of my own accent.

I lean forward and venture, "Is that a trace of a Southern accent?"

"I certainly hope not," she snaps—do I see a hint of a smile?—and quickly turns back to the famous translator beside her. I look down into my salad.

By the time Richard serves his lemon gelato made with mascarpone, the gathering is mellowing. Several empty wine bottles stand on a side table. The intense sun is now caught in the limbs of a chestnut. Ed and I join in where we can but this is a lively group of old friends with years of shared experiences. Fenella talks about her research trips to Bulgaria and Russia; her husband, Peter, tells a story about bringing a gray parrot in his coat pocket when he came back from an assignment in Africa. Cynthia talks about a family dispute over her famous mother's notebooks. Max makes us laugh over his unbelievable luck in sitting next to a film producer on a flight to New York, launching into a description of his script to this captive, who finally said to send him the script. Now the producer is coming to visit and has bought the option. Elizabeth looks bemused.

As the party breaks up she says, "You were supposed to call me. I've tried to get your number but there's no listing. Irby [a friend of my sister's] told me you've bought a house here. In fact, I met your sister at a dinner in Rome—Georgia, that is." I make excuses about the confusions of the house, then impulsively ask her to dinner on Sunday. Impulsively, because we don't have furniture, dishes, linen—only the rudimentary kitchen with a few pots and plates.

❋

I pick up a linen cloth at the market to cover the ram-shackle table left behind in the house, arrange wildflowers in a jar and place it in a flowerpot, plan dinner carefully but keep it simple: ravioli with sage and butter, sautéed chicken and *prosciutto* rolls, fresh vegetables and fruit. As Elizabeth arrives, Ed is moving the table out to the ter-race. The entire top and one leg fall off—either an ice-breaker or a disaster. She helps us piece the table together and Ed pounds in a few nails. Covered and set, it looks quite nice. We tour the big empty house and begin to talk drainpipes, wells, chimneys, whitewash. She com-pletely restored a noble *casa colonica* when she moved here. As a wall came down the first day, she found an angry sow left behind by the peasants. Quickly, it be-comes clear that she knows *everything* about Italy. Ed and I begin what is to become the ten thousand questions. Where do you get your water tested? How long was a Roman mile? Who's the best butcher? Can you buy old roof tiles? Is it better to apply for residency? She has been an intense observer of Italy since 1954 and knows an astonishing amount about the history, language, politics, as well as the telephone numbers of good plumbers, the name of a woman who prepares *gnocchi* with the lightest touch north of Rome. Long dinner under the moon, hoping the table won't keel over. Suddenly we have a friend.

Every morning, Elizabeth goes into town, buys a pa-per, and takes her espresso at the same café. I'm up early, too, and love to see the town come alive. I walk in with my Italian verb book, memorizing conjugations as I walk. Sometimes I take a book of poetry because walking suits poetry. I can read a few lines, savor or analyze them, read a few more, sometimes just repeat a few words of the poem; this meditative strolling seems to free the words. The rhythm of my walking matches the poet's cadence. Ed finds this eccentric, thinks I will be known as the weird American, so when I get to the town gate, I put away my book and concentrate on seeing Maria Rita arranging vegetables, the shopkeeper sweeping the street with one of those witch brooms made of twigs, the barber lighting his first smoke, leaning back in his chair with a tabby sleeping on his lap. Often I run into Elizabeth. Without plan, we begin to meet a morning or two a week.

✳

In town, too, Ed and I are beginning to feel more at home. We try to buy everything right in the local shops: hardware, electrical transformers, contact lens cleaner, mosquito candles, film. We do not patronize the cheaper supermarket in Camucia; we go from the bread store to the fruit and vegetable shop, to the butcher, loading everything into our blue canvas shopping bags. Maria Rita starts to go in back of her shop and bring out the just-picked lettuces, the choice fruit. "Oh, pay me tomorrow," she says if we only have large bills. In the post office, our letters are affixed with several stamps by the postmistress then individually hand-canceled with vengeance, *whack, whack, "Buon giorno, signori."* At the crowded little grocery store, I count thirty-seven kinds of dried pasta and, on the counter, fresh *gnocchi, pici,* thick pasta in long strands, fettuccine and two kinds of ravioli. By now they know what kind of bread we want, that we want the *bufala,* buffalo milk mozzarella, not the *normale,* regular cow's milk kind.

We buy another bed for my daughter's upcoming visit. Box springs don't exist here. The metal bed frame holds a base of woven wood on which the mattress rests. I thought of the slats in my spool bed when I was growing up, how the mattress, springs and all, collapsed when I jumped up and down on the bed. But this is securely made, the bed firm and comfortable. A very young woman with tousled black curls and black eyes sells old linens at the Saturday market. For Ashley's bed I find a heavy linen sheet with crocheted edges and big square pillowcases of lace and embroidery. Surely these accompanied a bride to her marriage. The condition is so good I wonder if she ever took them from her trunk. They have dusty lines where they've been folded, so I soak them in warm suds in the hip bath, then hang them out to dry in the midday sun, a natural strong bleach that turns them back to white.

Elizabeth has decided to sell her house and rent the former priest's wing attached to a thirteenth-century church called Santa Maria del Bagno, Saint Mary of the Baths. Although she won't move until winter, she begins to sort her belongings. Perhaps out of memory of that first dinner, she gives us an iron outdoor table and four curly chairs. Years ago, when she worked on a TV show about Moravia, he demanded a place to rest between shoots. She bought the set then. I give the "Moravia table" a fresh coat of that blackish green paint you see on park furniture in Paris. We also are the recipients of several bookcases and a couple of shopping bags full of books. The fourteenth-century hermits who lived on this mountain still might approve of our white rooms so far: beds, books, bookcases, a few chairs, a primitive table. Big willow baskets hold our clothes.

On the third Saturday of each month, a small antique market takes place in a piazza in the nearby castle town of Castiglione del Lago. We find a great sepia photograph of a group of bakers and a couple of chestnut coatracks. Mostly we browse around, astonished at the crazy prices on bad garage sale furniture. On the way home, we come upon an accident—someone in a tiny Fiat tried to pass on a curve—the Italian birthright—and rammed into a new Alfa Romeo. The upside-down Fiat still has one spinning wheel and two passengers are being extracted from the crumpled car. An ambulance siren blares. The smashed Alfa is standing, doors open, no passengers in the front seat. As we inch by, I see a dead boy, about eighteen, in the backseat. He is still upright in his seat belt but clearly is dead. Traffic stops us and we are two feet from his remote blue stare, the trickle of blood from the corner of his mouth. Very carefully, Ed drives us home. The next day, when we are back in Castiglione del Lago for a swim in the lake, we ask the waiter at the bar if the boy killed in the accident was local. "No, no, he was from Terontola." Terontola is all of five miles away.

*

We're expecting the permits soon. Meanwhile, the main project we hope to finish before we go home at the end of August is the sandblasting of the beams. Each room has two or three large beams and twenty-five or thirty small ones. A big job.

Ferragosto, August 15, is not just a holiday for the Virgin, it is a signal for work to cease and desist all over Italy both before and after that day. We underestimated the total effect of this holiday. When we began calling for a *sabbiatrice,* sandblaster, after the wall was finished, we found only one who would think of taking the job in August. He was to arrive on the first, the job to last three days. On the second we began to call and have been calling ever since. A woman who sounds very old shouts back that he is on *vacanze al mare,* he's over on the coast walking those sandy beaches instead of sandblasting our sticky beams. We wait, hoping he will appear.

Although we can't paint until after the central heating is installed, we begin to scrub down the walls in preparation. On Saturdays and odd days when they're not working elsewhere, the Poles come over to help us. The flaky whitewash brushes off on our clothes if we rub against it. As they clean the walls with wet cloths and sponges, they uncover the earlier paints, most prevalent a stark blue that must have been inspired by Mary's blue robes. Renaissance painters could get that rare color only from ground lapis lazuli brought from quarries in what is now Afghanistan. Faintly, we see a far-gone acanthus border around the top of the walls. The *contadina* bedroom used to be painted in foot-wide blue and white stripes. Two upstairs bedrooms were clear yellow, like the *giallorino* Renaissance painters favored, made from baked yellow glass, red lead, and sand from the banks of the Arno.

From the third floor, I hear Cristoforo calling Ed, then he calls me. He sound urgent, excited. He and Riccardo talk at once in Polish and point to the middle of the dining room wall. We see an arch, then he rubs his wet cloth around it and scumbles of blue appear, then a farmhouse, almond green feathery strokes of what may be a tree. They have uncovered a fresco! We grab buckets and sponges and start gently cleaning the walls. Every swipe reveals more: two people by a shore, water, distant hills. The same blue that's on the walls was used for the lake, a paler blue for sky and soft coral for clouds. The biscuit-colored houses are the same colors we see all around us. Vibrant when wet, the colors pale as they dry. An electrical line, buried at some point in the wall, mars a faux-framed classical scene of ruins in a panel over the door. We rub all afternoon. Water runs down our arms, sloshes on the floor. My arms feel like slack rubber bands. The lake scene continues on the adjoining wall and it is vaguely familiar, like the villages and landscape around Lake Trasimeno. The naive style reveals no newly discovered Giotto but it's charming. Someone didn't think so and whitewashed it. Luckily, they didn't use tougher paint. We will be able to live with this soft painting surrounding our dinners indoors.

✳

A hundred years may not be long enough to restore this house and land. Upstairs I rub the windows with vinegar, shining the green scallop of the hills along the sky. I spot Ed on the third terrace, waving a long spinning blade. He's wearing red shorts as bright as a banner, black boots against the locust thorns, and a clear visor to shield his eyes from flying rocks. He could be a powerful angel, coming to announce a late annunciation, but he is only the newest in an endless line of mortals who've worked to keep this farm from sliding back into the steep slope it once was, perhaps long before the Etruscans, when Tuscany was a solid forest.

The ugly whine of the weed machine drowns out the whinnies of the two white horses across the road and the multicultural birds that wake us up every morning. But the dry weeds must be cut in case of fire, so he works in the fiery sun without his shirt. Each day his skin darkens. We've learned the gravity of the hillside, the quick springs pulling down dirt and the thrust of the stone walls which must be sluices and must push back harder than the downward pull of the soil. He bends and slings olive prunings to a stack he's building for fires on cool nights. What a body of work this place is. Olive burns hot. The ashes then are returned to the trees for fertilizer. Like the pig, the olive is useful in every part.

The old glass sags in places—strange that glass which looks so solid retains a slow liquidity—distorting the sharp clarity of the view into watery Impressionism. Usually, if I am polishing silver, ironing, vacuuming at home, I am highly conscious that I am "wasting time," I should be doing something more important—memos, class preparation, papers, writing. My job at the university is all-consuming. Housework becomes a nuisance. My houseplants know it's feast or famine. Why am I humming as I wash windows—one of the top ten dreaded chores? Now I am planning a vast garden. My list includes sewing! At least a fine handkerchief linen curtain to go over the glass bathroom door. This house, every brick and lock, will be as known to me as my own or the loved one's body.

Restoration. I like the word. The house, the land, perhaps ourselves. But restored to what? Our lives are full. It's our zeal for all this work that amazes me. Is it only that once into the project, what it all means doesn't come up? Or that excitement and belief reject questions? The vast wheel has a place for our shoulders and we simply push into the turning? But I know there's a taproot as forceful as that giant root wrapped around the stone.

I remember dreaming over Bachelard's *The Poetics of Space,* which I don't have with me, only a few sentences copied into a notebook. He wrote about the house as a "tool for analysis" of the human soul. By remembering rooms in houses we've lived in, we learn to abide (nice word) within ourselves. I felt close to his sense of the house. He wrote about the strange whir of the sun as it comes into a room in which one is alone. Mainly, I remember recognizing his idea that the house protects the dreamer; the houses that are important to us are the ones that allow us to dream in peace. Guests we've had stop in for a night or two all come down the first morning, ready to tell their dreams. Often the dreams are way-back father or mother dreams. "I was in this car and my father was driving, only I was the age I am now and my father died when I was twelve. He was driving fast . . . ." Our guests fall into long sleeps, just as we do when we arrive each time. This is the only place in the world I've ever taken a nap at nine in the morning. Could this be what Bachelard meant by the "repose derived from all deep oneiric experience"? After a week or so, I have the energy of a twelve-year-old. For me, *house,* set in its landscape, always has been crypto-primo image land. Bachelard pushed me to realize that the houses we experience deeply take us back to the *first* house. In my mind, however, it's not just to the first house, but to the first concept of self. Southerners have a gene, as yet undetected in the DNA spirals, that causes them to believe that place is fate. Where you are is who you are. The further inside you the place moves, the more your identity is intertwined with it. Never casual, the choice of place is the choice of something you crave.

An early memory: Mine is a small room with six windows, all open on a summer night. I'm three or four, awake after everyone has gone to bed. I'm leaning on the windowsill looking out at the blue hydrangeas, big as beach balls. The attic fan pulls in the scent of tea olive and lifts the thin white curtains. I'm playing with the screen latch, which suddenly comes undone. I remember the feel of the metal hook and the eye I almost can stick my little finger into. Next, I'm climbing up on the sill and jumping out the window. I find myself in the dark backyard. I start running, feeling a quick rush of what I now know as freedom. Wet grass, glow of white camellias on the black bush, the new pine just my height. I go out to my swing in the pecan tree. I've just learned to pump. How high? I run around the house, all the rooms of my sleeping family, then I stand in the middle of the street I am not allowed to cross. I let myself in the back door, which never was locked, and into my room.

That pure surge of pleasure, flash flood of joy—to find the electric jolt of the outside place that corresponds to the inside—that's it.

In San Francisco, I go out on the flower-filled tiny back deck of my flat and look three stories down at the ground—a city-sized terrace surrounded with attractive low-maintenance flower beds on a drip system, cared for by a gardener. It does not lure me. That the jasmine on the high fences has climbed to my third floor and blooms profusely around the stair railing, I am thankful for. At night after work, I can step out to water my pots and watch for stars and find the tumbling vines sending out their dense perfume. Such flowers—jasmine, honeysuckle, gardenia—spell South, metabolic home, to my psyche. A fragmental connection though—my feet are three stories off the earth. When I leave my house, concrete separates my feet from the ground. The people who have bought the flats on the first and second floors are friends. We have meetings to discuss when to repair the steps or when to paint. I look into or onto the tops of trees, wonderful trees. My house backs onto the very private gardens unhinted at by the joined fronts of Victorian houses in my neighborhood. The center of the block is green. If all of us took down our fences, we could wander in a blooming green sward. Because I like my flat so much, I didn't know what I missed.

Was there really a *nonna,* a presiding spirit who centered this house? This three-story house rooted to the ground restores some levels in my waking and sleeping hours. Or is it the house? A glimmer: *Choice* is restorative when it reaches toward an instinctive recognition of the earliest self. As Dante recognized at the beginning of *The Inferno:* What must we do in order to grow?

At home I dream of former houses I've lived in, of finding rooms I didn't know were there. Many friends have told me that they, too, have this dream. I climb the stairs to the attic of the eighteenth-century house I loved living in for three years in Somers, New York, and there are three new rooms. In one, I find a dormant geranium, which I take downstairs and water. Immediately, Disney-style, it leafs and breaks into wild bloom. In house after house (my best friend's in high school, my childhood home, my father's childhood home), I open a door and there is more than I knew. All the lights are on in the New York house. I am walking by, seeing the life in every window. I never dream of the boxy apartment I lived in at Princeton. Nor do I dream of my flat I am so fond of in San Francisco—but perhaps that is because I can hear from my bed before I fall asleep foghorns out on the bay. Those deep voices displace dreams, calling from spirit to spirit, to some underlying voice we all have but don't know how to use.

In Vicchio, a house I rented a few summers ago brought the recurrent dream to reality. It was a huge house with a caretaker in a side wing. One day I opened what I'd assumed was a closet in an unused bedroom and found a long stone corridor with empty rooms on either side. White doves flew in and out. It was the second floor of the housekeeper's wing and I hadn't realized it was uninhabited. In many waking moments since, I've opened the door to the stony light of that hallway, oblong panels of sunlight on the floor, caught a glimpse and flutter of white wings.

Here, I am restored to the basic pleasure of connection to the outdoors. The windows are open to butterflies, horseflies, bees, or anything that wants to come in one window and out another. We eat outside almost every meal. I'm restored to my mother's sense of preserving the seasons and to *time,* even time to take pleasure in polishing a pane of glass to a shine. To the house safe for dreaming. One end of the house is built right against the hillside. An omen of reconnection? Here, I don't dream of houses. Here, I am free to dream of rivers.

✸

Though the days are long, the summer is somehow short. My daughter, Ashley, arrives and we have mad, hot days driving around to sights. When she first walked up to the house, she stopped and looked up for a while, then said, "How strange—this will become a part of all our memories." I recognized that knowledge we sometimes get in advance when travelling or moving to a new city—here's a place that will have its way with me.

Naturally, I want her to love it but I don't have to convince her. She begins talking about Christmas here. She chooses her room. "Do you have a pasta machine?" "Can we have melon every meal?" "A swimming pool could go up on that second terrace." "Where's the train schedule to Florence? I need shoes."

The minute she graduated from college, she lit out for New York. The artist's life, the odd-job life, the long hot summer, health problems—she's ready for the icy mountain-fed pool run by a priest back in the hills, for trips to the Tyrrhenian coast, where we rent beach chairs and bake all day, for strolls in stony hill towns at night after dinner in a strictly local *trattoria*.

The days stream by and soon it is time for both of us to leave. I must be at work but Ed will stay another ten days. Maybe the sandblaster will come.

FESTINA TARDE
(MAKE HASTE SLOWLY)

WALKING OUT OF THE SAN FRANCISCO AIRPORT, I'm shocked by cool foggy air, smelling of salt and jet fumes. A taxi driver crosses the street to help with luggage. After a few pleasantries, we lapse into silence and I'm grateful. I have been travelling for twenty-four hours. The last leg, from JFK, where Ashley and I said good-bye, to SF seems cruel and unusual, especially the extra hour it takes because of the prevailing wind. The houses on the hills are necklaces of light, then along the right, the bay almost laps the freeway. I watch for a certain curve coming up. After rounding it, suddenly the whole city rises, the stark white skyline. As we drive in, I anticipate the breath-stopping plunges over hills and glimpses between buildings where I know there's a wedge or slice or expanse of rough blue water.

Still, imprinted on my eyes are the stone towns, mown fields, and sweeping hills covered with vineyards, olives, sunflowers; this landscape looks exotic. I start to look for my house key, which I thought was in the zippered inside pocket of my bag. If I've lost it—what? Two friends and a neighbor have keys to my place. I imagine getting their answering machines, "I'm out of town until Friday . . ." We pass Victorian houses discreetly shuttered and curtained, porch lights shining on wooden banisters and pots of topiary. No one, not even a dog walker or someone running to the store for milk, is out. I feel a pang for the towns full of people who leave their keys dangling in their locks, for the evening *passeggiata* when everyone is out and about, visiting, shopping, taking a quick espresso. I've left Ed there because his university starts later than mine and the sandblasting still is a dream of accomplishment for the summer. The taxi lets me out and speeds off. My house looks the same; the climbing rose has grown and tried to wind around the columns. Finally I find the key mixed in with my Italian change. Sister comes to greet me with a plaintive meow and a quick brush of her sides against my ankles. I pick her up to smell her earthy, damp leaf smell. In Italy, I often wake up thinking she has leapt on the bed. She jumps on top of my bag and curls down for a nap. So much for having suffered in my absence.

Lamps, rugs, chests, quilts, paintings, tables—how amazingly comfortable and cluttered this looks after the empty house seven thousand miles away. Bookshelves, crammed, the glass kitchen cabinets lined with colorful dishes, pitchers, platters—so much of everything. The long hall carpet—so soft! Could I walk out of here and never look back? Virginia Woolf, I remember, lived in the country during the war. She rushed back to her neighborhood in London after a bombing and found her house in ruins. She expected to be devastated but instead felt a strange elation. Doubtless, I would not. When the earth quaked, I was shaken for days over my whiplashed chimney, broken vases, and wineglasses. It's just that my feet are used to the cool *cotto* floors, my eyes to bare white walls. I'm still *there,* partly here.

There are eleven messages on the answering machine. "Are you back?" I need to get your signature on my graduation form . . ." "Calling to confirm your appointment . . ." The housesitter has left a list of other calls on a pad and stacked the mail in my study. Three kneehigh stacks, mostly junk, which I compulsively begin to go through.

Because I have stayed away as long as possible, I must return to the university immediately. Classes begin in four days, and regardless of faxes from Italy and the good offices of an excellent secretary, I am chair of the department and need to be bodily present. By nine, I'm there, dressed in gabardine pants, a silk print blouse. "How was your summer?" we all say to one another. The start-up of a school year always feels exhilarating. Everyone feels the zest in the air. If the bookstore were not crowded with students buying texts, I probably would go over and buy a supply of fine-point pens, a notebook with five-subject index, and a few pads. Instead, I sign forms, memos, call a dozen people. I go into racing gear, ignoring jet lag.

Stopping for groceries after work, I see that the organic store has added a masseuse to the staff. I could pause in a little booth and get a seven-minute massage to relax me before I begin selecting potatoes. I'm temporarily overwhelmed by the checkout rows, the aisles and aisles of bright produce and the tempting cakes at the new bakery just installed in the front of the store. Mustard, mayonnaise, plastic wrap, baking chocolate—I buy things

I haven't seen all summer. The deli has crab cakes and stuffed baked potatoes with chives, and corn salad and tabouli. So much! I buy enough "gourmet takeout" for two days. I'm going to be too busy to cook.

It's eight A.M. at Bramasole. Ed probably is chopping weeds around an olive tree or pacing around waiting for the sandblaster. As I turn in my garage I see Evit, the one-toothed homeless man, rifling through our recycle bin for bottles and cans. My neighbor has posted a VISUALIZE BEING TOWED sign on his garage door.

The last message on the machine starts with static, then I hear Ed's voice; he sounds raspy. "I was hoping to catch you, sweetheart; are you *still* at work? The sandblaster was here when I got home from the airport." Long pause. "It's hard to describe. The noise is deafening. He's got this huge generator and the sand really does *blast* out and fall into every crack. It's like a storm in the Sahara. He did three rooms yesterday. You can't believe how much sand is on the floors. I took all the furniture out on the patio and I'm just camped in one room, but the sand is *all* over the house. The beams look *very good;* they're chestnut, except for one elm. I don't know *how* I'm going to get rid of this sand. It's in my *ears* and I'm not even in the room with him. Sweeping is out of the question. I *wish* you were here." He usually doesn't speak with so many italics.

When he calls next, he's on the *autostrada* near Florence, en route to Nice and home. He sounds exhausted and elated. The permits have come through! The blasting is over. Primo Bianchi, however, won't be able to do our work because he must have a stomach operation. Ed met again with Benito, the yellow-eyed Mussolini look-alike, and has worked out a contract with him. Work is to start immediately and to finish in early November, easily in time for Christmas. The clean-up goes slowly; the sand-blaster says to expect sand to trickle down for five years!

Ian, who helped us with the purchase, will oversee the work. We left diagrams of where electrical outlets, switches, and radiators should go, how the bathroom should be laid out, how the kitchen should be installed—even the height of the sink and the distance between the sink and the faucet—where to pick up the fixtures and tile we selected for the bathroom, everything we can think of. We are anxious for word that work is under way.

The first fax arrives September 15; Benito has broken his leg on the first day of the job and start-up will be delayed until he is able to walk.

✳

Festina tarde was a Renaissance concept: Make haste slowly. Often it was represented by a snake with its tail in its mouth, by a dolphin entwined with an anchor, or by the figure of a seated woman holding wings in one hand and a tortoise in the other: The great wall of Bramasole in one, the central heating, kitchen, patio, and bathroom in the other. The second fax, October 12, warns that "delays have occurred" and that "some changes in installation can be expected" but he has full confidence and not to worry.

We fax back our encouragement and ask that everything be covered well with plastic and taped.

Another fax, just after, says the opening of the three-foot-thick wall between the kitchen and dining room has begun. Two days later, Ian faxes us the news that when a very large boulder was pulled out, the whole house creaked and all the workers ran out because they feared a collapse.

We called. Didn't they brace the rooms? Had Benito used steel? Why hadn't they known what to do? How could this happen? Ian said stone houses were unpredictable and couldn't be expected to react the way American houses react and the door is now in and looks fine, although they didn't make it as wide as we wanted because they were afraid to. I vacillated between thinking that the workers were incompetent and fearing that they might have been crushed by an unstable house.

By mid-November, Benito has finished the upstairs patio and the opening of the infamous door, plus they've opened the two upstairs doors that connect to the *contadina* apartment. We decide to cancel the opening of the other large door that would join the living room to the *contadina* kitchen. The image of all Benito's men fleeing the premises does not inspire confidence. The next delays Ian mentions concern the new bath and the central heating. "Almost certainly," he advises, "there will be no heat when you come for Christmas. In fact, the house will not be habitable due to the fact that the central heating pipes must be inside the house, not on the back as we were originally told." Benito asks him to relay that his charges are higher than anticipated. Items listed on the contract have been farmed out to electricians and plumbers and their overlapping bills have become incomprehensible. We have no way of knowing who did what; Ian seems as confused as we are. Money we wire over takes too long to get there and Benito is angry. What is clear is that we are not there and our house's work is done between other jobs.

*

Hoping for miracles, we go to Italy for Christmas. Elizabeth has offered us her house in Cortona, which is partly packed for her move. She also wants to give us a great deal of her furniture, since her new house is smaller. As we drive out of the Rome airport, rain hits the windshield like a hose turned on full blast. All the way north we face foggier and foggier weather. When we arrive in Camucia, we head straight to the bar for hot chocolate before we go to Elizabeth's. We decide to unpack, have lunch, and face Bramasole later.

The house is a wreck. Canals for the heating pipes have been cut into the inside walls of every room in the house. The workers have left rock and rubble in piles all over the unprotected floors. The plastic we'd requested was simply tossed over the furniture so every book, chair, dish, bed, towel, and receipt in the house is covered in dirt. The jagged, deep, floor-to-ceiling cuts in the wall look like open wounds. They are just beginning on the new bathroom, laying cement on the floor. The plaster in the new kitchen already is cracking. The great long sink has been installed and looks wonderful. A workman has scrawled in black felt-tip pen a telephone number on the dining room fresco. Ed immediately wets a rag and tries to rub it clean but we're stuck with the plumber's number. He slings the rag onto the rubble. They've left windows open all over and puddles have collected on the floor from this morning's rain. The carelessness apparent everywhere, such as the telephone being completely buried, makes me so angry I have to walk outside and take gulps of cold air. Benito is at another job. One of his men sees that we are extremely upset and tries to say that all will be done soon, and done well. He is working on the opening between the new kitchen and the cantina. He's shy but seems concerned. A beautiful house, beautiful position. All will be well. His bleary old blue eyes look at us sadly. Benito arrives full of bluster. No time to clean up before we arrived, and anyway it's the plumber's responsibility, he has been held up himself because the plumber didn't come when he said he would. But everything is *perfetto, signori.* He'll take care of the cracked plaster; it didn't dry properly because of the rains. We hardly answer. As he gestures, I catch the worker looking at me. Behind Benito's back he makes a strange gesture; he nods toward Benito, then pulls down his eyelid.

The upstairs patio seems perfect. They've laid rose-colored brick and reattached the rusty iron railings so that the patio is secure but still looks old. Something was done well.

By four, twilight begins; by five, it's night. Still, the stores are opening after siesta. A morning of work, siesta, reopening at dark for several hours: the winter rhythm unchanged from the massively hot summer days. We stop by and greet Signor Martini. We're cheered to see him, knowing he'll say, *"Boh,"* and *"Anche troppo,"* one of his all-purpose responses that means yes, it's too bloody much. In our bad Italian we explain what's going on. As we start to go, I remember the strange gesture. "What does this mean?" I ask, pulling down my eyelid.

"Furbo," cunning, watch out, he answers. "Who's *furbo?"*

"Apparently our contractor."

✳

Warm house. Thank you, Elizabeth. We buy red candles, cut pine boughs and bring them in for some semblance of Christmas. Our hearts are not into cooking, although all the winter ingredients in the shops almost lure us to the kitchen. We love the furniture Elizabeth has given us. Besides twin beds, coffee table, two desks, and lamps, we'll have an antique *madia,* whose top part was used to knead bread and let it rise. Beneath the coffin-shaped bread holder are drawers and cabinet. The chestnut's warm patina makes me rub my hand over the wood. On the list she's left for us, we find her immense *armadio,* large enough to hold all the house linens, a dining room table, antique chests, a *cassone* (tall storage chest), two peasant chairs, and wonderful plates and serving pieces. Suddenly we will live in a furnished house. With all our rooms, there will be plenty of space, still, for acquiring our own treasures. Amid all the restoration horrors, this great act of generosity warms us tremendously. Right now, the pieces seem to belong to her orderly house, but before we leave we must move everything over to the house full of debris.

As Christmas nears, work slows then stops. We had not anticipated that they would take off so many holidays. New Year's has several holidays attached to it. We'd never heard of Santo Stefano, who merits one day off. Francesco Falco, who has worked for Elizabeth for twenty years, brings his son Giorgio and his son-in-law with a truck. They take apart the *armadio,* load everything into the truck except the desk, which is too wide to exit the study. Elizabeth has written all her books at that desk and it seems that it was not meant to leave the house. I'm taking boxes of dishes to our car when I look up and see them lowering a desk by rope out the second-floor window. Everyone applauds as it gently lands on the ground.

At the house, we cram all the furniture into two rooms we've shoveled out and swept. We cover everything with plastic and shut the doors.

There is absolutely nothing we can do. Benito does not answer our calls. I have a sore throat. We've bought no presents. Ed has grown silent. My daughter, sick with flu in New York, is spending her first Christmas alone because the construction debacle threw off her plans to come to Italy. I stare for a long time at an ad for the Bahamas in a magazine, the totally expected photo of a crescent of sugar-sand beach along clear, azure water. Someone, somewhere, drifts on a yellow striped float, trailing her fingers in a warm current and dreaming under the sun.

On Christmas Eve we have pasta with wild mushrooms, veal, an excellent Chianti. Only one other person is in the restaurant, for *Natale* is above all a family time. He wears a brown suit and sits very straight. I see him slowly drink wine along with his food, pouring out half glasses for himself, sniffing the wine as though it were a great vintage instead of the house carafe. He proceeds through his courses with care. We're through; it's only nine-thirty. We'll go back to Elizabeth's, build a fire, and share the *moscato* dessert wine and cake I bought this afternoon. While Ed waits for coffee, our dinner partner is served a plate of cheese and a bowl of walnuts. The restaurant is silent. He cracks a shell. He cuts a bit of cheese, savors it, eats a walnut, then cracks another. I want to put my head down on the white cloth and weep.

*

According to Ian, the work finished satisfactorily at the end of February. We paid for the amount contracted but not for the exorbitant extra amount Benito tacked on. He listed such charges as a thousand dollars for hanging a door. We will have to be there to determine exactly what extra work he did. How we'll settle the final amount is a mystery.

In late April, Ed returns to Italy. He has the spring quarter off. His plan is to clear the land and treat, stain, and wax all the beams in the house before I arrive on June first. Then we will clean, paint all rooms and windows, and restore the floors to the condition they were in before Benito's restoration. The new kitchen has in it only the sink, dishwasher, stove, and fridge. Instead of cabinets, we plan to make plastered brick columns with wide plank shelves and have marble cut for countertops. We have a major incentive: At the end of June, my friend Susan has planned to be married in Cortona. When I asked why she wanted her wedding in Italy, she replied cryptically, "I want to get married in a language I don't understand." The guests will stay with us and the wedding will take place at the twelfth-century town hall.

Ed tells me he's confined to the room on the second floor that opens onto the patio, his little haven amid the rubbish. He cleans one bathroom, unpacks a few pots and dishes, and sets up rudimentary housekeeping. Benito hauled several loads out of the house but only made it as far as the driveway, now a dump. On the front terrace he left a small mountain of stone that was taken out of the wall. The patio and bedroom brick form another small mountain. Even so, Ed is elated. They're gone! The new bathroom, with its foot square tiles, *belle époque* pedestal sink, and built-in tub, feels large and luxurious, a stark contrast to the former bucket-flush bathroom. Spring is astonishingly green and thousands of naturalized irises and daffodils bloom in long grass all over our land. He finds a seasonal creek pouring over mossy rocks where two box turtles sun themselves. The almond and fruit trees are so outrageously beautiful that he has to tear himself away from working outside.

We try not to call; we tend to get into long conversations, then decide that we could have done x at the house for the money the call has cost. But there is a great need to recount what you've done when you're working on a house. Someone needs to hear that the beams look really great after their final waxing, that your neck is killing you from working above your head all day, that you're on the fourth room. He relates that each room takes forty hours: beams, ceiling, walls. Floors will come last. Seven to seven, seven days a week.

Finally, finally, June—I can go. With all the work Ed has described, I expect the house to glow when I arrive. But, naturally enough, Ed has concentrated on telling me his progress.

When I first arrive, it's hard to focus on how far he has come. The beams look beautiful, yes. But the grounds are full of rubbish, plaster, the old cistern. The electrician has not shown up. Six rooms haven't been touched. All the furniture is piled into three rooms. It's strictly a war zone. I try not to show how horrified I am.

I'm ready for r & r. Unfortunate, because there's nothing to do but launch into this work. We have about three weeks to get ready for our first major onslaught of guests. The wedding! It seems ludicrous that anyone could stay here.

Ed is 6'2". I am 5'4". He takes the ceiling I take the floor. Biology is destiny—but which is better? He actually loves finishing the beams. Painting the brick ceiling is less fun but is rewarding. Suddenly the gunky beams and flaking ceiling are transformed into dark substantial beams, pristine white-brick ceiling. The room is defined. Painting goes quickly with the big brushes made of wild boar hair. Pure white walls—white on plaster is whiter than any other white. As each room is finished, my job is to paint the *battiscopa,* a six-inch-high gray strip along the bases of the walls, a kind of pseudo-moulding that is traditional in old houses of this area. Usually it's a brick color but we prefer the lighter touch. The word means broom-hit. The darker paint doesn't show the marks of the mops and brooms that must constantly pass over these floors. Almost upside down, I measure six inches in several places, tape the floor and wall, then quickly paint and pull off the tape. Naturally, the tape pulls off some white paint, which then has to be retouched. Twelve rooms, four walls each, plus the stairwell, landings, and entrance. We're leaving the stone cantina as is. Next, I decalcify the floor. The first step is to sweep up all the large chunks and dirt, then vacuum. With a special solution I spread, the residue from dirt, plaster, and paint drippings is dissolved. After that, I rinse the floor with a wet mop three times, the middle time with a mild soap solution. I'm on my knees. Next: mop again with water and a little muriatic acid. Rinse, then paint the floor with linseed oil, letting it soak in and dry. After it dries for two days, I wax. On the floor again, char style. My knees, totally unused to this, rebel and I suppress groans when I stand up. Last step: buff with soft cloth. The floors come back, rich and dark and shiny. Each room pops into place, looking very much as they did when we bought the house, only now the beams are right and the radiators are in place. *"Brutto,"* ugly, I said to the plumber when I saw them. "Yes," he replied, "but beautiful in winter."

As Ed told me, seven to seven: seven days a week. We spread the rubble down the driveway, which is chewed up anyway from all the trucks. We dig in the larger stones and bricks, spread grass cuttings on top. Gradually, it will settle in. We hire someone to take away a truckload that Benito failed to haul. On a walk a few days later, we see a pile of awful rubble dumped along a road about a mile from our house, and to our horror, spot our plaster with the madonna blue coat of paint underneath.

From high school through graduate school, Ed worked as a house mover, busboy, cabinetmaker, refrigerator hauler. A friend calls him "the muscular poet." He's thriving on this work, though he, too, is sapped at night. I never have done manual labor, except spurts of refinishing furniture, pruning, painting, and wallpapering. This is an order of bodily exertion to shock my system. Everything aches. What *is* water on the knee? I think I may get it. I die at night. In the mornings, we both have surges of new energy that come from somewhere. We plug right back in. We're consumed. I'm amazed: the relentlessness we've developed. I never will feel the same toward workers again; they should be paid fortunes.

When I seal the patio bricks with linseed oil, the sun feels especially deadly. I'm determined to finish and keep working until I start to reel with the fumes and the heat. Now and then I stand up and breathe in great draughts of the honeysuckle we've planted in an enormous pot, stare off into the great view, then dip the brush into the pot again. Who would think to ask, when paying a lot for a new patio, whether the job included finishing the brick's surface? It never occurred to either of us that we would have to treat the kitchen and patio bricks to several coats of this gloppy stuff.

After we clean up late in the day, we walk around assessing what's left, how we've done. We will not have any children together but decide that this is the equivalent of having triplets. As each room is finished, we get to bring in the furniture for it. Gradually, rooms are set up, still spare but basically furnished. I've brought over white bedspreads for the twin beds. We take a morning in Arezzo and buy a few lamps from a place that still makes the traditional majolica vases of the area into lamps. A fabulous feeling—things are shaping up, they're done, it's clean, we'll be warm in winter—we've done it! This feels giddy and fuels us to keep going.

A week before the wedding, our friends Shera and Kevin arrive from California. We see them get off the train way down the track. Kevin is maneuvering something enormous that looks like a coffin for two. His bicycle! We keep working while they go to Florence, Assisi, and on the Piero della Francesca trail. At night we make great meals together and they tell us all the wonders they've seen and we tell them about the new faucet we want to install for the hip bath. They fall instantly in love with the whole area and seem to want to hear our daily saga of cleaning the new bricks on the kitchen floor. When they're not travelling, Kevin is off on long bicycle trips. Shera, an artist, is captive here. She is painting milky blue half circles over the windows in a bedroom. We've picked a star from one of Giotto's paintings and she makes a stencil of it and fills the half domes with gold leaf stars. A few stars "fall" out of the dome and onto the white walls. We're preparing the bridal chamber. At an antique shop near Perugia, I buy two colored prints of the constellations with mythological beasts and figures. At the Cortona market, I find pretty linen and cotton sheets in pale blue with cutwork in white. We're preparing, too, for our first houseparty. We buy twenty wineglasses, linen tablecloths, pans for baking the wedding cake, a case of wine.

There is no way everything can be finished in time for the wedding (or ever?), but we manage an extraordinary amount. The day before everyone arrives, Kevin comes downstairs and asks, "Why does the toilet steam? Is there something peculiar about Italian toilets?" Ed brings in the ladder, climbs up to the wall-mounted tank, and dips in his hand. Hot water. We check the other bathrooms. The new one is O.K. but the other old one also has hot water. We hardly have used those bathrooms and had not let water run long enough for the hot water to arrive, so we had not noticed that neither bathroom had cold water at all. As soon as guests started using the baths, it became noticeable. Shera says she thought the shower was awfully hot, once it finally warmed up, but hadn't wanted to complain. The plumber cannot come for a few days, so we will go through the wedding with quick showers and smoking toilets!

The front terrace is still rough but we have potted geraniums along the wall to distract from the torn-up ground. At least we removed the rubble. Four rooms have beds. Susan's two cousins from England and Cole's brother and sister-in-law are arriving. Shera and Kevin will move to a hotel in town for a couple of days. Other friends are coming from Vermont.

By day, we are twelve in the house. Many hands to help with drinks and lunch. The cake must be improvised because the oven is small. I envisioned three tiers of sponge cake with a hazelnut butter-cream frosting, to be served with whipped cream and cherries steeped in sugared wine. We couldn't find a large pan for the bottom and finally bought a tin dog dish to bake it in. The cake is lovely, if a bit lopsided. We decorate it with flowers all around. Everyone is running off in different directions sightseeing and shopping.

We're having the prenuptial dinner here on a clear warm night, everyone in pale linens and cottons. Many photos are taken of us arm in arm on the steps and leaning over the balcony. Susan's cousin brings out champagne he has brought from France. After drinks with *bruschette* and dry olives, we start with cool fennel soup. I've made a rustic casserole of chicken, white beans, sausage, tomatoes, and onions. There are tiny green beans, baskets of bread, and a salad of arugula, radicchio, and chicory. Everyone tells wedding stories. Mark was to have married a Colorado girl who ran away on the wedding day and married someone else in a week. Karen was a bridesmaid on a boat wedding and the bride's mother, in teal chiffon, tipped into the drink. When I married at twenty-two, I wanted a midnight wedding with everyone wearing robes and carrying candles. The minister said absolutely not, that midnight was a "furtive hour." Nine was as late as he'd go. And instead of a robe, I wore my sister's wedding dress and carried a leatherbound Keats down the aisle. My mother pulled my skirt and I leaned over for her words of wisdom. She whispered, "It won't last six months." But she was wrong.

We should have an accordion player, à la Fellini, and maybe a white horse for the bride to ride, but we do well with the fabulous night, and the CD player inspires a little dancing in the dining room. The white peach tart with pine nuts should end this dinner but Ed's description of the *crema* and the hazelnut *gelati* in town sends everyone to the cars. They're amazed that such a small town is still hopping at eleven, everyone outdoors with coffee, ice cream, or perhaps an *amaro,* an after-dinner bitter. Babies in strollers still as wide-eyed as their parents, teenagers sitting on the town hall steps. The only thing sleeping is a cat on top of the police car.

The morning of the wedding Susan, Shera, and I pick a bouquet of lavender, pink, and yellow wildflowers for Susan to carry. When we're all dressed in silks and suits, we walk into town over the Roman road. Ed carries our good shoes in a shopping bag. Susan has brought Chinese painted paper parasols for everyone because of the midday sun. We walk through town and up the steps of the twelfth-century town hall. It's a dark, high-ceilinged room with tapestries and frescoes and high judicial-look-ing chairs, an impressive room to sign a treaty in. The city of Cortona has sent red roses and Ed has arranged for Bar Sport to come over right after the ceremony with cold *prosecco*. Susan's cousin Brian runs all around with his video camera, getting shots from every angle. After the brief ceremony, we cross the piazza to La Logetta for a Tuscan feast beginning with a selection of typical *antipasti: crostini,* little rounds of bread topped with olives, peppers, mushroom, or chicken liver; *prosciutto e melone,* fried olives stuffed with *pancetta* and spicy bread crumbs; and the local *finocchiona,* a salami studded with fennel seeds. Next they bring out a selection of *primi,* first courses to try, including ravioli with butter and sage, and *gnocchi di patate,* little "knuckles" of potato served here with pesto. Course after course arrives, culminating in platters of roast lamb and veal and the famous grilled Val di Chiana steak. Karen notices the grand piano in the corner under a massive vase of flowers and prevails upon Cole, who is a pianist, to play. Ed is at the other end of the table but he catches my eye as Cole begins Scarlatti. Three weeks ago this was a dream, a long shot, a frightening prospect. "Cheers!" the English cousins call out.

Back at home, we're all stunned by the food and heat and decide to postpone the wedding cake until late afternoon. I hear someone snoring. In fact, I hear two people snoring.

Though the cake lacks that professional touch, it may be the best cake I ever tasted. I'll credit our tree for the nuts. Shera and Kevin are dancing in the dining room again. Others stroll out to the point where our land ends for the view of the lake and valley. We can't decide whether to eat again or forget it. Finally we run down to Camucia for pizza. Our favorite places are closed, so we end up in a definitely downscale, unatmospheric place. The pizza is excellent, however, and no one seems to notice the dust gray curtains or the cat who has leapt on the adjoining table and is polishing off the remains of someone's dinner. At the end of the table our bride and groom, holding hands, are in a charmed circle of two.

Susan and Cole have headed to Lucca then back to France; their family guests are gone.

Shera and Kevin are here for a few more days. Ed and I visit the *marmista* and choose thick white marble for the countertops. The next day he cuts and bevels them and Ed and Kevin load them into the back of the car. Suddenly the kitchen looks the way I thought it would: brick floor, white appliances, long sink, plank shelves, marble counters. I sew a blue plaid curtain to go under the sink and hang a braid of garlic and some dried herbs from the wall shelves. In town we find an old peasant dish and cup rack. The dark chestnut looks great against the white walls. At last, a place for all the cups and bowls we're buying in the local ceramic patterns.

Everyone has gone. We eat the last of the wedding cake. Ed begins one of his many lists—we should paper a room with them—of projects he hopes to accomplish now. The kitchen is looking irresistible and we're moving into high season for vegetables and fruit. July fourth: Much of summer is left. My daughter is coming. Travelling friends will stop in for lunch or for a night. We're ready.

A LONG TABLE UNDER THE TREES

MARKET DAY FALLS ON THURSDAYS IN CAMUCIA, the lively town at the bottom of Cortona's hill, and I'm there early before the heat sets in. Tourists pass right through Camucia; it's just the modern spillover from the venerable and dominant hill town above it. But modern is relative. Among the *frutta e verdura* shops, the hardware and seed stores, you happen on a couple of Etruscan tombs. Near the butcher's shop are remnants of a villa, an immense curly iron gate and swag of garden wall. Camucia, bombed in World War II, has its share of chestnut trees, photographable doors, and shuttered houses.

On market day, a couple of streets are blocked to traffic. The vendors arrive early, unfolding what seems like whole stores or supermarket aisles from specially made trucks and wagons. One wagon sells local *pecorino,* the sheep's milk cheese that can be soft and almost creamy, or aged and strong as a barnyard, along with several wheels of *parmigiano.* The aged cheese is crumbly and rich, wonderful to nibble as I walk around the market.

I'm hunting and gathering food for a dinner for new friends. My favorite wagons belong to the two *porchetta* maestros. The whole pig, parsley entwined with the tail, apple—or a big mushroom—in its mouth, stretches across the cutting board. Sometimes the decapitated head sits aside at an angle, eyeing the rest of its body, which has been stuffed with herbs and bits of its own ears, etc. (best not to inquire too closely), then roasted in a wood oven. You can buy a *panino* (a crusty roll) with nothing on it but slabs of *porchetta* to take home, lean or with crispy, fatty skin. One of the lords of the *porchetta* wagons looks very much like his subject: little eyes, glistening skin, and bulbous forearms. His fingers are short and porky, with bitten-down nails. He's smiling, extolling his pig's virtues, but when he turns to his wife, he snarls. Her lips are set in a permanent tight half smile. I've bought from him before and his *porchetta* is delicious. This time I buy from the milder man in the next stand. For Ed, I ask for extra *sale,* salt, which is what the indefinable stuffing is called. I like it but find myself picking through to see if there's something peculiar in it. Though the pig is useful and tasty in all its parts and preparations, the slow-roasted *porchetta* must be its apogee. Before I move on to the vegetables, I spot a pair of bright yellow espadrilles with ribbons to wind around the ankles; I balance my shopping bags while I try on one. Perfect, and less than ten dollars. I drop them in with the *porchetta* and *parmigiano.*

Scarves (bright Chanel and Hermès copies) and linen tablecloths float from awnings; toilet cleaners, tapes, and T-shirts are stacked in bins and on folding tables. Besides buying food, you can dress, plant a garden, and stock a household from this market. There are a few local crafts for sale but you have to look for them. The Tuscan markets aren't like those in Mexico, with wonderful toys, weaving, and pottery. It's a wonder these markets continue at all, given the sophistication of Italian life and the standard of living in this area. I find the iron-working traditions still somewhat in evidence. Occasionally, I see good andirons and handy fireplace grills. My favorite is a holder for whole *prosciutto,* an iron grip with handle mounted on a board for ease in slicing; maybe someday I'll find I need that much *prosciutto* and buy one. One week I bought handwoven baskets made from dark supple willow twigs, the large ones perfect for kitchen supplies and the small round ones for the ripe-right-now peaches and cherries. One woman sells old table and bed linens with thick monograms, all of which must have been gathered from farms and villas. She has three mounds of yellowed lace. Perhaps some of it was made on the nearby island, Isola Maggiore in Lake Trasimeno. Women still sit in the doorways there, hooking lace in the afternoon light. I find two enormous square linen pillowcases with miles of inset lace and ribbons—ten thousand lire, same as the sandals, seems to be the magic number today. Of course, I will have to have the pillows especially made. When I buy some striped linen dishtowels, I notice several goat skins hanging from a hook. I have in mind that they would look terrific on the *cotto* floors at my house. The four the man has are too small but he says to come back next week. He tries to convince me that his sheepskins would be better anyway, but they don't appeal to me.

I'm wending my way toward the produce, but walk up to the bar for a coffee. Actually, I stop with an excuse to stare. People from surrounding areas come not only to shop but to greet friends, to make business arrangements.

The din around the Camucia market is a lovely swarm of voices, many speaking in the local Val di Chiana dialect; I don't understand most of what they're saying but I do hear one recurring habit. They do not use the *ch* sound for *c*, but slide it into an *s* sound. "Shento," they say for *cento* (one hundred), instead of the usual pronunciation "chento." I heard someone say "cappushino," for cappuccino, though the usual affectionate shortening of that is "cappuch." Their town is pronounced not "Camuchia," but "Camushea." Odd that the *c* is often the affected letter. Around Siena, people substitute an *h* sound for *c*—"hasa" and "Hoca-Hola." Whatever the local habit with *c*, they're all talking. Outside the bar, groups of farmers, maybe a hundred men, mill about. Some play cards. Their wives are off in the crowd, loading their bags with tiny strawberries, basil plants with dangling roots, dried mushrooms, perhaps a fish from the one stand that sells seafood from the Adriatic. Unlike the Italians who take their thimbleful of espresso in one quick swallow, I sip the black, black coffee.

A friend says Italy is getting to be just like everywhere else—homogenized and Americanized, she says disparagingly. I want to drag her here and stand her in this doorway. The men have the look of their lives—perhaps we all do. Hard work, their faces and bodies affirm. All are lean, not a pound of extra fat anywhere. They look cured by the sun, so deeply tan they probably never go pale in winter. Their country clothes are serviceable, rough— they don't "dress," they just get dressed. They wear, as well, a natural dignity. Surely some are canny, crusty, cruel, but they look totally present, unhidden, and alive. Some are missing teeth but they smile widely without embarrassment. I look in one man's eyes: The left one is white with milky blue veins like those in an exploded marble. The other is black as the center of a sunflower. A retarded boy wanders among them, neither catered to nor ignored. He's just there, living his life like the rest of us.

At home I plan a menu ahead, though I frequently improvise as I shop. Here, I only begin to think when I see what's ripe this week. My impulse is to overload; I forget there are not ten hungry people at home. At first I was miffed when tomatoes or peas had spoiled when I got around to cooking them a few days later. Finally I caught on that what you buy today is ready—picked or dug this morning at its peak. This also explained another puzzle; I never understood why Italian refrigerators are so minute until I realized that they don't store food the way we do. The Sub-Zero giant I have at home begins to seem almost institutional compared to the toy fridge I now have here.

Two weeks ago, small purple artichokes with long stems were in. We love those, quickly steamed, stuffed with tomatoes, garlic, yesterday's bread, and parsley, then doused with oil and vinegar. Today, not one. The *fagiolini,* slender green beans, are irresistible. Should I have two salads, because the beans also would be good with a shallot vinaigrette? Why not? I buy white peaches for breakfast but for tonight's dessert, the cherries are perfect. I take a kilo, then set off to find a pitter back in the other part of the market. Since I don't know the word, I'm reduced to sign language. I do know *ciliegia,* cherry, which helps. I've noticed in French and Italian country desserts that the cooks don't bother to pit the cherries, but I like to use the pitter when they're served in a dish.

These I'll steep in Chianti with a little sugar and lemon. I decide on some tiny yellow potatoes still half covered with dirt. Just a scrubbing, a dribble of oil and some rosemary and they'll roast in the oven.

I could complete my shopping for this meal right here. I pass cages of guinea hens, ducks, and chickens, as well as rabbits. Since my daughter had a black angora rabbit as a pet once, I can't look with cold eyes on the two spotted bunnies nibbling carrots in the dusty Alitalia flight bag, can't imagine them trembling in the trunk of my car. I intend to stop at the butcher's for a veal roast. The butcher's is bad enough. I admit it's not logical. If you eat meat, you might as well recognize where it comes from. But the drooped heads and closed eyelids of the quail and pigeon make me stop and stare. Rooster heads, chicken feet (with yellow nails like Mrs. Ricker's, my grand-mother's Rook partner), the clump of fur to show the skinned rabbit is not a cat, whole cows hanging by their feet with a square of paper towel on the floor to catch the last drops of blood—all these things make my stomach flip. Surely they're not going to eat those fluffy chicks. When I was a child, I sat on the back steps and watched our cook twist a chicken's neck then snap off the head with a jerk. The chicken ran a few circles, spurting blood, before it keeled over, twitching. I love roast chicken. Could I ever wring a neck?

I have as much as I can carry. The other stop I'll make is at the cooperative cantina for some local wine. Near the end of the sinuous line of market stalls, a woman sells flowers from her garden. She wraps an armful of pink zinnias in newspaper and I lay them under the straps of my bag. The sun is ferocious and people are beginning to close down for siesta. A woman who has not sold many of her striped lime and yellow towels looks weary. She dumps the dog sleeping in her folding chair and settles down for a rest before she begins to pack up.

On my way out, I see a man in a sweater, despite the heat. The trunk of his minuscule Fiat is piled with black grapes that have warmed all morning in the sun. I'm stopped by the winy, musty, violet scents. He offers me one. The hot sweetness breaks open in my mouth. I have never tasted anything so essential in my life as this grape on this morning. They even smell purple. The flavor, older than the Etruscans and deeply fresh and pleasing, just leaves me stunned. Such richness, the big globes, the heap of dusty grapes cascading out of two baskets. I ask for *un grappolo,* a bunch, wanting the taste to stay with me all morning.

✳

As I unload my cloth sacks, the kitchen fills with the scents of sunny fruits and vegetables warmed in the car. Everyone coming home from market must feel compelled to arrange the tomatoes, eggplants (*melanzane* sounds like the real name and even aubergine is better than dreary-sounding eggplant), zucchini, and enormous peppers into a still life in the nearest basket. I resist arranging the fruit in a bowl, except for what we'll eat today, because it's ripe this minute and all we're not about to eat now must go in the fridge.

I'm still amazed that the kitchen is finished. Though there still is the ghost of a circle above the outside door, where a saint or cross hung in a niche when this was the chapel for the house, there is no sign at all of the room's later inhabitants, oxen and chickens. When the mangers were ripped out, we found the remains of elaborate scroll designs on the crumbling plaster. As the nasty pen came down, we saw green faux marble designs. Now and then in the restoration we stopped and said, "Did you ever expect to be scraping decades of mold from animal's uric acid off a wall?" and "You realize we'll be cooking in a *chapel?*"

Now, oddly, it looks as though the kitchen always could have been this way. Like those in the rest of the house, the floors are waxed brick, the walls white plaster, and the ceiling has (oh, Ed's neck and back!) dark beams. We avoided cabinets. It was easy to construct the plaster-covered brick supports built for thick plank shelves we envisioned when we spent our evenings drawing on tablets of grid paper. Ed and I cut and painted them white. The baskets from the market hold utensils and staples. The two-inch-thick white Carrara marble tops are smooth to my eye and always cool to the touch or to the pizza dough and pastry I roll on it. We hung the same rough shelves on another wall for glasses and pasta bowls. To secure the brackets, Ed drilled toggle bolts into solid rock, spewing stones and straining the drill to its highest whine.

✳

The *signora* who lived here a hundred years ago could walk in now and start to cook. She'd like the porcelain sink, big enough to bathe a baby in, its drain board and the curved chrome faucet. I imagine her with a pointed chin and shiny black eyes, her hair swept up and twisted in a comb. She's in sturdy shoes that tie and a black dress with the sleeves pushed up, ready to roll out the ravioli. She'd be ecstatic, no doubt, to see appliances—the dishwasher, stove, and frost-free fridge (still a novelty in Tuscany), but otherwise, she'd feel quite at home. In my next life, when I am an architect, I always will design houses with kitchens that open to the outdoors. I love stepping out to head and tail my beans while sitting on the stone wall. I set dirty pots out to soak, dry my dishcloths on the wall, empty excess clean water on the arugula, thyme, and rosemary right outside the door. Since the double door is open day and night in summer, the kitchen fills with light and air. A wasp—is it the same one?—flies in every day and drinks from the faucet, then flies right out.

The one absolutely American feature is the lighting. Terrifically high utility costs explain the prevalence of forty-watt bulbs hanging in so many houses. I cannot bear a dim kitchen. We chose two bright fixtures and a rheostat, causing Lino, the electrician, extreme consternation. He'd never installed a rheostat, which intrigued him. But the lights! "One is enough. You are not performing surgery in here," he insisted. He needed to warn us that our electrical bill—he had no words, only the gesture of loosely shaking both hands in front of him and shaking his head at the same time. Clearly, we are headed for ruin.

On the brick ledge behind the sink, I've begun to accumulate local hand-painted majolica platters and bowls. I've thought of luring Shera back to paint a stencil of grapes, leaves, and vines around the top of the walls. But for the moment, the kitchen is *finito*.

✳

We poured so much energy into the kitchen because a dominant gene in my family is the cooking gene. No matter what occasion, what crisis, the women I grew up among could flat out hold forth in the kitchen, from delicate timbales and pressed chicken to steaming cauldrons of Brunswick stew. In summer, my mother and our cook, Willie Bell, went into marathons of putting up tomatoes, pickling cucumbers, stirring vats of scuppernongs for jelly. By early December they had made brandied cakes and shelled mountains of pecans for roasting. Never was our kitchen without tins of brownies and icebox cookies. Or without a plate of cold biscuits left over from dinner. I still miss toasted biscuits for breakfast. At one meal we already were talking about the next.

My daughter showed every sign of breaking the legacy of my mother and Willie, whose talents destined my sisters and me to shelves of cookbooks, constant plans for the next party, and—ultimate test—even the fate to cook when eating alone. Throughout her childhood, except for an occasional batch of obsidian-like fudge, Ashley disdained the kitchen. Shortly after she graduated from college, she began to cook and immediately started calling home for recipes for chicken with forty cloves of garlic, profiteroles, risotto, chocolate soufflé, potatoes Anna. Without meaning to, she seemed to have absorbed certain knowledge. Now, when we're together, we, too, go into paroxysms of planning and cooking. She has taught me a great marinated pork tenderloin recipe and a buttermilk lemon cake. These familial connections give me a helpless feeling: Cooking is destiny.

This inexorable inheritance notwithstanding, in recent years, I've worked more and more. In our normal life in San Francisco, everyday cooking becomes, at times, a chore. I confess to an occasional supper of ice cream from the carton, eaten with a fork while leaning against the kitchen counter. Sometimes we both get home late and find in the fridge celery, grapes, withered apples, and milk. No problem, since San Francisco has great restaurants. On weekends we try to roast two chickens or make minestrone or a big pasta sauce to get us to Tuesday. On Wednesday: a stop at Gordo's for super carnitas burritos with sour cream, guacamole, extra hot sauce, and a thousand grams of fat. In rushes of super organization, I freeze plastic tubs of soup and chili and stew and stock.

The leisure of a summer place, the ease of prime ingredients, and the perfectly casual way of entertaining convince me that this is the kitchen as it's meant to be. I think of my mother's summer tables often. She *launched* meals, seemingly with ease. Finally it dawns on me—maybe I'm not simply inadequate. It was easier then. She had people around her, as we do here. I sat on the ice cream churn while my sister turned the handle. My other sister shelled peas. Willie was totally capable. My mother directed kitchen traffic, arranged the table. I use her recipes often, and have a measure of her ease with guests but, please, no fried chicken. Here, I have that prime ingredient, time. Guests really do want to pit the cherries or run into town for another wedge of *parmigiano*. Also, cooking seems to take less time because the quality of food is so fine that only the simplest preparations are called for. Zucchini has a real taste. Chard, sautéed with a little garlic, is amazing. Fruit does not come with stickers; vegetables are not waxed or irradiated, and the taste is truly different.

Nights turn cool at fifteen hundred feet. That suits us because we can prepare some of the hearty foods that are not at all suitable in the sun. While *prosciutto* with figs, chilled tomato soup, Roman artichokes, and pasta with lemon peel and asparagus are perfect at one, the fresh evenings fuel the appetite. We serve spaghetti with *ragù* (I finally learned that the secret ingredient of a *ragù* is chicken liver), minestrone with globes of pesto, *osso buco,* grilled polenta, baked red peppers stuffed with ricotta and herb custard, warm cherries in Chianti with hazelnut pound cake.

When tomatoes are ripe, nothing is better than cold tomato soup with a handful of basil and a garnish of polenta croutons. *Panzanella,* little swamp, is another to-mato favorite, a salad of oil, vinegar, tomatoes, basil, cu-cumber, minced onion, and stale bread soaked in water and squeezed dry—a true invention from necessity. Since bread must be bought every day, Tuscan cooking makes good use of leftovers. The rough loaves work perfectly for bread puddings and for the best French toast I've ever had. We go for days without meat and don't even miss it, then a roasted *faraona* (guinea hen) with rosemary, or sage-stuffed pork loin, remind us of how fabulous the plainest meats can be. I cut a small basketful of thyme, rosemary, and sage, wishing I could beam one of each plant to San Francisco, where I keep a window box of faltering herbs going. Here, the sun doubles their size every few weeks. The oregano near the well quickly spreads to a circle about three feet wide. Even the wild mint and lemon balm I dug up on the hill and moved have taken off. Mint thrives. Vergil says deer wounded by hunters seek it for wounds. In Tuscany, where hunters long since have driven out most wildlife, the mint is more plentiful than deer. Maria Rita, at the *frutta e verdura,* tells me to use lemon balm in salads and vegetables, as well as in my bathwater. I think I would like cutting herbs even if I weren't cooking. The pungency of just-snipped herbs adds as much to the cook's enjoyment as to taste. After weeding the thyme, I don't wash my hands until the fragrance fades from my hands. I planted a hedge of sage, more than I ever could use, and let most flower for the butterflies. Sage flowers, along with lavender, look pretty in wildflower bouquets. The rest I dry or use fresh, usually for white beans with chopped sage and olive oil, a favorite of Tuscans, who are known as "bean eaters."

Anytime we grill, Ed tosses long wands of rosemary on the coals and on the meat. The crispy leaves not only add flavor, they're good to nibble, too. When he grills shrimp, he threads them on rosemary sticks.

I have pots of basil by the kitchen door because it is supposed to keep out flies. During the wall-building and well-drilling weeks, I saw a worker crush leaves in his hand and smear his wasp sting. He said it took away all the pain. A larger patch grows a few feet away. The more I cut off, the more seems to grow. I use whole leaves in salad, bunches for pesto, copious amounts in sautéed summer squashes and tomato dishes. Of all herbs, basil holds the essence of Tuscan summer.

✳

The long stretch of summer lunches calls for a long *tavola*. Now that the kitchen is finished, we need a table outdoors, the longer the better, because inevitably the abundance at the weekly market incites me to buy too much and because inevitably guests gather—friends from home, a relative's friends from somewhere who thought they'd say hello since they were in the area, and new friends, sometimes with friends of *theirs*. Add another handful of pasta to the boiling pot, add a plate, a tumbler, find another chair. The table and the kitchen can oblige.

I have considered my table, its ideals as well as its dimensions. If I were a child, I would want to lift up the tablecloth and crawl under the unending table, into the flaxen light where I could crouch and listen to the loud laughs, clinks, and grown-up talk, hear over and over *"Salute"* and *"Cin-cin"* travelling around the chairs, stare at kneecaps and walking shoes and flowered skirts hiked up to catch a breeze, the table steady under its weight of food. Such a table should accommodate the wanderings of a large dog. At the end, you need room for an enormous vase of all the flowers in bloom at the moment. The width should allow platters to meander from hand to hand down the center, stopping where they will, and numerous water and wine bottles to accumulate over the hours. You need room for a bowl of cool water to dip the grapes and pears into, a little covered dish to keep the bugs off the Gorgonzola (*dolce* as opposed to the *piccante* type, which is for cooking) and *caciotta,* a local soft cheese. No one cares if olive pits are flung into the distance. The best wardrobe for such a table runs to pale linens, blue checks, pink and green plaid, not dead white, which takes in too much glare. If the table is long enough, everything can be brought out at once, and no one has to run back and forth to the kitchen. Then the table is set for primary pleasure: lingering meals, under the trees at noon. The open air confers an ease, a relaxation and freedom. You're your own guest, which is the way summer ought to be.

In the delicious stupor that sets in after the last pear is halved, the last crust scoops up the last crumbles of Gorgonzola, and the last drop empties into the glass, you can ruminate, if you are inclined that way, on your participation in the great collective unconscious. You are doing what everyone else in Italy is doing, millions of backsides being shined by chairs at millions of tables. Over each table, a miniature swarm of gnats is gathering. There are exceptions, of course. Parking attendants, waiters, cooks—and thousands of tourists, many of whom made the mistake of eating two wedges of great sausage pizza at eleven and now have no inclination to eat anything. Instead, they wander under the unbearable sun, peeking through metal grates covering shop windows, pusing at the massive doors of locked churches, sitting on the sides of fountains while squinting into minuscule guidebooks. Give it up! I've done the same thing. Then, later, it's hard to deny yourself the luscious *melone* ice cream cone at seven, when the air is still hot and your sandals have rubbed your heels raw. Those weak ones (*mea culpa*) who succumb possibly will have another wedge, artichoke this time, on the way to the hotel; then, when Italy begins eating at nine, the foreign stomach doesn't even mumble. That happens much later, when all the good restaurants are full.

The rhythm of Tuscan dining may throw us off but

after a long lunch outside, one concept is clear—siesta. The logic of a three-hour fall through the crack of the day makes perfect sense. Best to pick up that Piero della Francesca book, wander upstairs and give in to it.

I know I want a wooden table. When I was growing up, my father had dinners for his men friends and a few employees on Fridays. Our cook, Willie Bell, and my mother spread a long white table under a pecan tree in our yard with fried chicken cooked right there on our brick barbecue, potato salad, biscuits, iced tea, pound cake, and bottles of gin and Southern Comfort. The noon meal often lasted most of the day, sometimes ending with the swaying men, arm in arm singing "Darktown Strutter's Ball" and "I'm a Ramblin' Wreck from Georgia Tech" slowly as if on a tape that warped in the sun.

From the very first weeks we lived in the house, we used the abandoned worktable, a crude prototype of the table I imagined us eventually setting under the line of five *tigli* trees. At a market stall, I bought tablecloths, long to keep splinters from digging into our knees. With napkins to match, a jar of poppies, Queen Anne's lace, and blue bachelor's buttons on the table, our yellow plates from the COOP, we served forth, mainly to each other.

My idea of heaven is a two-hour lunch with Ed. I believe he must have been Italian in another life. He has begun to gesture and wave his hands, which I've never seen him do. He likes to cook at home but simply throws himself into it here. For a lunch he prepares, he gathers *parmigiano,* fresh mozzarella, some *pecorino* from the mountains, red peppers, just-picked lettuces, the local salami with fennel, loaves of *pane con sale* (the bread that isn't strictly traditional here since it has salt), *prosciutto,* a glorious bag of tomatoes. For dessert, peaches, plums, and, my favorite, a local watermelon called *minne di monaca,* nun's tits. He piles the bread board with our cheeses, salami, peppers, and on our plates arranges our first course, the classic *caprese:* sliced tomatoes, basil, mozzarella, and a drizzle of oil.

In the *tigli* shade, we're protected from the midday heat. The cicadas yammer in the trees, that deeply heart-of-summer sound. The tomatoes are so intense we go silent as we taste them. Ed opens a celebratory bottle of *prosecco* and we settle down to recap the saga of buying and restoring the house. Oddly, we now omit the complications and panic; we've begun the selection process, the same one that insures the continuance of the human race: forgetting the labor. Ed starts drawing up plans for a bread oven. We dream on about other projects. The sun through the flowering trees bathes us in gold sifted light. "This isn't real; we've wandered into a Fellini film," I say.

Ed shakes his head. "Fellini is a documentary film-maker—I've lost my belief in his genius. There are Fellini scenes everywhere. Remember the brilliant motorcycle that comes around and around in *Amarcord?* It happens *all* the time. You're nowhere in a remote village, no one in sight, and suddenly a huge Moto Guzzi streaks by." He peels a peach in one long spiral and just because this was all too pleasant we open a second bottle of *prosecco* and wile away another hour before we drift in to rest and revive our energy for a walk into town to case out the restaurants, stroll along the parterre overlooking the valley, and, hard to contemplate, begin the next meal.

✳

We have called the shy and silent carpenters, Marco and Rudolfo. They seem amused no matter what work they do here. The idea of a painted table seating ten seems to stun them. They're used to chestnut stain. Are we certain? I see them swap a glance with each other. But it will have to be repainted in two years. Too impractical. We've sketched what we want and have the paint sample, too—primary yellow.

They return four days later with the table, sealed and painted—a miracle turnaround time anywhere but especially for two as busy as they are. They laugh and say the table will glow in the dark. It does pulsate with color. They haul it to the spot with the broadest view into the valley. In the deep shade, the yellow shines, luring us to come forth from the house with jugs and steaming bowls, baskets of fruit and fresh cheeses wrapped in grape leaves.

✳

Dinner tonight is for an Italian couple, their baby, and our compatriot writers. This Italian baby girl, at seven months, chews on piquant olives and looks longingly at the food. Our friends have been amused by our adventures in restoration, safely amused since their houses were restored before workmen disappeared and before the dollar dove. Each knows an astonishing amount about wells, septic systems, gutters, pruning—minute technical knowledge acquired by years under the roofs of quirky old farmhouses. We're awed by their fluency with Italian, their endless knowledge of the intricacies of telephone bills. Though I imagine conversations about the currents in Italian literature, opera, and controversial restorations, we seem to discuss most passionately olive pruning, grease traps, well testing, and shutter repair.

The menu: with drinks, *bruschette* with chopped tomatoes and basil, *crostini* with a red pepper confit. The first course, *gnocchi,* not the usual potato but light semolina *gnocchi* (small servings—it's rich), followed by veal roasted with garlic and potatoes, then garnished with fried sage. The little green beans, still crisp, warm, with fennel and olives. Just before they arrive, I pick a huge basket of lettuces. At the start of summer, I scattered two envelopes of mixed lettuces as an edging along a flower bed. They were up in a week and in three, bolted the border. Now they're everywhere; it feels odd to be weeding the flower bed and accumulating dinner at the same time. Some look unfamiliar; I hope we're not eating just-sprouting calendula or hollyhocks. The cherries, simmered and cooled, have attracted bees to them all afternoon. One of the tiny hummingbirds made a quick foray into the kitchen, drawn possibly by the scent of the deep red wine syrup.

When they arrive it will be the soft, slow Tuscan twilight, fading after drinks from transparent to golden to evening blue, then, by the end of the first course, into night. Night happens quickly, as though the sun were pulled in one motion under the hill. We light candles in hurricane shades all along the stone wall and on the table. For background music, a hilarious chorus of frogs tunes up. *Molte anni fa,* many years ago, our friends begin. Their stories weave an Italy around us that we know only through books and films. *In the sixties . . . In the seventies . . . A true paradise.* That's why they came—and stayed. They love it but it's downhill now in comparison to the four armoires from that nutty contessa. *How alive the streets of Rome were with people, and remember the theater with the roof that rolled back, how sometimes it would rain?* Then the talk shifts to politics. They know everyone. We're all horrified at the car bombing in Sicily. Is there a Mafia here? Our questions are naive. The fascist leaning in recent elections disturbs everyone. Could Italy go back? I tell them about the antique dealer in Monte San Savino. I saw a photo of Mussolini over his shop door and he saw me looking at it. With a big smile he asks if I know who that is. Not knowing if the photo is a campy object or one of veneration, I give him the fascist salute. He goes crazy, thinking I approve. He's all over me, talking about what a bold and *bravo* man Il Duce was. I want to get out with my strange purchases—a big gilt cross and the door to a reliquary—but now the prices come down. He invites me back, wants me to meet his family. Everyone advises me to take full advantage.

I feel immersed here; my "real life" seems remote. Odd that we're all here. We were given one country and we've set ourselves up in another—they much more radically than we; they defined their lives and work by *this* place, not *that*. We feel so much at home, pale and American as we are. We could just stay here, go native. Let my hair grow long, tutor local kids in English, ride a Vespa into town for bread. I imagine Ed on one of those tiny tractors made for terraced land. Imagine him starting a little vineyard. Or we could make tisanes of lemon balm. I look at him but he is pouring wine. I almost feel our strange voices—English, French, Italian—spreading out around the house, over the valley. Sound carries on the hills. *(Stranieri,* foreigners, we're called, but it sounds more dire, more like strangers, an oddly chilling word.) Often we hear parties of invisible neighbors above us. We've shifted an ancient order of things on this hillside, where the tax collector, the police captain, and the news-stand owner (our nearest neighbors although we can't see any of them) heard only Italian until we encamped here.

The Big Dipper, clear as a dot-to-dot drawing, seems about to pour something right on top of the house, and the Milky Way, so pretty in Latin as the *via lactia,* sweeps its bridal train of scattered stars over our heads. The frogs go silent all at once, as if someone shushed them. Ed brings out the *vin santo* and a plate of *biscotti* he made this morning. Now the night is big and quiet. No moon. We talk, talk, talk. Nothing to interrupt us except the shoot-ing stars.

SUMMER KITCHEN NOTES

ONE SPRING WHEN I STUDIED COOKING WITH SI-
mone Beck at her house in Provence, she said some
things I never forgot. Another student, a caterer and
cooking teacher, kept asking Simca for the technique for
everything. She had a notebook and furiously wrote
down every word Simca said. The other four of us were
mainly interested in eating what we'd prepared. When
she asked one time too many, Simca said crisply, "There
is no technique, there is just the way to do it. Now, are
we going to measure or are we going to cook?"

I've learned here that simplicity is liberating. Simca's
philosophy applies totally to this kitchen, where we no
longer measure, but just cook. As all cooks know, ingredients of the moment are the best guides. Much of what
we do is too simple to be called a recipe—it's just the way
to do it. I vary the ubiquitous *prosciutto e melone* with
halved figs. The cold tomato soup I make is simply
chopped herbs—mainly basil—and ripe tomatoes stirred
into clear chicken stock and popped in the freezer until
chilled. I roast whole heads of garlic in a terra-cotta dish
with a little olive oil—great to squeeze the cloves onto

bread. One of the best pastas is spaghetti tossed with chopped arugula, cream, and minced *pancetta,* then sprinkled with *parmigiano.* Green beans served with black olives, sliced raw fennel, spring onions, and a light vinaigrette or lemon juice must be one of the nicest things ever to happen to a bean. Ed's invention couldn't be easier: He splits figs, pours on a little honey, runs them under the broiler, then drizzles them with cream. Sliced peaches with sweetened mascarpone and a crumbling of *amaretti* cookies have become a standby. Some favorites are a bit more involved, though nothing to make me wonder what madness led me to get involved.

Growing such a plethora of herbs induces me to squander them. All platters are garnished with what's left in the basket: a bunch of flowering thyme scattered over vegetables, the roast presented on a bed of sage, sprigs of oregano around the pasta. Lavender, grape and fig leaves, and airy fennel greens are fun to use as garnishes, too. With a few wildflowers, cut herbs in a terra-cotta pot look right at home on the table.

Here are a few quick, personal recipes that guests have raved over or that have sent us secretly to the fridge the next morning to taste the leftovers. Italians wouldn't consider risotto or pasta a main course, but for us, often it is. The oil of choice is, of course, olive oil, unless otherwise specified. All herbs in these recipes are fresh.

ANTIPASTI

❋

Red Peppers (or Onions) Melted with Balsamic Vinegar

The immense, convoluted, lustrous peppers in primary red, green, and yellow are my favorite vegetable of summer because they wake up so many dishes. A quick sauté of a mixture of the three adds zip to any plate. And there's red pepper soup, mousse of yellow peppers, old-fashioned stuffed green ones . . .

Seed and slice 4 peppers thinly and cook slowly in a little olive oil and 1/4 cup of balsamic vinegar until very soft, about an hour. Stir occasionally; peppers should almost "melt." Season with salt and pepper. Add oil and balsamic vinegar once or twice if they look dry. Run under the broiler (or grill) about 25 rounds of bread sprinkled with olive oil. Rub a cut clove of garlic over each piece. Spoon peppers onto bread and serve warm. Try the same method with thinly sliced onions, adding a teaspoon of brown sugar to the balsamic and letting the onions slowly carmelize. Both versions of this are rich accompaniments for roast chicken. Leftovers are good on pasta or polenta. With cheese and/or grilled eggplant, very savory sandwiches can be made quickly.

❋

Pea and Shallot Bruschetta

New peas pop right out of the crisp pods. I thought shelling them was a meditative act until I saw a woman in town sitting outside her doorway with her cat sleeping at her ankles. She was shelling an immense pile of peas and already had filled a large dishpan. She looked up and said something rapidly in Italian and I smiled, only to realize as I walked on that she'd said, "It shouldn't happen to a dog."

Mince 4 shallots. Shell enough peas to fill 1 cup. Mix and sauté in butter until the peas are done and the shallots are wilted. Add a little chopped mint, salt, and pepper. Chop coarsely in a food processor or by hand and spoon onto 25 rounds of bread as prepared in the recipe above.

❋

Basil and Mint Sorbet

I tasted this unlikely but tantalizing sorbet at the ancient *fattoria*-turned-restaurant Locanda dell'Amorosa in nearby Sinalunga. The next day I tried to duplicate it at home. At the restaurant, it was served after the pasta and fish courses and before the main course. More informally, it starts out a dinner on a warm summer night.

Make a sugar syrup by boiling together 1 cup of water and 1 cup of sugar, then simmering it for about 5 minutes, stirring constantly. Cool in the fridge. Purée $1/2$ cup of mint leaves and $1/2$ cup of basil leaves in 1 cup of water. Add another cup of water, 1 tablespoon of lemon juice, and chill. Mix the sugar syrup and the herbal water well and process in an ice cream maker according to manufacturer's instructions. Scoop into martini glasses or any clear glass dishes and garnish with mint leaves. Serves 8.

PRIMI PIATTI

✳

Cold Garlic Soup

As in chicken with 40 cloves of garlic, the amount of garlic in this recipe is no cause for alarm. The cooking process attenuates the strength but leaves the flavor.

Peel 2 whole heads of garlic. Chop 1 small onion and peel and dice 2 medium potatoes. Sauté the onion in 1 tablespoon of olive oil and, when it begins to turn translucent, add the garlic. The garlic should soften but not brown; cook gently. Steam the diced potatoes and add to the onion and garlic, along with 1 cup of chicken stock. Bring just to a boil, then quickly lower heat and simmer for 20 minutes. Purée in a food processor, then pour back into the pot and add 4 more cups of stock and 1 tablespoon of chopped thyme. (If you don't have a food processor, mince the garlic and onion before you cook them; after steaming, put the potatoes through a ricer.) Whisk in $1/2$ cup of heavy cream. Season with salt and pepper, then chill. Stir before serving with chopped thyme or chives on top. Serves 6.

✳

Fennel Soup

Thinly slice 2 fennel bulbs and 2 bunches of spring onions. Sauté briefly in a little olive oil. Add 2 cups of chicken stock to the pan and simmer until the fennel is cooked. Stir frequently. Purée until smooth. Whisk in $2\text{-}1/2$ more cups of stock. Season with salt and pepper and cover. Bring to a boiling point, then lower the heat and simmer for 10 minutes. Whisk in $1/2$ cup of mascarpone or heavy cream. Remove from heat immediately.

*Serve cold or warm, garnished with toasted fennel seeds.
Serves 6.*

*

Pizza with Onion Confit and Sausage

Pizza is endless in variety. Ed's favorite is Napoli: capers,
anchovies, mozzarella. I like fontina, olives, and *prosciutto*.
Another favorite is arugula and curls of *parmigiano*. We're
also enamored of potato pizza, as well as all the standard
ones. When we cook outside, we always grill lots of extra
vegetables and sausages for salads and pizza the next day.
A great vegetarian combination is grilled eggplant with
sundried tomatoes, olives, oregano, basil, and mozzarella.

*Thinly slice 3 onions and "melt" in a frying pan on low
heat, using a small amount of olive oil and 3 tablespoons of
balsamic vinegar. Onions should be caramel colored and limp.
Season with marjoram, salt and pepper. Grill or sauté 2 large
sausages. Here we use the local pork sausage seasoned with
fennel seeds. Slice. Grate 1 cup of mozzarella or parmigiano.*

*Dough: Dissolve 1 package of yeast in ¹/₄ cup of warm water
for 10 minutes. Mix the following: ¹/₂ teaspoon of salt, 1 teaspoon of sugar, 3 tablespoons of olive oil, 1 cup of cool water,
and pour into a mound of 3-¹/₄ cups of flour. Knead on a flat
surface until elastic and smooth. If you're using a food processor,
pulse until the dough forms a ball, then remove and knead by
hand. Place dough in a buttered and floured bowl and let rest for
30 minutes. Roll into 1 large or 2 smaller circles and brush with
oil. Scatter cheese, onions, and sausage over the surface and bake
at 400° for 15 minutes. Cut into 8 pieces.*

✳

Semolina Gnocchi

Gnocchi's usual knuckle shape changes in this grand and rich dish. Unlike the potato *gnocchi* or the light spinach and ricotta *gnocchi,* the *gnocchi* made with semolina are biscuit-sized. I used to buy these from a woman down in the valley until I found out how easy they are to make.

Bring 6 cups of milk almost to a boil in a large saucepan. Pour in 3 cups of semolina in a steady stream, stirring constantly. Cook on low, as you would cook polenta, continuing to stir for 15 minutes. Remove from heat, beat in 3 egg yolks, 3 tablespoons of butter and 1/2 cup of grated parmigiano. *Season with salt, pepper, and a little nutmeg. Beat briefly, lifting the mixture to incorporate air. Spread mixture in a circle 1 inch thick on the lightly floured counter or cutting board and let it cool. Cut into biscuit-sized circles with the rim of a glass or a cookie cutter. Place in a well-buttered baking dish. Pour 3 tablespoons of melted butter over the top, then sprinkle with 1/4 cup of* parmigiano. *Bake, uncovered, at 400° for 15 minutes. Serves 6.*

✳

Everything Pasta Salad with Baked Tomatoes

When making soups, ratatouille, or this salad, I steam everything separately. This keeps the flavors distinct and allows me to cook each vegetable to its first point of doneness. I've never seen pasta salad on an Italian menu, but it's a marvelous American import. This goes easily to a picnic in a big plastic container.

Prepare vinaigrette: 3/4 cup of olive oil, red wine vinegar to taste (about 3 tablespoons), 3 cloves of crushed garlic, 1 table-spoon of chopped thyme, salt, and pepper. Shake in a jar.

Fresh vegetables: 8 medium carrots, 5 slender zucchini, 2 big red peppers, 2 hot peppers, about one-half pound of green beans, and one bunch of spring onions. Cut in small pieces, except for hot peppers—mince these. Steam one by one until just done. Cool.

Chicken: Rub 2 whole breasts with olive oil and place in an oiled pan. Season with thyme, salt, and pepper. Roast at 350° for about 30 minutes. Cool and slice into julienne strips.

Pasta: Fusilli, the short, spiraled pasta, is best for salad. Cook two 1-pound packages and drain; immediately toss with 2 tablespoons of olive oil. Season and cool.

Mix everything well in a large container, such as a turkey roasting pan, and chill until an hour before serving. Toss again and divide between two large bowls.

For the tomatoes: Select one for each person (plus a few more for leftovers). Cut a cone-shaped hollow from the stem end and spoon out seeds. Trim off the bottom. Sprinkle with salt and pepper, then stuff tomato with a mixture of bread crumbs, chopped basil, and toasted pine nuts. Drizzle with olive oil. Bake at 350° for about 15 minutes.

To serve, place tomato in the center of the plate, surround with pasta salad, garnish with black olives and thyme sprigs and/or basil leaves. Makes 16–20 very pretty servings.

SECONDI

❋

Risotto with Red Chard

Risotto has become soul food to me. Like pasta, pizza, and polenta, it's another dish of infinite variety. In spring, barely cooked asparagus, tiny carrots, and a little lemon make a light risotto. I especially like it with fava beans that have been sautéed with minced shallots in a covered pan, then stirred into the risotto. Other good choices: chopped fennel, barely cooked, with rock shrimp; sautéed fresh mushrooms or dried *porcini* soaked in tepid water until plumped; grilled radicchio and pancetta. In Italy, you can buy *funghi porcini* bouillon cubes in grocery stores. They're excellent for risotto when no stock is at hand. Many recipes call for too much butter; if you have a good stock, butter is unnecessary and only a little olive oil is needed to start things off. If any risotto is left the next day, heat a tablespoon of olive oil in a nonstick pan, spread and pat down the risotto, and cook over a medium flame until crisp on the bottom. Flip over with a large spatula and crisp the other side. A fine lunch.

Chop, then sauté, 1 medium onion in 1 tablespoon of oil for about 2 minutes. Add 2 cups of Arborio rice and cook for a couple of minutes. Meanwhile, in another pot, heat 5-1/2 cups of seasoned stock (chicken, veal, or vegetable) and 1/2 cup of white wine to a boil and reduce heat to a simmer. Ladle the stock and wine gradually into the rice, stirring each ladle into the rice until it is absorbed before adding more. Keep both the stock mixture and the rice at a simmer. Stir and stir until rice is done. It should be al dente *and rather soupy. Add 1/2 cup of grated* parmigiano. *Thoroughly wash a bunch of chard, preferably red. Chop in shreds and quickly sauté in a little olive oil and minced garlic. Stir into risotto. Serve and pass a bowl of grated* parmigiano. *Serves 6.*

*

Rich Polenta Parmigiana

This is more of a California polenta than a traditional Italian one. So much butter and cheese! Classic polenta is cooked by the same method—don't stop stirring—with two or even three more cups of water. You then pour the polenta out on a cutting board and let it rest until firm. Often it's served with a *ragù* or with *funghi porcini*. I've served this version to Italians and they've loved it. Left-over polenta, either plain or this richer one, is sublime when sautéed until crisp.

Soak 2 cups of polenta in 3 cups of cold water for 10 minutes. In a stock pot, bring 3 cups of water to a boil and stir in the polenta. Let it come to a boil again, then turn down the heat immediately and stir for 15 minutes on a gentle flame that is strong enough to keep slow, big bubbles rising. Add salt and pepper, 8 tablespoons of butter, and 1 cup of grated parmigiano. *Add more water if the polenta is too thick. Stir well and pour into a large buttered baking dish. Run in the oven at 300° for about 15 minutes. Serves 6.*

*

A Sauce of Porcini

When available, fresh *porcini* are a treat. They're at their finest simply brushed with olive oil and grilled, a dish that is as substantial as steak, which they're often paired with on the grill. Out of season, the dried ones have many talents. Though they seem expensive, a little bit adds a lot of flavor. Spoon this sauce over polenta or serve as a risotto or pasta sauce.

Soften about 2 ounces of dried porcini in 1-1/2 cups of warm water. This takes about one half hour. Peel and dice five cloves of garlic and gently sauté in 2 tablespoons of olive oil. Add 1 tablespoon each finely chopped thyme and rosemary, 1 cup of tomato sauce, and salt and pepper. Strain the mushroom water through cheesecloth and add it to the tomato mixture. Chop and add the mushrooms and simmer the sauce until thick and savory, about 20 minutes. 6 servings for polenta, 4 for pasta.

❋

Chicken with Chickpeas, Garlic, Tomatoes, and Thyme

One of those recipes that can expand to accommodate any number.

Simmer 2 cups of dried chickpeas in water with 2 cloves of garlic, salt, and pepper until tender but with plenty of bite, about 2 hours. In hot olive oil, quickly brown 6 breasts that have been shaken in a bag of flour. Arrange pieces in a baking dish. Drain chickpeas and scatter over chicken. Add a little olive oil to the same pan and sauté 1 coarsely chopped onion and 3 cloves of minced garlic; add 4 ripe tomatoes, also chopped coarsely, 1 teaspoon of cinnamon, and 2 tablespoons of thyme. Simmer 10 minutes. Spread over the chicken. Season with salt, pepper, sprigs of fresh thyme, and 1/2 cup of black olives. Bake, uncovered, at 350° for about 30 minutes, depending on the size of the chicken breasts. This is attractive in a terra-cotta dish. Serves 6.

❋

Basil and Lemon Chicken

A last-minute favorite, this chicken, served with a platter of summer squash and sliced tomatoes, tempers the hottest July night.

In a large bowl, mix ¹/₂ cup each of chopped spring onions and basil leaves. Add the juice of 1 lemon, salt and pepper. Mix and rub onto 6 chicken pieces and place in a well-oiled baking pan. Dribble with a little olive oil. Roast, uncovered, at 350° for about 30 minutes, depending on the size of the chicken. Garnish with more basil leaves and lemon slices. Serves 6.

❋

Turkey Breast with Green and Black Olives

Turkey is popular here, though the whole bird is rare except at Christmas. In this recipe, the breast is sliced into cutlets, like *scaloppine.* You can use flattened chicken breasts instead of turkey. If you don't pit the olives, warn your guests. I use the rest of the breast for distinctly un–Tuscan stir-fry with peppers.

In a large pan, sauté 6 turkey cutlets in olive oil until almost done and remove to a platter. Add a little more oil to the pan and sauté 1 finely chopped onion and 2 cloves of crushed garlic. Add 1 cup of vermouth and bring to a boil, then quickly reduce heat to a simmer. Cover for 2 or 3 minutes, then add the turkey again, as well as the juice of 1 lemon and 1 cup of mixed green and black olives. Cook for 5 minutes or until the turkey is done. Season with salt and pepper and stir in a handful of chopped parsley. Serves 6.

CONTORNI

❊

Fried Zucchini Flowers

When this is good it's very, very good and when it's limp it's a disaster. I've made it both ways. The mistake was in the oil, which must be hot. Peanut or sunflower are the best oils for these delicate summer flowers.

Choose a fresh bunch of flowers, about a dozen. If they're slightly droopy, don't bother. Don't wash the blossoms; if moist, pat dry. Place a thin strip of mozzarella inside each one, dip in batter. To prepare the batter, beat 2 eggs with ¼ teaspoon of salt and pour in 1 cup of water and 1-¼ cups of flour. Mix well, breaking any lumps with a fork. Make sure the oil is hot (350°) but not smoking. Fry until golden and crispy. Drain quickly on paper towels and serve immediately.

❊

Baked Peppers with Ricotta and Basil

Stuffed peppers were my favorite dorm food in college. This ricotta filling is the polar opposite of the "mystery meat" we faced at Randolph-Macon. Fresh ricotta, made from ewe's milk, is a treat. The special baskets for making it imprint the sides of the cheese with a woven pattern. We often buy it at farms around Pienza, which is sheep country and also the source of *pecorino*.

Singe 3 large yellow peppers quickly over a gas flame or a grill. The peppers should char all over, but don't cook them so long that they turn limp. Cool in a plastic bag, then slide off the burned skin. Cut in half and clean out ribs and seeds. Drizzle with olive oil. In a bowl, mix 2 cups of ricotta, ½ cup of *chopped basil, $^1/_2$ cup of finely sliced green onions, $^1/_2$ cup minced Italian parsley, salt and pepper. Beat in 2 eggs. Fill peppers and bake at 350° for 30 minutes. Garnish with basil leaves. Serves 6.*

✳

Fried Sage

Too often sage is associated with that green dust that comes in little jars and makes you sneeze. Fresh sage has an assertive punch that complements meat.

Wash 20 or 30 sprigs of sage, pat with paper towels, and allow to dry completely. Heat 2 inches of sunflower or peanut oil until it is very hot but not smoking. Dip sprigs in batter (see recipe for Fried Zucchini Flowers, on page 161) and drop them in hot oil (350°) for about 2 minutes or until the leaves are crisp. Drain on paper towels. A splendid garnish for lamb, pork, or any meat.

✳

Sage Pesto

I found a pestle of olive wood at the monthly antique market in Arezzo and put it to use with an old stone mortar rescued from a friend who used it as a copious ashtray. These big mortars, she explained, originally were used for grinding coarse salt. Until recently, salt, a heavily taxed and government-controlled monopoly, was sold only in tobacco shops. The cheaper coarse salt was widely used. The large old mortars are handy for pesto; the pestle and rough stone release oils from the herbs and bind the essences of all the ingredients. Extrapolating on the basic basil pesto, I've made a lemon-parsley pesto for fish, an arugula pesto for pasta and *crostini,* and a mint pesto for shrimp. I've come to prefer the texture of these pestos to the smoother ones I'm used to. Traditional Tuscan white beans with sage and olive oil taste even better with a daub of this sage pesto. I like it on *bruschetta.* Passed separately in a bowl, it's a good accompaniment for grilled sausages.

Chop a big bunch of sage leaves, 2 cloves of garlic, and 4 tablespoons of pine nuts. Grind together in the mortar (or food processor), slowly adding olive oil to form a thick paste. Transfer to a bowl, mix again, add salt and pepper and a handful of grated parmigiano. *Makes about 1-1/2 cups.*

DOLCI

❋

Hazelnut Gelato

Super rich, this gelato makes me want to give up my citizenship and decamp permanently. Even people who claim not to like ice cream slip into a swoon over this one.

Toast 1-1/2 cups of hazelnuts in a moderate oven for five minutes. Watch the nuts carefully; they burn easily. Remove, wrap in a dish towel, and rub off the fine brown skin. Chop coarsely. Beat 6 egg yolks and gradually stir in 1-1/2 cups of sugar, beating until nicely incorporated. Heat 1 quart of half-and-half until almost boiling, then remove from the heat and quickly whisk in the egg and sugar mixture. In a double boiler, cook the mixture gently until it thickens and coats a wooden spoon. Cool in the fridge. Whisk in 2 tablespoons Fra Angelico (hazelnut liqueur) or vanilla, and 2 cups of heavy cream. Add hazelnuts and the juice and zest of one lemon. Pour the mixture into an ice cream maker and process according to manufacturer's instructions. Makes about 2 quarts.

❋

Cherries Steeped in Red Wine

All through June we buy cherries by the kilo and start eating them in the car on the way home. Almost nothing you can invent improves the taste of the plain cherry. We've planted three cherry trees and have uncovered three more from the ivy and brambles. Two neighboring trees are necessary for fruit production.

Stem and pit 1 pound of cherries. Pour 1 cup of red wine and the zest of a lemon over them and simmer for 15 minutes, stirring occasionally. Cover and let stand for 2 or 3 hours. Serve in bowls with plenty of juice and a big dollop of sweetened whipped cream or mascarpone. Little slices of hazelnut pound cake or cookies also might be served. You can use plums or pears instead of cherries. Serves 4.

❋

Folded Peach Tart with Mascarpone

I first learned to make folded pie crusts from a Paula Wolfert cookbook. On a cookie sheet, you spread the crust, pile the filling in the middle, then loosely fold the edges toward the center, forming a rustic tart with a spontaneous look. The peaches here—both the yellow and the white varieties—are so luscious that eating one should be a private act.

Roll out your favorite crust a little larger than you normally do for a pie pan. Slide to a nonstick cookie sheet or baking dish.

Slice 4 or 5 peaches. Mix 1 cup of mascarpone, $^1/_4$ cup of sugar, and $^1/_4$ cup of toasted almond slices. Combine this gently with peaches. Spoon into the center of the crust, and flop the pastry edges over, pressing them down a bit into the fruit mixture. Don't seal over the top—leave a four- or five-inch hole. Bake at 375° for about 20 minutes. Serves 6.

❋

Pears in Mascarpone Custard

This is an Italian version of the fruit cobblers I must have first tasted at the age of six months in the South, where they almost always were made of peaches or blackberries.

Peel and slice 6 medium pears (or peaches or apples) and arrange in a buttered baking dish. Sprinkle with 1 teaspoon of sugar. Cream 4 tablespoons of butter and $^1/_2$ cup of sugar until light. Beat in 1 egg, then $^2/_3$ cup of mascarpone. Stir in 2 tablespoons of flour last and mix well. Spoon over the fruit. Bake at 350° until just set, about 20 minutes. Serves 6 generously.

CORTONA, NOBLE CITY

ITALIANS ALWAYS HAVE LIVED OVER THE STORE. The *palazzi* of some of the grandest families have bricked-in arches at ground level, with remains of waist-high stone counters where someone used to ladle out preserved briny fish from a vat to customers, or carve the stuffed pig, a job now performed in sleek open-sided trucks that ply the weekly markets or sell from roadsides. I run my hand over these worn stone counters when I pass them. From odd windows at ground level, the *palazzo's* house wine was sold. First floors of some grand houses were warehouses. Today, my bank in Cortona is the bottom of the great Laparelli house, which rests on Etruscan stones. On the top floors, windows open to the night show antique chandeliers, big armfuls of light. Often the residents are leaning out, two, sometimes three to a window, watching one more day pass in the history of this piazza. The main shopping streets, lined with great houses, are everywhere converted on the ground floor to the businesses of hardware, dishes, food, and clothing. For many buildings, probably it always has been so.

On the facades, I notice how many times previous

occupants have changed their minds. The door should be here—no, here—and the arch should be a window, and shouldn't we join this building to the next one or add a continuous new facade across all three medieval houses now that the Renaissance is here? The medieval fish market is a restaurant, the Renaissance private theater is an exhibition space, the stone clothes-washing sinks still just await the flow of water, the women with their baskets.

But the clock repairer in his four-by-six-foot shop under the eleventh-century stairway of the city offices has been there for all this time, though he may now be changing the battery on the Swatch watch of an exchange student. He used to blow the glass and sift the white sand from the Tyrrhenian at Populonia for his hourglasses. He studied the water clocks drip by drip. I never have seen him stand; his back must be a hoop from slouching over the tiny parts for so many centuries. His face is lost behind the lenses he wears, so thick that his eyes seem to lunge forward. As I stop in front of his shop, he is working by the light that always angles in just so on the infinitesimal wheels and gold triangles, the numbers of the hours that sometimes fall off the white face, four and five and nine sprinkled on his table.

Perhaps my own teaching activities are immortal and I just don't see it because the place doesn't have this backdrop of time; in fact, my building at the university is a prime earthquake hazard, slated to be demolished. We're to move to a new building next fall, one with a flexible structure suited to a foundation that is partly sand dune. A postwar structure, the current Humanities Building already is obsolete: fifty-year turnaround.

The cobbler, however, seems permanent in his cave-shaped shop, which expands around him only enough for his bench, his shelf of tools, the shoes to be picked up, and one customer to squeeze into. A red boot like one on an angel in the Museo Diocesano, Gucci loafers, a yard of navy pumps, and a worn work shoe that must weigh more than a newborn baby. A small radio from the thirties still brings in the weather from the rest of the peninsula as he polishes my repaired sandal and says it should last for years.

At the *frutta e verdura,* it is the same, the same white peaches at the end of July. The figs that are perfect now and overripe by the time I get them to the kitchen. Apricots, a little basket of rising suns, and bunches of field lettuce still wet with dew. The Laparelli girl, who became a saint and now lies uncorrupted in her venerated tomb, stopped here for her grapes before she gave up eating, in order to feel His suffering more clearly. "From my garden this morning," she heard, as I do when Maria Rita holds up the melon for me to smell the fruit's perfume and her clean hand so often in the earth. When she takes me in the back of her shop to show me how much cooler it is, I step back into the medieval rabbit warren many buildings still are, behind their facades and windows filled with camcorders, silk skirts, and Alessi gadgets. We're under stone stairs, where she has a sink to wash the produce, then, another step down, we're in a narrow stone room with a twist into darkness at the end. *"Fresca,"* she says, fanning herself, and she shows me her chair among the wooden crates, where she can rest between customers. She doesn't get much rest. People shop here for her cascades of laughter, as well as for the uncompromising quality of her produce. She's open six and a half days a week, plus she cares for a garden. Her husband has been ill this year, so she's shifting crates every day as well. By eight, she's smiling, washing down her stoop, wiping a speck off a pyramid of gargantuan red peppers.

We shop here every day. Every day she says, *"Guardi, signori,"* and holds up a misshapen carrot that looks obscene to her, a luscious basket of tomatoes, or a cunning little bunch of radishes. Every garlic head, lemon, and watermelon in her shop has been lavished with attention. She has washed and arranged. She makes sure her best customers get the most select produce. If I pick out plums (touching is a no-no in produce shops and I sometimes forget), she inspects each, points out any deficiency she detects, mumbles, takes another. Each purchase comes with cooking tips. You can't make minestrone without *bietola;* chard is what makes minestrone. And toss in a heel of *parmigiano* for flavor. Just melt these onions for a long time in olive oil, a dash of balsamic vinegar, serve them on *bruschetta.*

Many of her customers are tourists, stopping in for some grapes or a few peaches. A man buys fruit and makes motions of washing his hands. He points to the fruit. She figures out that he's asking her where he can wash it. She explains that it is washed, no one has touched it, but, of course, he can't understand, so she leads him by the elbow down the street and points to the public water fountain. She finds this amusing. "Where is he from that he thinks the fruit isn't clean?"

All along the streets, artisans open their shop doors to the front light. As I glimpse the work inside, I think medieval guilds might still be practicing their crafts. A

young man works on elaborate fruit and flower mar-
quetry of a seventeenth-century desk. As he trims a sliver
of pear wood, he's as intent as a surgeon reattaching a
severed thumb. In another shop near the Porto
Sant'Agostino, Antonio of the dark intent gaze is framing
botanical prints. I step in to look and spot a lovely old
mirror on his shelf. *"Posso?"* May I, I ask before I touch
it. When I lift it, the top of the frame comes loose in my
hand and the fragile, silver-backed antique mirror crashes
to the floor. I want to dissolve. But his main concern is
my seven years of bad luck. I insist on paying for the
mirror, over his protests. He will make a couple of small
mirrors with the old foxed shards and he will repair my
frame and put in a new mirror. As I leave, I see him
carefully picking up the pieces.

Most fascinating to look into is the place where paintings are restored. Strong fumes emanate from this workshop where two women in white deftly clean layers of
time off canvases and rework spots that have been punc-
tured or damaged. Renaissance painters used marble dust,
chalk, and eggshells as paint bases. Sometimes they applied gold leaf onto a mordant made of garlic. Their black
paint came from lampblack, burned olive sticks, and nut-
shells; some reds from insect secretions, often imported
from Asia. Ground stones, berries, peach pits, and glass
yielded other colors, which were applied with brushes
made from boar, ermine, feathers, and quills: spiritual art
coming directly out of nature. To duplicate the colors of
those mulberry dresses, mauve cloaks, azurite robes,
modern alchemical processes must go on in this shop.

In holes in the wall all over town, the refinishing of
furniture goes on. Many men make tables and chests from

old wood. There's no subterfuge involved, no attempt to pass them off as antiques; they know the aged wood won't crack, will take the stain and wax, in short, will look *right,* that is, old. We take our tools to be sharpened in a blackened room where the *fabbro* apologizes because he can't get them back before tomorrow. When we pick up the ten hoes, scythes, sickles, etc., their knife edges gleam. Tempting, but I do not run my finger across the edge.

The tailor does not wear glasses and his stitches could be done by mice. In his dark shop with the sewing machine by the window and the spools lined up on the sill, I see a new white bicycle, a water bottle attached for long trips, nifty leather saddlebags over the back wheel. When I see him later, though, he is only in the town park, feeding three stray cats food from his saddlebags. He unwraps the scraps they are so clearly expecting. He and I are the only ones out on Sunday morning, when most people who live here are doing something else. When I gave him my pants to hem last week, he showed me a circle of photos tacked up on the back wall. His young wife with parted lips and wavy, parted hair. *Morta.* His mother like an apple doll, also dead. His sister. There was one of him, too, as a young soldier for the Pope, restored to youth, with black hair, his legs apart and shoulders back. He was twenty-five in Rome, the war just ended. Now fifty more years have passed, everyone gone. He pats the white bicycle. *I never thought I'd be the one left.*

✳

Cortona merits almost seven pages in the excellent *Blue Guide: Northern Italy.* The writer meticulously directs the walker up each street, pointing out what's of interest. From the gates to the city, further excursions into the surrounding countryside are recommended. Each side altar in the *duomo* is described according to its cardinal orientation, so that, if you happen to know which way east is, after travelling the winding roads, you can locate yourself and self-guide through the nooks and crannies. The writer has even identified all the murky paintings in the choir area. Reading the guide, I'm overwhelmed once again by all the art, architecture, history in one little hill town. This is only one of hundreds of such former marauder lookouts, perched picturesquely for views now.

Now that I know this one place a little, I read with doubled perception. The guide directs me to the acacia-shaded lane along the inside wall of the town, and I immediately remember the modest stone houses on one side, the view over the Val di Chiana on the other. I see, too, the three-legged dog I know lives in the house that always has the enormous underpants drying on a line. I see the cane-bottomed chairs all the people who live along that glorious stretch of wall pull out at evening when they view the sunset and check in with the stars. Yesterday, walking there, I almost stepped on a still soft dead rat. Inside one of the doorways that opens right out onto the narrow street, I glimpsed a woman holding her head in her hands at the kitchen table. Whether she was weeping or catching a catnap, I don't know.

Whatever a guidebook says, whether or not you leave somewhere with a sense of the place is entirely a matter of smell and instinct. There are places I've been which are lost to me. When I was there, I followed the guide faithfully from site to site, putting check marks in the margins at night when I plotted my route for the next day. On my first trip to Italy, I was so excited that I made a whirl-wind, whistlestop trip to five cities in two weeks. I still remember everything, the revelation of my first espresso under the arcades in Bologna, remarking that it stung my throat. Climbing *every* tower and soaking my blistered feet in the bidet at night. The candlelit restaurant in Florence where I first met ravioli with butter and sage. The pastries I bought to take to the room, all wrapped and tied like a present. The dark leather smell of the shoe store where I bought (inception of a lifelong predilection) my first pair of Italian shoes. Discovering Allori in a corner of the Uffizi. The room at the foot of the Spanish Steps where Keats died, and dipping my hand in the boat-shaped fountain just outside, thinking Keats had dipped his hand there. I kept no record of that trip. On later trips, I began to carry a travel journal because I realized how much I forgot over time. Memory is, of course, a trickster. I remember little of three days in Innsbruck—the first bite of autumn air, a beautiful woman with red hair at the next table in a restaurant—but I can still touch every stone of Cuzco; little is left of Puerto Vallarta but the Yucatan is bright in memory. I loved the Mayan ruins seen through waves of hallucinatory heat, a large iguana who slept on the porch of my thatched room, the dogged solitude of the people, crazy storms that blew out the lights, mosquito netting waving around the bed, and candles melting astonishingly fast.

Although a getaway weekend may be just that, most trips have an underlying quest. We're looking for something. What? Fun, escape, adventure—but then what? "This trip is life-changing," my nephew said. Did he know that at the outset, come to Italy looking for affirmation of a change he felt rising in him? I suspect not; he discovered this in travelling. Another guest compared the water, the architecture, the landscape, the wine—all she saw to her hometown's more excellent version. It irritated me to the point of surliness. I wanted to tape her mouth, point her to an eleventh century monastery and say "Look." I felt she went home having seen nothing. Shortly after, she wrote that she was getting a divorce (no word of this while she was here) after a fourteen-year marriage to a man who has decided he is gay. When I thought back on her attitudes here, I understood that she desperately had looked for the comfort of a home which was no longer there. A guest earlier in the summer was on one of those marathon seven countries in three weeks trips. It's tempting to mock that impulse but to me it's extremely interesting when one chooses to power through that many miles. First of all, it's very American. Just *drive,* please. And far and quickly. There's a strong "get me out of here" impetus behind such trips, even when they're disguised as "seeing the lay of the land so I'll know the places I want to come back to." It's not the destinations; it's the ability to be on the road, happy trails, out where no one knows or understands or cares about all the deviling things that have been weighing you down, keeping you frantic as a lizard with a rock on its tail. People travel for as many reasons as they don't travel. "I'm so glad I went to London," a friend told me in college, "Now I don't ever have to go again." The opposite end of that spectrum is my friend Charlotte who crossed China in the back of a truck, an alternate route

into Tibet. In his poem "Words from a Totem Animal,"
W.S. Merwin cuts to the core:

> *Send me out into another life*
> *lord because this one is growing faint*
> *I do not think it goes all the way.*

Once *in* a place, that journey to the far interior of the
psyche begins or it doesn't. Something must make it
yours, that ineffable *something* no book can capture. It can
be so simple, like the light I saw on the faces of the three
women walking with their arms linked when the late
afternoon sun slanted into the Rugapiana. That *light*
seemed to fall like a benison on everyone beneath it. I,
too, wanted to soak my skin under such a sun.

✳

The ideal approach to my new hometown is first to see
the Etruscan tombs down in the flatland below the town.
There are tombs from 800 to 200 B.C. near the train
station in Camucia and on the road to Foiano, where the
custodian never likes the tip. Maybe he's in a bad mood
because he spends eerie nights. His small farmhouse, with
a bean patch and yard-roaming chickens, coexists with
this *tomba* that would appear strangely primordial in the
moonlight. A little uphill, a rusted yellow sign is all that
points to the so-called tomb of Pythagoras. I pull over
and walk along a stream until I reach a short lane, cypress
lined, leading to the tomb. There's a gate but it doesn't
look as if anyone ever bothers to close it. So there it is,
just sitting on a round stone platform. Niches for the
upright sarcophagi look like the shrine at the bottom of

my driveway. The ceiling is partially gone but enough of the curve is left that I can see the dome shape. I'm standing inside a structure someone put together at least two thousand years ago. One massive stone over the door is a perfect half moon.

The mysterious Etruscans! My knowledge of them, until I started to come to Italy, was limited to the fact that they preceded the Romans and that their language was indecipherable. Since they built with wood, little remained. I was almost all wrong. Not much of their written language has been found, but much has been translated by now, thanks to the crucial find of some strips of linen shroud from an Egyptian mummy that travelled to Zagreb as a curio and were preserved later in the museum there. How the Etruscan linen, inscribed with text in ink made from soot or coal, became the wrapping for a young girl is still unknown. Possibly Etruscans migrated to Egypt after they were conquered by Rome around the first century B.C. and the girl was actually Etruscan. Or perhaps the linen was simply a convenient remnant, torn into strips by embalmers who used whatever was at hand. The mummy carried enough Etruscan text to provide several key roots, although the language still isn't totally translated. It's too bad what they left written on stone is gravestone information and government fact. A friend told me that last year a local *geometra* discovered a bronze tablet covered with Etruscan writing. He kicked it up in the dirt of a farmhouse where he was overseeing a renovation and took it home. The police heard about this and called on him that night; presumably, it is in the hands of archaeologists.

Of the local Etruscan culture, an astonishing amount

continues to be unearthed. Beside one of the local tombs, a seven-step stairway of stone flanked with reclining lions intertwined with human parts—probably a nightmare vision of the underworld—was discovered in 1990. Nearby Chiusi, like Cortona one of the original twelve cities of Etruria, only recently found its town walls. Both Cortona and Chiusi have extensive collections of Etruscan artifacts found both by archeological digs and by farmers turning up bronze figures in their furrows. In Chiusi, the museum custodian will take you out to see some of the dozens of tombs found in that area. The Romans considered Etruscans warlike (the Romans weren't?), so they come down to us with that rap on them, but the tombs, enormous clay horses, bronze figures, and household objects reveal them to be a majestic, inventive, humorous people. Certainly, they must have been strong. Everywhere they've left remains of walls and tombs constructed of stupendous stone.

In the land around Cortona, tombs that have been found are called *meloni* locally, for the curved shape of the ceilings. To stand under one of these for a few moments is all you need to absorb the sense of time that prepares you for Cortona.

Leaving the tombs, I start uphill, gently at first, then in a series of switchbacks, I begin to climb, glimpsing through the windshield terraced olives, the crenelated tower of Il Palazzone, where Luca Signorelli fell off scaffolding and died a few months later, a broken watchtower and tawny farmhouses. A soft palate: the mellow stone, olive trees flickering moss green to platinum; even the sky may be veiled by thin mist from the lake nearby. In July, small mown wheat fields bordering the olives turn the color of lion's fur. I glimpse Cortona, noble in profile as Nefertiti. At first I'm below the great Renaissance church of Santa Maria del Calcinaio, then, for a 280-degree loop of the road, level with its solid volumes, then above, looking down on the silvery dome and the Latin cross shape of the whole. The shoe tanners built this church, after the common occurrence of the appearance of the Virgin's face on their tannery wall. She is Saint Mary of the Lime Pits because they used lime in tanning leather and the church is erected on their quarry grounds. Odd how often sacred ground remains sacred: The church rests on Etruscan remains, possibly of a temple or burial ground.

A quick look back—I see how far I have climbed. The wide-open Val di Chiana spreads a fan of green below me. On clear days I can spot Monte San Savino, Sinalunga, and Montepulciano in the distance. They could have sent smoke signals: big *festa* tonight, come on over. Soon I've reached the high town walls, and to get one more brush with the Etruscans, drive all the way to the last gate, Porta Colonia, where the big boggling Etruscan stones support the base, with medieval and later additions built on top.

Whizzing past, I love the fast glimpses into the gates. In town, they sell old postcards of these views and they look exactly the same as now: the gate, the narrow street sloping up, the *palazzi* on either side. When I enter the town, the immediate sense is that I am *inside* the gates—a secure feeling if hoards of Ghibellines, Guelfs, or whoever is the current enemy, are spotted in the distance waving their lances, or even if I've only managed to survive the *autostrada* without getting my car mirror "kissed" by a demon passing in a car half the size of mine.

If I come by car, I walk in on Via Dardano, a name from deep in time. Dardano, believed to have been born here, was the legendary founder of Troy. Right away on the left, I pass a four-table trattoria, open only at midday. No menu, the usual choices. I love their thinly pounded grilled steak served on a bed of arugula. And love to watch the two women at the wood-fired stove in the kitchen. Somehow they never appear to be sweltering.

I'm fascinated by the perfect doors of the dead on this street. Traditionally, they're considered to be exits for the plague dead—bad juju for them to go out the door the living use. If this is so, the custom must have come from some superstition much older than Christianity, which was firmly the religious preference of that time. Some suggest that the raised, narrow doors were used in times of strife when the *portone,* the main door, was barricaded. I've wondered if they were not simply doors used when stepping out of a carriage or off a horse and right into the house in bad weather—rather than stepping down into the wet, probably filthy, street—or even in good weather to protect a long silk skirt. George Dennis, nineteenth-century archaeologist, described Cortona as "squalid in the extreme." That the doors are rather coffin shaped, however, lends a certain visual reinforcement to the door of the dead theory.

The *centro* consists of two irregular piazzas, joined by a short street. No town planner would design it this way but it is charming. A fourteenth-century town hall with twenty-four broad stone steps dominates the Piazza della Repubblica. The steps serve as ringside seats at night when everyone is out having *gelato*—a fine place to take in the evening spectacle below. From here, you can see a loggia on the level above across the piazza, where the fish market used to be. Now it's terrace seating for a restaurant and another perch for viewing. All around are harmonious buildings, punctuated by streets coming up from three gates. The life in the street buzzes, thrives. The miracle of no cars—how amazingly that restores human importance. I first feel the scale of the architecture, then see that the low buildings are completely geared to the body. The main street, officially named Via Nazionale but known locally as Rugapiana, the flat street, is only for walking (except for a delivery period in the morning) and the rest of the town is inhospitable to drivers, too narrow, too hilly. A street connects to a higher or lower one by a walkway, a *vicolo*. Even the names of the *vicoli* make me want to turn into each one and explore: Vicolo della Notte, night, Vicolo dell'Aurora, dawn, and Vicolo della Scala, a long rise of shallow steps.

In these stony old Tuscan towns, I get no sense of stepping back in time that I've had in Yugoslavia, Mexico, or Peru. Tuscans are of this time; they simply have had the good instinct to bring the past along with them. If our culture says burn your bridges behind you—and it does—theirs says cross and recross. A fourteenth-century plague victim, perhaps once hauled out of one of the doors of the dead, could find her house and might even find it intact. Present and past just coexist, like it or not. The old Medici ball insignia in the piazza until last year had a ceramic hammer and sickle of the Communist party right beside it.

I walk through the short connecting leg of street to

Piazza Signorelli, named for one of Cortona's hometown boys. Slightly larger, this piazza swarms on Saturday, market day, year round. It hosts an antique fair on the third Sunday in summer months. Two bars' outdoor tables extend into the piazza. I always notice the rather forlorn-looking Florentine lion slowly eroding on a column. No matter how late I go into town, people are gathered there; one last coffee before the strike of midnight.

Here, too, the *comune* sometimes sponsors concerts at night. Everyone is out anyway, but on these nights the piazza fills up with people from the nearby *frazioni* and farms and country villas. In this town of dozens of Catholic churches, a black gospel choir from America is singing tonight. Of course, this is no spontaneous Baptist group from a Southern church but a highly produced, professional choir from Chicago, complete with red and blue floodlights and cassettes for sale for twenty-thousand lire. They belt out "Amazing Grace" and "Mary Don't You Weep." The acoustics are weird and the sound warps around the eleventh-and twelfth-century buildings surrounding this piazza, where jousts and flag throwers have performed regularly, and where on certain feast days, the bishops hold aloft the relics of saints, priests swing braziers of burning myrrh, and we walk through town on flower petals scattered by children. The sound engineer gets the microphones adjusted and the lead singer begins to pull the crowd to him. "Repeat after me," he says in English, and the crowd responds. "Praise the Lord. Thank you, Jesus." The English and American forces liberated Cortona in 1944. Until tonight, this many foreigners may never have gathered here since, certainly not this many black ones. The choir is big. The University of

Georgia's students from the art program in Cortona are all out for a little down-home nostalgia. They, a smattering of tourists, and almost all the Cortonese are crushed into Piazza Signorelli. "Oh, Happy Day," the black singers belt out, pulling an Italian girl onstage to sing with them. She has a mighty voice that easily matches any of theirs, and her small body seems all song. What are they thinking, this ancient race of Cortonese? Are they remembering the tanks rolling in, oh happy, happy day, the soldiers throwing oranges to the children? Are they thinking, Mass in the duomo was never like this? Or are they simply swaying with the crude American Jesus, letting themselves be carried on his shoulders by the music?

The piazza's focus is the tall Palazzo Casali, now the Etruscan Academy Museum. The most famous piece inside is a fourth-century B.C. bronze candelabrum of intricate design. It's remarkably wild. A center bowl fed oil to sixteen lamps around the rim. Between them, in bold relief, are animals, horned Dionysus, dolphins, naked crouching men *in erectus,* winged sirens. One Etruscan word, *tinscvil,* appears between two of the lamps. According to *The Search for the Etruscans* by James Wellard, *Tin* was the Etruscan Zeus and the inscription translates "Hail to Tin." The candelabrum was found in a ditch near Cortona in 1840. In the museum, it is hung with a mirror above so you can get a good look. I once heard an English woman say, "Well, it is interesting, I suppose, but I wouldn't buy it at a jumble sale." In glass cases, you see chalices, vases, bottles, a wonderful bronze pig, a two-headed man, many lead soldier-sized bronze figures from the sixth and seventh centuries B.C., including some in *tipo schematico,* an elongated style that reminds the contemporary viewer of Giacometti. Besides the Etruscan collection, this small museum has a surprising display of Egyptian mummies and artifacts. So many museums have excellent Egyptian exhibits; I wonder sometimes if anything from ancient Egypt ever was lost. I always visit several paintings I like. One, a portrait of the thoughtful Polimnia wearing a blue dress and a laurel crown, was long thought to be Roman, from the first century A.D. She's the muse of sacred poetry and looks quite pensive with the responsibility. Now she's believed to be an excellent seventeenth-century copy. The museum has not changed the more impressive date.

Appealing family crests emblazoned with carved swans, pears, and fanciful animals cover the side of the Palazzo Casali. The short street below leads to the Duomo and the Museo Diocesano, formerly the Chiesa del Gesù, which I sometimes pop into. Upstairs, the treasure is the Fra Angelico *Annunciation,* with a fabulous neon orange-haired angel. The Latin that comes out of the angel's mouth heads toward the Virgin; her reply comes back to him upside down. This is one of Fra Angelico's great paintings. He worked in Cortona for ten years and this triptych and a faded, painted lunette over the door of San Domenico are all that remain from his years here.

Just to the right of Palazzo Casali is Teatro Signorelli, the new building in town, 1854, but built in a quasi-Renaissance style with arched portico, perfect to shade the vegetable sellers from sun or rain. Inside is an opera house straight out of a Márquez novel: oval, tiered, little boxes and seats upholstered in red, with a small stage on which I once witnessed a ballet troupe from Russia thump around for two hours. It serves now as the movie theater in winter. Midway through the movie, the reel winds down. Intermission. Everyone gets up for coffee and fifteen minutes of talk. It's hard, when you really love to talk, to shut up for an entire two hours. In summer, the movies are shown *sotto le stelle,* under the stars, in the town park. Orange plastic chairs are set up in a stone amphitheater, kind of like the drive-in with no cars.

Off both of these piazzas, streets radiate. This way to the medieval houses, that to the thirteenth-century fountain, there to the tiny piazzas, up to the venerable convents and small churches. I walk along all of these streets. I never have not seen something new. Today, a *vicolo* named Polveroso, dusty, though why it should be more or less dusty than others was impossible to see.

If you're in great shape, you'll still huff a little on a walk to the upper part of town. Even in the mad-dog sun right after lunch, it's worth it. I pass the medieval hospital, with its long portico, saying a little prayer that I never have to have my appendix out in there. At mealtimes, women dash in carrying covered dishes and trays. If you're hospitalized, it's simply expected that your family will bring meals. Next is the interminably closed church of San Francesco, austerely designed by Brother Elias, pal of Saint Francis. At the side the ghost of a former cloister arcs along the wall. Up, up, streets utterly clean, lined with well-kept houses. If there are four feet of ground, someone has planted tomatoes on a bamboo tepee, a patch of lettuces. In pots, the neighborhood hands-down favorite, besides geraniums, is hydrangeas, which grow to bush size and always seem to be pink. Often, women are sitting outside, along the street on chairs, shelling beans, mending, talking with the woman next door. Once, as I approached, I saw a crone of a woman, long black dress, black scarf, hunched in a little cane chair. It could have been 1700. When I got closer, I saw she was talking on a cellular phone. At Via Berrettini, 33, a plaque proclaims it to be the birthplace of Pietro Berrettini; I finally figured out that's Pietro da Cortona. A couple of shady piazzas are surrounded by townhouse-style old houses, with pretty little gardens in front. If I lived here, I'd like *that* one, with the marble table under the arbor of Virginia creeper, the starched white curtain at the window. A woman with an elaborate swirl of hair shakes out a cloth. She is laying plates for lunch. Her rich *ragù* smells like an open invitation, and I look longingly at her green checked tablecloth and the capped bottle of farm wine she plunks down in the center of the table.

The church of San Cristoforo, almost at the top, is my favorite in town. It's ancient, ancient, begun around 1192 on Etruscan foundations. Outside, I peer into a small chapel with a fresco of the Annunciation. The angel, just landed, has chalky aqua sleeves and skirts still billowing from flight. The door to the church is always open. Actually, it's always half open, just ajar, so that I pause and consider before I go in. Basically a Romanesque plan, inside the organ balcony of curlicued painted wood is a touching country interpretation of Baroque. A faded fresco, singularly flat in perspective, shows Christ crucified. Under each wound, a suspended angel holds out a cup to catch his falling blood. They're homey, these neighborhood churches. I like the jars (six today) of droopy garden flowers on the altar, the stacks of Catholic magazines under another fresco of the Annunciation.

This Mary has thrown up her hands at the angel's news. She has a you've-got-to-be-kidding look on her face. The back of the church is dark. I hear a soft honking snore. In the privacy of the last pew, a man is having a nap.

Behind San Cristoforo is one of the staggering valley views, cut into diagonally by a slice of fortress wall, amazingly high. What has held them up all these centuries? The Medici castle perches at the top of the hill, and this part of its extensive walls angles sharply down. I walk up the road to the Montanina gate, the high entrance to town. Etruscan, too; isn't this place ancient? I often walk this way into town. My house is on the other side of the hill and from there the road into this top layer of Cortona remains level. I like to go through the upper town without having to climb. One pleasure of my walk is Santa Maria Nuova. Like Santa Maria del Calcinaio, this church is situated on a broad terrace below the town. From the Montanina road, I'm looking down at its fine-boned shape, rhythmic curves, and graceful dome, a deeply glazed aquamarine and bronze in the sun. Though Calcinaio is more famous, having been designed by Francesco di Giorgio Martini, Santa Maria Nuova pleases my eye more. Its lines counter a sense of weight. The church looks as though it alighted there and easily could fly, given the proper miracle, to another position.

Turning back from the gate toward town, I walk to the other treasure of a church, San Niccolò. It's newer, mid-fifteenth century. Like San Cristoforo's, the decorations are amateurish and charming. The serious piece of art is a Signorelli double-sided painting, a deposition on one side and the Madonna and baby on the other. Meant to be borne on a standard in a procession, it now can be reversed by the custodian. On a hot day, this is a good rest. The eye is entertained; the feet can cool on the stone floor. On the way out, almost hidden, I spot a small Christ by Gino Severini, another Cortona boy. As a signer of the Futurist manifesto and an adherent to the slogan "Kill the moonlight," Severini doesn't readily associate in my mind with religious art. The Futurists were down on the past, embraced velocity, machines, industry. Around town, in restaurants and bars, I've seen posters of Severini's paintings, all color, swirl, energy. Then, over a table in Bar Sport, I noticed that the modern Madonna nursing a baby is his. The woman, unlike any Madonna I've seen, has breasts the size of cantaloupes. Usually a Madonna's breasts look disassociated from the body; often they're as round as a tennis ball. The Severini original in the Etruscan museum just escapes being lugubrious by being tedious. A separate room devoted to Severini is filled with an interesting hodge-podge of his work. Nothing major, unfortunately, but a taste of the styles he ran through: Braque-like collages with the gears, pipes, speedometers the Futurists loved, a portrait of a woman rather in the style of Sargent, art school-quality drawings, and the more well-known Cubist abstractions. A couple of glass cases hold his publications and a few letters from Braque and Apollinaire. None of this work shows the verve and ambition he was capable of. Of course, all the Futurists have suffered from their early enthusiasm for Fascism; baby went out with the bathwater. They've suffered more from the tendency we have had, until recently, to look to France for the news about art. Many astounding paintings from the Futurists are unknown. For whatever reasons, Severini, in his later years, returned to his roots for subjects. I think there's a microbe in Italian painters' bloodstreams that infects them with the compulsion to paint Jesus and Mary.

As I leave San Niccolò, walking down, I pass several almost windowless convents (they must have large courtyards), one of which is still cloistered. If I had lace needing of repair, I could place it on a Catherine wheel, where it is spun in to a nun to mend. Two of the convents have chapels, strangely modernized. On down the hill, I encounter Severini again in a mosaic at San Marco; if I climb this street, I'm on a Crucifixion trail he designed. A series of stone-enshrined mosaics traces Christ's progress toward the Crucifixion and then the Deposition. At the end of that walk (on a hot day I feel I've carried a cross), I'm at Santa Margherita, a large church and convent. Inside, Margherita herself is encased in glass. She has shrunk. Her feet are creepy. Most likely, a praying woman will be kneeling in front of her. Margherita was one of the fasting saints who had to be coaxed to take at least a spoon of oil every day. She shouted of her early sins in the streets. She would be neurotic, anorectic today; back then they understood her desire to suffer like Christ. Even Dante, it is believed, came to her in 1289 and discussed his "pusillanimity." Margherita is so venerated locally that when mothers call their children in the park, hers is the name most often heard. A plaque beside the Bernada gate (now closed) proclaims that through it she first entered the city in 1272.

The major street off the Piazza della Repubblica leads to the park. The Rugapiana is lined with cafés and small shops. The proprietors often are sitting in chairs outside or grabbing an espresso nearby. From the *rosticceria,* tempting smells of roasting chicken, duck, and rabbit drift into the street. They do a fast business in lasagne at lunch and all day in *panzarotti,* which means rolled bread but loses something in the translation. It's rolled around a variety of stuffings, such as mushrooms or ham and cheese. Sausage and mozzarella is one of the best. Past the circular Piazza Garibaldi—almost every Italian town has one—you come to the proof, if you have not intuited it before, that this is one of the most civilized towns on the globe. A shady park extends for a kilometer along the parterre. Cortonese use it daily. A park has a timeless quality. Clothing, flowers, the sizes of trees change; otherwise it easily could be a hundred years ago. Around the cool splash of the fountain of upside-down nymphs riding dolphins, young parents watch their children play. The benches are full of neighbors talking. Often a father balances a tiny child on a two-wheeler and watches her wobble off with a mixture of fear and exhilaration on his face. It's a peaceful spot to read the paper. A dog can get a long evening walk. Off to the right, there's the valley and the curved end of Lake Trasimeno.

The park ends at the *strada bianca* lined with cypresses commemorating the World War I dead. After walking along that dusty road toward home for about a kilometer, I look up and see, at the end of the Medici walls, the section of Etruscan wall known as Bramasole. My house takes its name from the wall. Facing south like the temple at Marzabotto near Bologna, the wall may have been part of a sun temple. Some local people have told us the name comes from the short days in winter we have on this side of the hill. Who knows how old the name, indicating a yearning for the sun, might be? All summer the sun strikes the Etruscan wall directly at dawn. It wakes me up, too. Behind the pleasure and fresh beauty of sunrise, I detect an old and primitive response: The day has come again, no dark god swallowed it during the night. A sun temple seems the most logical kind anyone ever would build. Perhaps the name does go back twenty-six or so centuries to the ancient purpose of this site. I can see the Etruscans chanting orisons to the first rays over the Apennines, then slathering themselves with olive oil and lying out all morning under the big old Mediterranean sun.

Henry James records walking this road in his *The Art of Travel*. He "strolled forth under the scorching sun and made the outer circuit of the wall. There I found tremendous uncemented blocks; they glared and twinkled in the powerful light, and I had to put on a blue eye-glass in order to throw into its proper perspective the vague Etruscan past . . ." A blue eye-glass? The nineteenth-century equivalent of sunglasses? I can see Henry peering up from the white road, nodding wisely to himself, dusting off his uppers, then, no doubt, heading back to his hotel to write his requisite number of pages for the day. I take the same stroll and attempt the same mysterious act, to throw the powerful light of the long, long past into the light of the morning.

RIVA, MAREMMA:
INTO WILDEST TUSCANY

FINALLY, WE'RE READY TO LEAVE BRAMASOLE, IF only for a few days. The floors are waxed and gleaming. All the furniture Elizabeth gave us shines with beeswax polish and the drawers are lined with Florentine paper. The market supplied us with antique white coverlets for the beds. Everything works. We even oiled the shutters one Saturday, took each one down, washed it, then rubbed in a coat of the ubiquitous linseed oil that seems to get poured onto everything. The can of mixed garden flowers I flung along the Polish wall bloom with abandon, ready to bolt at any moment. We live here. Now we can begin the forays into the concentric circles around us, Tuscany and Umbria this year, perhaps the south of Italy next year. Our travels are still somewhat housebased: We are ready to stock a wine cellar, to begin to build up a collection of wines associated with places where we have enjoyed them with local food. Many Italian wines are meant to be drunk immediately; our "cellar" under the stairs will be for special bottles. In the cantina off the kitchen, we'll keep our demijohn and the cases of house wine.

Along the way we plan to taste as much of the Maremma cuisine as possible, bake in the sun, track down other Etruscan sites. Ever since reading D.H. Lawrence's *Etruscan Places* years ago, I have wanted to see the ancient diving boy, the flute player in his sandals, the crouching panthers, to experience the mysterious verve and palpable *joie de vivre* hidden underground all those centuries. For several days we've plotted our route. This seems like a journey into the far interior, though, in reality, it's only about a hundred miles from our house to Tarquinia, where acres and acres of Etruscan tombs are still being explored. Time keeps bending on me here. The *density* of things to see in Tuscany makes me lose sight of our California sense of distance and freeway training, where Ed drives fifty miles to work. A week will be short. The area called the Maremma, moorland, is no longer swampy. The last of the marshy waters were long since drained off. Its history of killing malaria, however, kept this south-western stretch of Tuscany relatively unpopulated. It's the land of the *butteri,* cowboys, of the only unsettled piece of coast along the Tyrrhenian, and of wide-open spaces interrupted only by small stone huts where shepherds used to shelter.

Soon we arrive in Montalcino, a town built for broad views along a bony ridge of hills. The eye seems to stop before the waving green landscape does. Small wine shops line the street. A table with white cloth and a few wineglasses waits right inside each door, as though inviting you in for an intimate drink with the proprietor and a toast to the great vintages.

The hotel in town is modest, indeed, and I'm alarmed that the electrical switches for the bathroom are located in the shower. I aim the showerhead as far into the opposite corner as possible and splash as little as possible. I do not want to fry before tasting the local wines! Compensation is our panorama of the tile rooftops and into the countryside. The *belle époque* café in the center of town doesn't appear to have changed an iota since 1870—marble tables, red velvet banquettes, gold mirrors. The waitress polishing the bar has cupid-bow lips and a starchy white blouse with ribbons on the sleeves. What could be more sensuous than a lunch of *prosciutto* and truffles on *schiacciata,* a flat bread like *focaccia,* with salt and olive oil, along with a glass of Brunello? The utter simplicity and dignity of Tuscan food!

After siesta, we walk to the fourteenth-century *fortezza,* now a fantastic *enoteca.* In the old lower part, which used to store crossbows and arrows, cannons and gunpowder, all the wines of the area are available for tasting. It's brilliantly sunny outside. In the *fortezza,* the light is dim, the stone walls musky and cool. Vivaldi is playing while we try a couple of good whites from Banfi and Castelgiocondo vineyards. Appropriately, the music changes to Brahms as we taste the dark Brunellos from several vineyards: Il Poggiolo, Case Basse, and the granddaddy of all Brunello, Biondi. Brilliant, totally evolved wines that make me want to rush to a kitchen and prepare the kind of hearty food they deserve. I can't wait to cook for these wines—rabbit roasted with balsamic vinegar and rosemary, chicken with forty cloves of garlic, pears simmered in wine and served with mascarpone. The man serving us insists that we try some dessert wines.

We fall for one called simply "B" and another Moscadello from Tenuta Il Poggione. The enologist must have been a former perfume maker. No dessert would be needed with these, except perhaps a white peach, just ripe. On second thought, a lemon soufflé might be just the touch of heaven. Or my old Southern favorite, crème brûlée. We buy a few bottles of the luxurious Brunellos. Just the memory of the price at home makes us indulgent. At Bramasole, we have good wine storage in two spaces under the stone stairs. We can shove cases in, lock the door, and start taking them out in a few years. Since long-term planning is not a strong suit of either of us, we buy a couple of cases of less costly Rosso di Montalcino, drinkable now, in fact, smooth and full bodied. I doubt if the dessert wines will be around by the end of summer.

In late afternoon we drive the few miles to Sant'Antimo, one of those places that feels as if it must be built on sacred ground. From a distance, you see it over in a field of manicured olives, a pale travertine Romanesque abbey, starkly simple and pure in style. It does not look Italian. When Charlemagne passed this way, his soldiers were struck by an epidemic and Charlemagne prayed for it to stop. He promised to found an abbey if his prayer was granted and in 781 he built a church. Perhaps it is the heritage that gives the present church, built in 1118, its slender French lines. We arrive as vespers begin. Only a dozen people are here and three of these are women fanning themselves and chatting just behind us. Usually, the habit of regarding the church as an extension of the living room or piazza charms me, but today I turn and stare at them because the five Augustinian monks who strode in and took up their books have begun the Gregorian chant of this hour. The lofty, unadorned church amplifies their voices and the late lambent sun turns the travertine translucent. The music is piercing to my ear, as some birds' songs that almost can hurt. Their voices seem to roll and break, then part and converge on downward humming tones. The chanting disengages my mind, releases it from logic. The mind goes swimming and swims through large silence. The chant is buoyant, basic, a river to ride. I think of Gary Snyder's lines:

> *stay together*
> *learn the flowers*
> *go light*

I glance at Ed and he is staring up into the pillars of light. But the women are unmoved; perhaps they come every day. In the middle, they saunter noisily out, all three talking at once. If I lived here, I'd come every day, too, on the theory that if you don't feel holy here, you never will. I'm fascinated by the diligence of the monks performing this plainsong for the six liturgical hours of every day, beginning with *lodi,* prayers of praise, at seven A.M., and ending with *compieta,* compline, at nine. I would like to come back for a whole day and listen. I see in the brochure that those on spiritual retreat can stay in guest quarters and eat at a nearby convent. We walk around the outside, admiring the stylized hooved creatures supporting the roof.

A cool evening to ride over dirt roads admiring the land, sniffing like a dog out the window the fresh country smells of dry hay. We arrive at Sant'Angelo in Colle, a restaurant operated by Poggio Antico vineyards. A wedding party is in uproarious progress and all the waitresses are enjoying the action. We're put in a back room alone, with the rousing party echoing around us. We don't mind. A stone sink is piled with ripe peaches, scenting the room. We order thick onion soup, roast pigeon, potatoes with rosemary, and what else, the house's Brunello.

*

Wildest Tuscany is somewhat of an oxymoron. The region, as a whole, has been tamed for centuries. Every time I dig in the garden, I'm reminded of how many have gone before me on the land. I have a big collection of fragments of dishes, dozens of patterns, so many that I wonder if other women fling their dishes into the garden. Crockery colanders, edges of lids, delicate cup handles, and assorted pieces of plates gradually have collected on an outdoor tabletop, along with jawbones of a boar and a hedgehog. The land has been trod and retrod. A glance at terraced farming shows how the hills have been reshaped for the convenience and survival of humans. Still, the Maremma area remained, until less than a hundred years ago, a low coastal plain inhabited by cowboys, shepherds, and mosquitoes. Its *mal aria* was definitely associated with chills and fever. Farmhouses are occasional whereas the rest of Tuscany is dotted with them. The Renaissance touched lightly here; towns, generally, are not permeated with monumental examples of architecture and adorned by the great names in painting. The bad air, now soft and fresh, probably kept the extensive Etruscan tombs safer. Although many were recklessly pillaged, an astonishing number remain. Were Etruscans immune to malaria? All evidence shows that the area was quite populated in their time.

Our next base is a villa, now a small hotel, on the Acquaviva vineyard property outside Montemerano. Ed has cased the *Gambero Rosso* guide and spotted this tiny village with three excellent restaurants. Since it is central for most of what we want to see, we decide to stay put for a few days rather than checking in and out of hotels. A tree-lined drive leads to a park-sized garden with shady places to sit outside and look over the rolling vineyards. We have a room right on the garden. I push open the shutters and the window fills with blue hydrangea. We quickly unpack and take off again; we can relax later.

Pitigliano must be the strangest town in Tuscany. Like Orvieto, it sits on top of a tufa mass. But Pitigliano looks like a drip castle, a precipitous one looming above a deep gorge. Who could look down, while trying to see the town and the road at the same time? Tufa isn't the strongest rock in the world, and sections of it sometimes weaken, erode, or veer off. Pitigliano's houses rise straight up; they're literally living on the edge. The tufa beneath the houses is full of caves—perhaps for the storage of the area's Bianco di Pitigliano, a wine that must derive its astringent edge from the volcanic soil. In town, the bartender tells us that many of the caves were Etruscan tombs. Besides wine, oil is stored and animals are housed. Medieval towns have a dark and twisted layout; this town's feels darker, more twisted. Many Jews settled here in the fifteenth century; it was outside the realm of the Papal States, who were busy persecuting. The area where they lived is called a ghetto. Whether there was a strict ghetto here, as there was in Venice, where Jews had to keep to a curfew, had their own government and cultural life, I don't know. The synagogue is closed for reconstruction but it does not appear that anything much is happening. Almost everything seems to be for sale. In this life or the next, some of the rim houses are going to find themselves in the gorge. Perhaps this contributes to the gloomy feel the town gives me. On the way out, we buy a few bottles of the local white for our growing collection. I ask how many Jews lived there during World War II. "I don't know, signora, I'm from Naples." Winding downhill, I read in a guidebook that the Jewish community was exterminated in the war. I'd never trust a guidebook on a fact and hope that this is wrong.

Tiny Sovana, nearby, has the feeling of a ghost town in California, except that the few houses along the main street are immensely old. People are outnumbered, it seems, by Etruscan tombs built into the hillsides. We spot a sign and pull over. A path takes us into a murky wooded area with a stagnant stream just made for female anopheles mosquitoes. Soon we're scrambling on slippery paths, up along a steep hillside. We begin to see the tombs—tunnels into the hills, stony passageways leading back, probably to vipers. The entrances in that wildness look undisturbed for the centuries. Nothing is attended—no tickets sold, no guides waiting; it is as though you discover these strange haunted sepulchers yourself. Vines dangle, as in the Mayan jungles around Palenque, and the eroded carvings in the tufa also have that strangely Eastern aspect that many of the Mayan carvings have, as though long ago art was the same everywhere. It's very clear that becoming an Etruscan archaeologist is a good move. Endless areas are awaiting further investigation. We climb for hours, encountering only a large white cow standing up to its knees in the stream. When we emerge, I have bleeding scratches on my legs but not a single mosquito bite. I have the feeling that this is a place I will think about on nights of insomnia. Down the road, we see another sign. This points to the remains of a temple, which looks carved out of the tufa hillside. We walk among eerie arches and columns, partly excavated and looking quite abandoned. Those Etruscans are going to stay mysterious. What did they do here? An Art in the Park summer concert series? Strange rites? The guidebooks refer to this as a temple, and perhaps here in the center a wise person practiced haruspication, the art of divining by reading a sheep's liver. A bronze model of one was found near Piacenza, with the liver divided into sixteen parts. It is thought that the Etruscans similarly divided the sky, and that the way the liver was sectioned also determined the layout of Etruscan towns. Who knows? Perhaps the forerunners of talk shows held forth here or it was the market for seafood. In places such as Machu Picchu, Palenque, Mesa Verde, Stonehenge, and now here, I always have the odd and somber consciousness of how time peels us off, how irretrievable the past really is, especially in these hot spots where you sense some matrix of the culture took place. We can't help but push our own interpretations on them. It's a deep wish of philosophers and poets to search for theories of eternal return and time past being time present. Bertrand Russell was closer when he said the universe was created five minutes ago. We can't recover the slightest gesture of those who chopped out this rock, not the placing of the first stone, the lighting of a fire to make lunch, the stirring of a pot, the sniffing of an underarm, the sigh after lovemaking, *niente*. We can walk here, the latest little dots on the time line. Knowing that, it always amazes me that I am intensely interested in how the map is folded, where the gas gauge is pointed, whether we have withdrawn enough cash, how everything matters intensely even as it is disappearing.

We've seen enough for the day but can't resist a walk through ancient Sorano, also poised on an endangered tufa mass. There seem to be no tourists in this whole area. Even the roads are empty. Sorano looks the same way it did in 1492, when Columbus found America. The last building must have gone up around then. There's a somber feel to the narrow streets, a gray light that comes off the dark stone, but the people seem extraordinarily friendly. A potter sees us looking in and insists that we visit his workshop. When we buy two peaches, the man rinsing off his crates of grapes with a hose gives us a bunch. *"Speciale!"* he tells us. Two people stop to help us out of a tight parking place, one gesturing come on, the other gesturing stop.

We're dusty and worn out as we pull into our parking spot near Acquaviva's garden. Before dinner, we shower, change, and take glasses of their own white wine, a Bianco di Pitigliano, out to the comfortable chairs and watch the sun drop behind the hill, just as two Etruscans might have in this exact place.

Montemerano is only a few minutes away, a high castle town, beautiful and small.

It has its requisite fifteenth-century church with the requisite Madonna—this one with a difference. It's entitled *Madonna della Gattaiola, Madonna of the Cat Hole*. The bottom part of the painting had a hole to let the cat out of the church. Everyone in town seems to be outside. A few local boys and men are playing some jazz right in the center of town. The woman running the bar slams the door. Apparently she's heard enough. Absolutely everyone stares when a tall and gorgeous man in riding boots and a tight T-shirt strides by. But he's aloof, takes no notice. I see him check out his image in the shop windows he passes.

We're ravenous. As soon as the magic hour of seven-thirty arrives and the restaurant opens the door, we rush in. We're the only ones in Enoteca dell'Antico Frantoio, a former olive mill, now remodeled to the extent that it looks like a reproduction of itself. Although it has lost its authentic feel, the result is rather like an airy Napa Valley restaurant, so we feel quite at home. The menu, however, reveals the Maremma roots: *Acquacotta,* served all over Tuscany, is a particular local specialty, the "cooked water" soup of vegetables with an egg served on top; *testina di vitella e porcini sott'olio,* veal head and porcini mushrooms under olive oil; *pappardelle al ragù di lepre,* broad pasta with *ragù* made of hare; *cinghiale in umido alle mele,* smoked boar with apples. In *trattorie* over most of Tuscany, menus are almost interchangeable: the usual pastas with *ragù,* butter and sage, pesto, or tomato and basil, the standard selection of grilled and roasted meats, the *contorni* usually consisting of fried potatoes, spinach, and salad. No one seems interested in varying the classics of the cuisine. In this less settled, less travelled region, the cuisine of Tuscany is closer to its origins, the hunter bringing home the kill, the farmer using every part of the animal, the peasant woman making soup with a handful of vegetables and an egg. Usually you do not find the above items; nor do you see *capretto,* kid, or *fegatello di cinghiale,* boar liver sausage, on menus. The Frantoio has its more delicate side, too: *ravioli di radicchio rosso e ricotta,* ravioli with red radicchio and ricotta, and *sformato di carciofi,* a mold of baked artichoke. We start with *crostini di polenta con pure di funghi porcini e tartufo,* polenta squares with a purée of porcini and truffles—rich and savory. Ed orders the rabbit, roasted with tomatoes, onions, and garlic, and I bravely order the kid. It's delicious. The wine of the region is the Morellino di Scansano, black as the wine of Cahors, a discovery for us. This enoteca's own is the Banti Morellino, big and accomplished. Now I'm really happy.

In the morning, I have one of the favorite experiences of my life. We get up at five and go to the hot waterfall near Saturnia. No one is there at that hour, although the hotel manager warned us of crowds later in the day. Pale blue but clear water cascades over tufa, which the falls have hollowed out in many places, forming perfect places to sit down and let the warm water flow over and around you. When I first heard of the falls, I thought we might emerge smelling like old Easter eggs, but the sulphur is mild. The current has enough force so that you feel massaged, not enough to sweep you away. Bliss. Where are the water nymphs? Whatever it is supposed to cure, I'm sure it does. After an hour I feel as though I have no bones in my body. I am utterly relaxed, limp, speechless. We leave just as two cars pull up. Back at Acquaviva, we have breakfast on the terrace: fresh orange juice, nut bread, toast, something like pound cake, and pots of coffee and warm milk. It's hard to leave. Only the lure of the Etruscans stirs us to pick up our map and go.

Tarquinia is out of Tuscany, a few miles into Lazio. It gets ugly along the way, industrial and crowded. I'm less able to visualize the Etruscans here than in the green and dreamy Maremma. Traffic annoys us after so many empty roads. Soon we're in the busy town of Tarquinia, where hoards of items from the tombs are exhibited in a fifteenth-century palazzo. Staggering, amazing, fantastic, and worth the trip alone are two terra-cotta winged horses from the fourth or third century B.C. These were found in 1938 near the steps leading to a temple, now just a two-level base of square limestone blocks. The horses must have been ornaments. I wonder about their connection to Pegasus, who started the flow of the sacred Hippocrene with a dash of his hoof, who always is linked with poetry and the arts. These are fabulously vigorous horses with muscles, genitals, ribs, perky ears, and feathered wings. The chronological arrangement of the museum is useful for sorting out when there were Attic influences, when they began using stone sarcophagi, how design changed. Everything from cinerary urns to perfume burners makes you feel the creative energy and spirit behind these objects. Several tomb paintings have been brought here to prevent deterioration. The tomb of the Triclinium, with its prancing musician and young dancer swathed in what looks like a chiffon throw, would melt the heart of a stone. In almost any museum, I fade after a couple of hours and can wander by with a glance at something that would have stopped me for minutes when I first arrived. We resolve to come back, though, because there is so much to linger over.

The field of tombs could be any field, the necropoli like outhouses attached to sheds. The structures built over tombs open to the public are simply entrances with a flight of steps leading down. The tombs are lit. We're disappointed to find that only four a day are open. Why? No one seemed to know; they're on a rotation system, that's all. Now we know we'll come back because the Hunting and Fishing Tomb is not on view today. We see the Lotus Flower one, with decorations that have almost a Deco style, then the Lionesses one, famous for the reclining man holding up an egg—symbolic of resurrection, as in Christian belief, the shell like the tomb broken open. Dancers cavort here, too. I notice their elaborate sandals with straps crossed and wound around the ankles just like the ones I'm wearing—did the Italians always love shoes? We're lucky to see the Jugglers' tomb, rather Egyptian looking, except for what appears to be a Middle Eastern belly dancer about to go into her act. In the two-chambered tomb of the Orcas remains, amid much faded scenes of a banquet, a startling portrait of a woman in profile with a crown of olive leaves.

After a quick bite, we drive the few kilometers to Norchia, which we've heard is the site of many recent finds. It does not appear that anyone has been about in decades. The broken sign points up to the sky. After we wander about, a farmer points us in the right direction. At the end of a dirt road we park and set out along the edge of a wheat field. A few meters down the path, we encounter a severed goat head covered with flies. Here, indeed, is a sign—a primitive one of sacrifice. "This is getting spooky," I say as we step around it. The terrain becomes precipitous. We're climbing down and all I can think about is the climb back up. A few rusted hand railings indicate we're going in the right direction. The declivity becomes sharper; we're skidding, holding on to vines. Haven't we seen enough of these tombs? When it levels out, we start to see the openings into the hillside, dark mouths, vines, and brush. We venture into two, breaking through impressive spiderwebs with sticks. Inside, it's as black as, well, a tomb. We see slabs and pits where the bodies and urns lay. Vipers must coil here now. We walk about half a mile along this level. The tombs are more numerous than at Sovana and poke into the hillside at various levels. There's an oppressive feeling of danger I can't identify. I just want to leave. I ask Ed if he thinks this is a weird place and he says, "Definitely, let's go." The way out is as awful as I expected. Ed stops to empty dirt out of his loafer and a sliver of bone falls out. We come to the place where we saw the goat head; it is no longer there. When we get back to the car, another one is parked near us. A young couple is kissing and rolling around with such intensity that they don't hear us. This dispels the bad aura and we head back to the hotel, saturated with Etruscan voodoo.

Ah, dinner, the favorite hour. Tonight it's Caino, which we expect to be the gastronomic highlight of our trip. Before driving into Montemerano, we take a little detour to Saturnia, perhaps the oldest town in Italy if Cortona isn't. It would have to be if, as legend has it, Saturn, son of sky and earth, founded it. The warm waterfall, legend also tells us, first poured forth when the horse of Orlando (Roland in English) pawed the ground with his hoof. A town on Via Clodia has to be older than anything I can grasp. I practice saying "I live on Via

Clodia," imagining a life on such an ancient street. The town is shady and active, not at all lost in time. A few highly bronzed people from the expensive hotel near the falls seem to be looking for something to buy but the shops are plain. They settle at an outdoor café and order colorful drinks in tall glasses.

Caino, a jewel: two gracious small rooms with flowers on the tables, pretty china and wineglasses. With glasses of *spumante,* we settle into the menu. Everything looks good and I have a hard time deciding. They, too, have a combination of sophisticated choices and the rustic Maremma specialties, such as *zuppa di fagioli,* white bean soup, pasta with rabbit sauce, *cinghiale all'aspretto di mora,* boar with blackberry sauce. For our *antipasti,* we're attracted to *flan di melanzane in salsa tiepida di pomodoro,* eggplant flan with tepid tomato sauce, and *mousse di formaggi al cetriolo,* a mousse of cheeses and cucumber. We both want *tagliolini all'uovo con zucchine e fiori di zucca,* egg pasta with zucchini and squash blossoms, for first courses. After that, it's roast lamb for Ed and duck breast in a sauce of grape must vinegar for me. We take the waiter's suggestion for tonight's Morellino, the Le Sentinelle Riserva 1990 by Mantellassi. Praise Allah! What a wine. The dinner is superb, every bite, and the service attentive. Everyone in the small restaurant has noticed the young couple at the table in the middle from the moment they were seated. They look like twins. Both have that curly, magnificent black hair and hers has jasmine flowers caught in its ripples. Both have the sultry eyes my mother used to refer to as "bedroom eyes" and lips like those on archaic Greek statues. They're dressed out of Milan or Rome boutiques, he in a somewhat rumpled tan linen suit and she in a yellow puckered silk sundress that was melted onto her. The waiter pours champagne for them, an oddity in an Italian restaurant. We all avert our eyes as they toast each other and seem to disappear into each other's eyes. Our salads look as if someone picked them from a field this afternoon, and perhaps they did. We're falling into a deep relaxation and exhilaration by now, just what a vacation is supposed to be. "Would you like to go to Morocco?" Ed asks out of nowhere.

"What about Greece? I never intended not to go to Greece." Seeing new places always brings up the possibility of other new places. We're riveted again by the beautiful couple. I see the other diners discreetly staring, too. He has moved from his chair across from her to the one next to her and has taken her hand. I see him reach into his pocket and take out a small box. We turn back to our salads. We will have to forego *dolci* but with our coffee they bring a plate of little pastries anyway, which we manage to eat. This is one of the best dinners I've had in Italy. Ed proposes that we stay a few more days and eat here every night. The lustrous girl now is holding out her hand, admiring a square emerald surrounded by diamonds I can see from here. They both smile at everyone, who they suddenly realize has followed this engagement. Spontaneously we all lift our glasses in a toast and the waiter, sensing the moment, rushes in to refill. The girl shakes back her long hair and little white flowers fall on the floor.

When we leave, the village is dark and silent until we get to the bar at the end of the street, where the whole town must be playing cards and having a last coffee.

In the morning we drive over to Vulci, another ancient-sounding name, with a humpbacked bridge and a castle turned museum. The bridge is Etruscan, with Roman and medieval repairs and additions. Why it's so highly arched is impossible to know because the Fiora, little more than a mighty stream, runs far below in a gorge. But humped it is. Whatever road it once joined has disappeared, so the bridge has a strangely surreal aspect. The castle fortress at one end was built much later. A Cistercian monastery surrounded by a moat, it now serves as a museum, like Tarquinia's, full of astonishing things. Too bad the glass separates us from the objects. They are extremely appealing to the touch. I want to pick up each little votive hand, fawn-shaped perfume bottle, to rub the monumental stone sculptures, such as the boy on the winged horse. Here's the real news about the Etruscans—their art is fortifying, the remains of people who lived in the moment. D.H. Lawrence certainly caught that—but who could not, having seen as much as he did. Rereading him along the way, I'm struck often with what an *ass* he was. The peasants are dullards because they do not immediately see to the wishes of this obnoxious foreigner. No one is just waiting to take him miles into the country to see ruins. No one is equipped with candles the minute he asks. What an inconvenient country! The train schedules are unlike those at Victoria Station; the food is not to his liking. I forgive him now and then, when he totally disappears from the text and just writes what he sees.

Remains of the Etruscan, then Roman, town lie out in the field—stone foundations and bits of floor, some with black and white mosaic, subterranean passageways and remnants of baths: a floor plan of the town, actually, so that you walk around imagining the walls around you, the activities, the views across to the bridge. Off to the side, we see the stark Roman remains of a brick building, walls, a few windows, and holes for beams to hold up a floor. Vulci, a lavish archeological area. Unfortunately, the area's painted tombs are closed today—another reason to return.

We're amazed by the restaurants, too. Enoteca Passaparola, on the road leading up to Montemerano, serves robust food in a very casual ambience—paper napkins, chalkboard menu, plank floors. If there are cowboys left in the Maremma, I think they would head here. We order big plates of grilled vegetables and wonderful green salads with a bottle of Lunaia, a Bianco di Pitigliano made by La Stellata, another gorgeous local wine. The waiter tells us about the area's Cantina Cooperativa del Morellino di Scansano, then brings over a glass for us to taste. We find our house wine for the rest of the summer. At about $1.70 a bottle, it has a deep mellifluous taste that surprises us. More straightforward than the *reserve* Morellinos we've tried, this wine definitely stands up to be counted. We still have the backseat where we can pile a couple of cases.

At the next table an artist draws caricatures of us. Mine looks like Picasso's Dora Maar. When we toast him and begin to chat, he opens a satchel and starts showing us catalogues of his shows. Soon we're nodding politely. He pulls out reviews, pours more wine. His wife looks not mortified but resigned; she's been to restaurants with him before. They're at the *terme,* taking the waters for his liver. I can imagine him cornering people there as they sip their measures of mineral water. He slides his chair over, leaving her at their table. I'm torn between the pleasure of the berry tart listed on the chalkboard and the pleasure of getting the check and leaving. Ed asks for the check and we exit. Up in town we have coffee, then on the way back to the car, we look in the window and see that Signor Picasso is gone. So we have the berry tart after all. The waiter brings us a complimentary *amaro*. "They come here every night," he complains. "We're counting the days until he goes back to Milano with his liver."

Saturated with the Etruscans, well fed, pleased with the hotel, we pack and take off for Talamone, a high-walled town over the sea. The water must be pure here. It's clear as far out as I can wade and quite cold. At our modern hotel, there's no beach, just rocks jutting straight up, with concrete platforms on the water where you can sit in a striped chair and sunbathe. We chose Talamone because it is adjacent to the Maremma's preserved sea-shore, the only long stretch of Tuscan coast unblemished by development. Most sand beaches are a series of con-cessions for umbrellas and rows of chairs as deep as the beach is wide, leaving only a strip along the water for walking. Often these concessions have changing rooms, showers, and snack bars. Italians seem to like this way of being at the beach. So many people to talk to! And, usually, families or groups of friends are together. As a Californian, I'm unhappy to be surrounded. Beaches I grew up on in Georgia and my years of loving the raw windy stretches of sand at Point Reyes unequip me for the Old World beaches. Ed and my daughter like the umbrellas. They've dragged me to Viareggio, Marina di Pisa, Pietrasanta, insist it's just different; you have to get into it. I like to lie on the beach and listen to the waves, to walk with no one in sight. The Tuscan beaches are as crowded as streets. The Maremma preserve, however, even has wild horses, foxes, boar, and deer, according to the brochure. I love the smell of the *macchia,* the wild salty shrubs sailors say they can smell when still out of sight of land. Mostly there's nothing—trails with wild rosemary and sea lavender through sandy hills, the vacant beaches. We walk and sit on the beach all morning. Tyrrhenian, Tyrrhenian the waves say, that ancient sea. We've brought mortadella sandwiches, a hunk of *parmigiano,* and iced tea. Except for a small group of people down the beach, I have my wish to be in nature alone. What color is the sea? Cobalt is close. No, it's lapis lazuli, exactly the color of Mary's dress in so many paintings, with a tesselated sheen of silver. It's good to walk, after days of chasing sites in the car. I'm trying to read but the sun is blaring—perhaps an umbrella *would* be nice.

In the morning we move on to Riva degli Etruschi, coast of the Etruscans. We can't get away from them. This beach does have the rented chairs but, since it joins the preserve, it's not as crowded. We're able to take a long, long walk on the beach followed by a siesta in our tiny individual cottage. We're near San Vicenzo, where Italo Calvino summered. The town shops sell rubber beach balls, rafts, and sand pails. At evening, everyone strolls around buying postcards and eating ice cream. Beach towns are beach towns. We find an outdoor restaurant and order *cacciucco,* a big fish stew. Several kinds of fish, filleted at the cart, are piled in a large white bowl and a hot broth is poured over them. The waiter spreads creamy roasted garlic on slices of toasted bread and we float them in the soup, breathing in the heady aroma. Two fierce little bug-eyed lobsters eye us from our bowls. The waiter keeps coming around, ladling in enough to keep the bread afloat. When he brings the salad, he wheels over a cart of olive oils in crocks, clear bottles, colorful ceramic ones, dozens of choices for our salad. We ask him to select for us and he pours from on high a thin stream of pale green oil onto a bowl of red and green radicchio.

En route to Massa Marittima, we detour to Populonia, simply because it is close and it sounds too ancient to miss. Every little pause makes me want to linger for days. In a café where we stop for coffee, two fishermen bring in buckets of fish, their night's catch. Lunch is not for hours, unfortunately. A woman from the kitchen starts writing up the menu of the day on a blackboard. We drive on into town and park under an immense fortress, the usual castle and wall like those in old books of hours. Ah, another Etruscan museum and I must see every object. Ed is through, for now, with anything that happened before the last millennium, so he goes off to buy honey from bees that have buzzed around in the coastal shrubs. We meet in a shop where I find an Etruscan clay foot for sale. Whether it's genuine or fake, I don't know. I decide to think about it while we take a walk but when we come back to buy it, the shop is closed. As we leave, I see a sign to an Etruscan site but Ed presses on the accelerator; he's tombed out.

Last overnight—the town I have chronically mispronounced. The accent, I find, is on Marit'tima. I've said Maritti'ma. Will I ever, ever learn Italian? Still so many basic errors. Once close to the sea, the town gradually became surrounded by silt, which eventually filled in, leaving Massa Marittima far inland but with a sense of outlook as it rises high over the grassy plain. We could be in Brazil, a remote outpost that appeals to magic realist novelists. It's two towns really, the old town and the older town, both austere, with deep shadows and sudden sunlight. We're a little tired. We check in and for the first time, our room has a TV. A World War II film, faded and in odd Italian, is on and we get hooked. A village, occupied by Germans, depends on an American soldier hiding in the countryside to help them. They must evacuate. They pile everything on a few donkeys and set out, for where we don't know. I doze. Someone is trying to open the shutters at Bramasole. I wake up. Another soldier is in the hayloft. Something is burning. Is Bramasole all right? Suddenly I realize this is our one day in Massa Marittima.

In two hours, we've covered every street. The Maremma keeps reminding me of the American West, its little out of the way towns the freeway missed by fifty miles, the shop owner staring out the window, the wide sky in his gaze. Certainly the piazza and fabulous cathedral are nothing like the West—the similarity is under the skin of the place: a loneliness, an eye on the stranger.

✳

En route home, we pause at San Galgano, loveliest of ruins, a graceful French Gothic church that lost its floor and roof centuries ago, leaving the open-windowed skeleton to grass and clouds. A romantic wedding could take place here. Where the large rose window was, only the imagination can color the space scarlet and blue; where monks lit candles at side altars, birds nest in the corners.

A stone stairway leads nowhere. A stone altar remains, so disassociated from Christian function that human sacrifice could have taken place on it. The place fell into ruin when an abbot sold the lead in the roof for some war. Now it's a home for several cats. One has a litter of multicultural kittens; several fathers must have contributed to the ginger, black, and striped pile curled around the large white mother.

Home! Hauling in the wine, throwing open the shutters, running to water the drooping plants. We settle the wine into crates in the dark wedge of closet under the stairs. The spirit of all the grapes we saw ripening, now bottled and mellowing for those occasions we hope to celebrate. Ed closes the door, leaving them to dust and scorpions for now. Only a week away. We missed the house and come back understanding the next few circles around us. Qualities those of us with northern blood envy—that Italian insouciance and ability to live in the moment with gusto—I now see came down straight from the Etruscans. All the painted images from the tombs seem charged with meaning, if we only had the clues to read it. I close my eyes and look at the crouching leopards, the deft figure of death, the endless banqueting. Sometimes Greek myths come to mind, Persephone, Actaeon and the dogs, Pegasus, but the instinct I have is that the tomb images—and the Greek ones—each came from further back, and those further back came from something even earlier. The archetypes keep appearing and we find in them what we can, for they speak to our oldest neurons and synapses.

When I lived in Somers, New York, I had a large herb garden beside the eighteenth-century house I still dream of. Often I turned up brown and amber medicine bottles. As I was planting a border of santolina, the branches of which used to be spread on church floors in the Middle Ages to keep the human scents down, my trowel unearthed a small iron horse, rusty, stretched into full-out running position. I propped the horse on my desk as my private totem. Earlier this summer, I was digging up stones and my shovel sent flying a small object. When I picked it up, I was stunned to find that it was a horse. Is it Etruscan or is it a toy from a hundred years ago? This horse, too, is running.

A few years ago I read a section in the *Aeneid* about the decision to found Carthage on the spot where the wanderers dug up an omen:

> *the head of a spirited horse, for by this sign*
> *it was shown that the race would be distinguished*
> *in war and abound with the means of life*
>
> (I, 444)

The war in the line doesn't thrill me but "means of life" does. The hoof of Orlando opened the hot spring. The winged horses at Tarquinia, unearthed from stone rubble and dirt, keep appearing in my vision. I prop a postcard photo of them next to my own two horses. Means of life. The Etruscans had it. In certain times and places, we find it. We can run full out, if not fly.

TURNING ITALIAN

THE ITALIAN ED IS A LIST MAKER. ON THE DINING room table, the bedside table, the car seat, in shirt and sweater pockets, I find folded pieces of notepaper and crumpled envelopes. He makes lists of things to buy, things to accomplish, long-range plans, garden lists, lists of lists. They're in mixed English and Italian, whichever word is shorter. Sometimes he knows only the Italian word if it's a special tool. I should have saved the lists during the restoration and papered a bathroom with them, as James Joyce did with his rejection slips. We've exchanged habits; at home, he rarely makes even a grocery list—I make lists there, letters to write, chores, and especially of my goals for each week. Here, I usually don't have any goals.

It is hard to chart such changes of one's own in response to a new place but shifts are easy to spot in another person. When we first started coming to Italy, Ed was a tea drinker. As an undergraduate, he took a semester off to study on his own in London. He lived in a cold-water bed-sitter near the British Museum and sustained himself on cups of tea with milk and sugar while reading Eliot and Conrad. Espresso, of course, is pandemic in Italy; the *whoosh* of steam is heard in every piazza. During our first summer in Tuscany, I remember seeing him eye the Italians as they stepped up to the bar and ordered, in a clipped voice, *"un caffe."* At that time, espresso was rarely seen in America. When he ordered like the Italians, at first the bartenders asked him, *"Normale?"* They thought surely a tourist was making a mistake. We require big cups of brown coffee, as the Italians, with a touch of wonder, call it.

"Sì, sì, normale," he answered, with a slight tone of impatience. Soon he was ordering with authority; no one asked again. He saw the locals down it at once, instead of sipping. He noticed the brands different bars used: Illy, Lavazza, Sandy, River. He began commenting on the *crema* on top. Always he took it black.

"Your life must be sweet," one *barrista* told him, "to take your coffee so bitter." Then Ed began to notice the sugar boats all the bars have, to notice how when the bartender put down the saucer and spoon, the sugar bowl would be pushed over and opened with a flourish. The Italians shoveled in an incredible amount—two, three mounded spoons. One day, I was shocked to see Ed, too, pouring in the sugar. "It makes it almost a dessert," he explained.

The second year we visited Italy, he went home at the end of the summer carrying a La Pavoni, purchased in Florence, a gleaming stainless-steel machine with an eagle on top, a hand-operated classic. I was the beneficiary of cappuccino in bed, our guests of after dinner espresso served in tiny cups he bought in Italy.

Here, he also has bought a La Pavoni, this one automatic. Before going to bed, he has his final cup of elixir, either at home or in town. There is something he likes about ordering in bars. Sometimes they have curvy Deco-era La Faema machines, sometimes chic Ranchillios. He examines the *crema,* swirls the cup once, and gulps it down. It gives him, he says, the strength to sleep.

The second major cultural experience he took to with zest is driving. Most travellers here feel that driving in Rome qualifies as an experience that can be added to one's *vita,* that everyday *autostrada* trips are examinations in courage and that the Amalfi coast drive is a definition of hell. "These people really know how to drive," I remember him saying as he swung our no-power rented Fiat into the passing lane, turn signal blinking. A Maserati zooming forward in the rearview mirror blasted us back to the right lane. Soon he was admiring daring maneuvers. "Did you see *that*? He had two wheels dangling in thin air!" he marveled. "Sure, they have their share of duffers riding the center lane but most people keep to the rules."

"What rules?" I asked as someone in a tiny car like ours whizzed by going a hundred. Apparently there *are* speed limits, according to the size of the engine, but I never have seen anyone stopped for speeding in all my summers in Italy. You're dangerous if you're going sixty. I'm not sure what the accident rate is; I rarely see one but I imagine many are caused by slow drivers (tourists perhaps?) who incite the cars behind them.

"Just watch. If someone starts to pass and it's at all dicey, the person behind him won't pull out until the person has passed—he gives him the chance to drop back. No one ever passes on the right, ever. And they stay out of the left lane entirely except to pass. You know how at home someone figures he's going at the speed limit, he can stay in whatever lane he wants."

"Yes, but—look!—they pass on curves all the time. Here comes a curve, time to pass. They must learn that in driving school. I bet the instructor has an accelerator instead of a brake on his side of the car. You just *know,* if someone is behind you, he's planning to pass—it's his obligation."

"Yes, but all the oncoming traffic knows that. They adjust because they know cars are coming out."

He's delighted to read what the mayor of Naples says about driving there. Naples is the most chaotic city for drivers on earth. Ed loved it—he got to drive on the sidewalk while the pedestrians filled the street. "A green light is a green light, *avanti, avanti,*" the mayor explained. "A red light—just a suggestion." And yellow? he was asked. "Yellow is for gaiety."

In Tuscany, people are more law abiding. They may jump the gun but they do stop for signals. Here, the challenge is the medieval streets with inches to spare on either side of the car and the sudden turn a bicycle barely could make. Fortunately, most towns have closed their historic centers to cars, a boon all around because the scale of piazza life is restored. A boon for my nerves, too, as the twisted streets lured Ed and we have backed out of too many when they became impassable, all the locals stopping and staring as we reverse through their town.

He was most impressed that the police drove Alfa Romeos. The first year after we went home he bought a twenty-year-old silver GTV in perfect condition, surely one of the prettiest cars ever made. He got three speeding tickets in six weeks. One he protested. He was harassed, he told the judge. The highway patrol picks on sports cars and this time he was not speeding. In a simple miscarriage of justice, the judge told him to sell the car if he didn't like the system and he doubled the fine on the spot.

For a while, we exchanged cars. We had to. He was in danger of losing his license. I drove the silver arrow to work and never got a ticket; he drove my vintage Mercedes sedan, unaffectionately known as the Delta Queen. "It lumbers," he complained.

"It's very safe, though—and you haven't been stopped."

"How could I in the gutless wonder?"

When we returned to Italy, he was back in his element. Most of our trips are on small roads. We've learned not to hesitate to take the unpaved roads if the route looks appealing. Usually, they're well maintained or at least navigable. We've been known to go off road to get to an abandoned thirteenth-century church and, as in the tiny towns, to back up when necessary. No problem to one who has ice water in his veins. To back uphill on a curvy one-lane road is an experience to delight the manic driver. "Whoa!" he shouts. He's turned around, one hand on the back of my seat, the other on the wheel. I'm looking down—straight down—into a lovely valley far below. There are perhaps five inches between the wheel and the edge. We encounter a car coming down. They jump out to confer, then they, too begin to back up; now we are a convoy of idiots. They're in a red Alfa GTV like Ed's at home. We all get out where the road widens and they discuss the car at length, going over its particular kind of mirror, the problem with the turn signal, value today, ad infinitum. I've spread the ordinance map on the hot hood of the Fiat, trying to figure how we can escape this ravine where, obviously, the collapsed monastery is not located.

One reason Ed likes the *autostrada* so much is that he gets to combine his pleasures. Autogrills appear every thirty or so miles. Sometimes they're quick stop places with a bar and gas. Others arch over the freeway and have a restaurant and shop, even a motel. He appreciates the clean efficiency of the bars. He nips his espresso, often has a quick *panino* of thick bread and mortadella. I will have a capuccino, unorthodox in afternoon, and he patiently waits. He never would malinger at the bar. In and out. That's the way it's done. Then back on the road, with the fully leaded espresso zinging through him, the speedometer climbing to cruising speed. *Paradiso!*

At a more fundamental level, he has been changed by the land. At first we thought we wanted twenty or thirty acres. Five seemed small, until we started clearing it of jungle, until we started maintaining it. The *limonaia* is full of tools. At home we have our tools in a shiny red metal toolbox—the small size. We did not expect to have pole digger, chain saw, hedge clippers, weed machine, a whole line of hoes, rakes, a corner for stakes, innumerable hand tools that look pre-Industrial Revolution—sickles, grape cutters, and scythe. If we thought, I suppose we thought we'd clear the land, prune the trees, and that was it. An occasional mowing, fertilizing, trimming. What we never knew is the tremendous resurgent power in nature. The land is implausibly regenerative. My experience with gardening led me to think plants must be coaxed along. Ivy, fig, sumac, acacia, blackberry can't be stopped. A vine we call "evil weed" twines and chokes. It must be dug out down to its carrot-sized root; so must nettles. It's a wonder nettles have not taken over the world. Digging them out, even with heavy gloves, it's almost impossible not to get "stung" by their juices. Bamboo, too, has its runners constantly sending shoots into the driveway. Limbs fall. New olives must be restaked after storms. The terraces must be plowed, then disced. The olives must be hoed around, fertilized. The grapes still need weeks of attention. In short, we have a little farm here and we must have a farmer. Without constant work, this place would revert in months to its previous state. We could either feel burdened by this or enjoy it.

"How's Johnny Appleseed?" a friend asks. She, too, has seen Ed up on a high terrace examining each plant, fingering the leaves of a new cherry tree, picking up stones. He has come to know every ilex, boulder, stump, and oak. Perhaps it was the clearing that forged the bond.

Now he walks the terraces daily. He has taken to wearing shorts, boots, and a "muscle shirt," one of those cutaway undershirts my father used to wear. His biceps and chest muscles bulge like "after" pictures on the backs of old comic books. His father was a farmer until the age of forty, when he had to give up and work in town. His ancestors must have come out of the Polish fields. They,

I'm certain, would recognize him across a field. Although he never remembers to water the houseplants in San Francisco, he hauls buckets up to the new fruit trees in dry spells, babies a special lavender with scented foliage, reads into the night about compost and pruning.

*

How Italian will we ever be? Not very, I'm afraid. Too pale. Too unable to gesture as a natural accompaniment to talking. I saw a man step outside the confining telephone booth so he could wave his hands while talking. Many people pull over to the side of the road to talk on their car phones because they simply cannot keep a hand on the wheel, one on the telephone, and talk at the same time. We never will master the art of everyone talking at once. Often from the window, I see groups of three or four strolling down our road. All are talking simultaneously. Who's listening? Talking can be about talking. After a soccer game, we'll never gun through the streets blowing the horn or drive a scooter around and around in circles in the piazza. Politics always will passeth understanding.

Ferragosto, at first, baffled us as a holiday until we began to understand it as a state of mind. We, gradually, have entered this state of mind ourselves. Simply put, *ferragosto*, August 15, marks the ascension of the corporeal body and soul of the Virgin Mary into heaven. Why August 15? Perhaps it was too hot to remain on earth another day. The domed ceiling of the cathedral in Parma depicts her glorious skyward rise, accompanied by many others. From the perspective below, you're looking up their billowing skirts as they balloon above the cathedral floor.

This is a triumph of art—no one's underwear shows. But the day itself is only a marker in the month, for the broader meaning of the word is August holidays and a period of intense *laissez-faire*. We're coming to understand that everyday work life is suspended for *all* of August. Even though throngs of tourists descend on a town, the best *trattoria* may have tacked up a *chiuso per ferie* sign, closed for vacation, and the owners have packed and taken off for Viareggio. American business logic does not bear up; they do not necessarily rake in money during tourist season and take their holiday during April or November when tourists are gone. Why not? Because it is August. The accident rates soar on the highways. The beach towns are mobbed. We have learned to forget all projects more complicated than putting up jam. Or to abandon even that—I fill my hat with plums then sit down under the tree, suck the juice, and toss skin and seed over the wall. All over Italy, the feast of the Assumption calls for a celebration. Cortona throws a grand party: the *Sagra della bistecca,* a *festa* for the great beefsteaks of the area.

Sagra is a wonderful word to look for in Tuscany. Foods coming into season often cause a celebration. All over the small towns, signs go up announcing a *sagra* for cherries, chestnuts, wine, *vin santo,* apricots, frog legs, wild boar, olive oil, or lake trout. Earlier this summer, we went to the *sagra della lumaca,* the snail, in the upper part of town. About eight tables were set up along the street and music blared over them, but because of no rain the snails had disappeared and a veal stew was served instead. At the *sagra* in a mountain *borgo,* I came within one number of winning a donkey in the raffle. We ate pasta with *ragù,* grilled lamb, and watched a dignified old couple, him in a starched collar and her in black to her ankles, dance elegantly to the accordion.

Preparations for Cortona's two-day feast start several days in advance. Town employees construct an enormous grill in the park—a knee-high brick foundation about six by twenty feet and a foot high, with iron grills placed over the top, somewhat like the barbecue pits I remember from home. On the same spot, the grill is used later in the year for the town's *festa* for the autumn *porcini.* (Cortona claims to use the largest frying pan in the world for the mushrooms. I've never been here for that *festa* but can imagine the savory aroma of *porcini* filling the whole park.) The men arrange tables for four, six, eight, twelve under the trees and decorate with lanterns. Little booths for serving go up near the grill, then the ticket booth is taken out of a shed, dusted off, and set up at the entrance to the park. Walking through, I glimpse stacks of charcoal in the shed.

The park, normally closed to cars, is opened these two days of the year to accommodate all the people arriving for the *sagra.* Bad news for our road, which links to the park. Traffic pours by starting at around seven, then pours by again from eleven on. We decide to walk in over the Roman road to avoid clouds of white dust. Our neighbor, one of the grill volunteers, waves.

Big steaks sizzle over the huge bed of red coals. We join the long line and pick up our *crostini,* our plates and salad and vegetables. At the grill, our neighbor spears two enormous steaks for us and we lurch to a table already almost full. Pitchers of wine pass round and round. The whole town comes out for the *sagra* and, oddly, there seem to be no tourists here, except for a long table of English people. We don't know the people we're with. They're from Acquaviva. Two couples and three children. The baby girl is gnawing on a bone and looks delighted. The two boys, in the well-behaved way of Italian children, focus on sawing their steaks. The adults toast us and we toast back. When we say we're Americans, one man wants to know if we know his aunt and uncle in Chicago.

After dinner, we walk through town, along with throngs of people. The Rugapiana is jammed. The bars are jammed. We manage to obtain hazelnut ice cream cones. A bunch of teenagers is singing on the steps of the town hall. Three small boys toss firecrackers, then try to look innocent of the act without succeeding. They double over with laughter. I wait outside listening to them while Ed goes in a bar for a shot of the black elixir he loves. On the way home, we pass back through the park. It's almost ten-thirty and still the grill is smoking. We see our neighbor dining with his gorgeous wife and daughter and a dozen friends. "How long has the town had this *sagra*?" Ed asks them.

"Always, always," Placido answers. Scholars think the first commemoration of Mary's feast day was celebrated in Antioch back in 370 A.D. That makes this year's the 1,624th event for her. Old as Cortona is, perhaps killing the white cow and serving it forth in honor of some deity goes back even farther than that.

✳

After *ferragosto,* Cortona is unusually quiet for a few days. Everyone who was coming to town has been. The shop-keepers sit outside reading the paper or looking absently down the street. If you've ordered something, it won't be coming until September.

❋

Our neighbor, the grill master, is also the tax collector. We know the time by when he passes our house on his Vespa in the morning, at lunch, after siesta, and as he comes home at night. I have begun to idealize his life. It is easy for foreigners to idealize, romanticize, stereotype, and oversimplify local people. The drunk who staggers down the road after unloading boxes at the market in the mornings easily falls into the Town Drunk character from central casting. The hunched woman with blue-black hair is known as The Abortionist. The red and white terrier who visits three butchers to beg for scraps each morning turns into Town Dog. There's the Mad Artist, the Fascist, the Renaissance Beauty, the Prophet. Once the person is really known, of course, the characterization blessedly fades. Placido, the neighbor, however, owns two white horses. He sings as he rides by on his Vespa. We hear him clearly because he coasts by our house on his way in. Starts the motor down the road where the hill levels out. He keeps peacocks and geese and white doves. In early middle age, he wears his light hair long, some-times tied with a bandanna. On horseback, he looks to-tally at home, a born rider. His wife and daughter are unusually pretty. His mother leaves flowers in our shrine and his sister refers to Ed as that handsome American. All this—but what I idealize is that Placido seems utterly happy. Everyone in town likes him. "Ah, Placi," they say, "you have Placi for a neighbor." He walks through town to greetings from every door. I have the feeling that he could have lived in any era; he is independent of time there in his stone house on the olive terraces with his peaceable kingdom. To reinforce my instinct, he has appeared, my Rousseau paradigm neighbor, at our door with a hooded falcon on his wrist.

With my bird phobia, left from some forgotten childhood transference, the last thing I want to see at the door is a predatory bird. Placido has a friend with him and they are beginning to train the falcon. He asks if they can go out on our land to practice. I try not to show the extent of my fear. *"Ho paura,"* I admit, thinking how accurate the Italian is: I *have* fear. Mistake. He steps forward with the twitchy bird, inviting me to take it on my arm; surely I won't be afraid if I see the magnificence of this creature. Ed comes downstairs and steps between us. Even he is somewhat alarmed. My phobia gradually has rubbed off on him. But we are happy that our Placido feels neighborly enough toward the *stranieri* to come over, and we walk out to the far point of land with him. His friend takes the bird and stands about fifty feet away. Placido removes something from his pocket. The falcon extends its wings—a formidable span—and flaps madly, rising up on his talons.

"A live quail. Soon I'll take pigeons from the piazza," he laughs. The friend unfastens the cunning little leather hood and the bird shoots like an arrow to Placido. Feathers start to fly. The falcon devours quickly, making bloody work of the former quail. The friend signals with a whistle and the falcon flies back to his wrist and takes the hood. A chilling performance. Placido says there are five hundred falconers in Italy. He has bought his bird in Germany, the little hood in Canada. He must train it every day. He praises the bird, now immovable on his wrist.

This sport certainly does nothing to subtract from my impression that Placido lives across time. I see him on the white horse, falcon on his wrist, and he is en route to some medieval joust or fair. Walking by his house, I see the bird in its pen. The stern profile reminds me of Mrs. Hattaway, my seventh-grade teacher. The sudden swivel of its head brings back her infallible ability to sense when notes were tossed across the room.

✻

I'm packing for my flight home from Rome when a stranger calls me from the United States. "What's the downside?" a voice asks on the telephone. She's read an article I wrote in a magazine about buying and restoring the house. "I'm sorry to bother you but I don't have anyone to discuss this with. I want to do *something* but I don't know exactly what. I'm a lawyer in Baltimore. My mother died and . . ."

I recognize the impulse. I recognize the desire to surprise your own life. "You must change your life," as the poet Rilke said. I stack like ingots all I've learned in my first years as a part-time resident of another country. Just the satisfaction of feeling many Italian words become as familiar as English would be pleasure enough: *pompelmo, susino, fragola*—the new names of everything. What I feared was that with the end of my marriage, life would narrow. A family history, I suppose, of resigned disappointed ancestors, old belles of the country looking at the pressed roses in their world atlases. And, I think, for those of us who came of age with the women's movement, there's always the fear that it's not real, you're not really allowed to determine your own life. It may be pulled back at any moment. I've had the sensation of surfing on a big comber and soon the spilling wave will curl over, sucking me under. But, slow learner, I'm beginning to trust that the gods are not going to snatch my firstborn if I happen to enjoy my life. The woman on the other end of the line has somehow, through the university, obtained my number in Italy.

"What are you thinking of doing?" I ask this total stranger.

"The islands off the coast of Washington, I've always loved them. There's this place for sale, my friends think I'm crazy because it's all the way across the country. But you go by ferry . . ."

"There's no downside," I say firmly. The waterfall of problems with Benito, the financial worries, the language barriers, the hot water in the toilet, the layers of gunk on the beams, the long flights over from California—this is *nothing* compared to the absolute joy of being in possession of this remarkable little hillside on the edge of Tuscany.

I have the impulse to invite her over to visit. Her desire makes her familiar to me so that we would immediately be friends and talk long into the night. But I'm leaving soon. As I speak to her in her highrise office, the half moon rises above the Medici fortress. Way up, I see the bench Ed made for me under an oak tree. A plank over two stumps. I like to zigzag up the terraces and sit there in late afternoons when the gilded light starts to sift over the valley and shadows stretch between the long ridges. I was never a hippie but I ask her if she ever heard the old motto "Follow your bliss."

"Yes," she replies, "I was at Woodstock twenty-five years ago. But now I handle labor disputes for this transnational conglomerate . . . I'm not sure this makes sense."

"Well, does it seem that you'd be moving into a larger freedom? I've had an incredible amount of fun here." I don't mention the sun, how when I'm away and picture myself here, it's always in full light; I feel *permeable* now. The Tuscan sun has warmed me to the marrow. Flannery O'Connor talked about pursuing pleasure "through gritted teeth." I sometimes must do that at home but here pleasure is natural. The days right themselves one after another, as easily as the boy holding up the jingling scale easily balances the fat melon and the rusty iron discs.

I am waiting to hear if she took the clapboard cottage with its own deep-water pier.

I see her blue bicycle leaning against a pine tree, morning glories climbing up the porch railing.

❊

Brave girl! Placido is walking with his daughter out to the point. She holds up the falcon on her wrist. Her long curls bounce as she walks. Even something to fear is layering into memory; I'm going to dream about this over the winter. Perhaps the falcon will fly through a nightmare. Or perhaps it only will accompany these neighbors in late afternoon as they walk up the cypress drive and out to where they release the bird, allowing it to fly farther each time. So much more to take home at the end of summer. "The Night," by Cesare Pavese, ends:

> At times it returns,
> in the motionless calm of the day, that memory
> of living immersed, absorbed, in the stunned light.

GREEN OIL

"DON'T PICK TODAY—TOO WET." MARCO OB-
serves us taking down the olive baskets. "And the moon's
wrong. Wait until Wednesday." He's hanging the doors,
two original chestnut ones he oiled and repaired, and
new ones, virtually indistinguishable from the old, that he
has made during the fall while we were gone. They re-
place the hollow-core doors our great improver in the
fifties preferred.

We're already late for the olive harvest. All of the mills
close before Christmas and we've arrived with a week to
spare. Outside, a gray drizzle blurs the intense green
grasses that thrived on November rains. I put my hand on
the window. Cold. He's right, of course. If we pick today, the wet olives might mildew if we don't finish and
get them to the mill. We gather our osier baskets that
strap around the waist—so handy for stripping a
branch—and the blue sacks the olives are loaded into, the
aluminum ladder, our rubber boots. Still jet-lagged and
dazed, we're up early, thanks to Marco's arrival at seven-

thirty when it barely was light. He tells us to go make an appointment at a mill; maybe it will clear up later. If so, the sun will dry the olives quickly.

"What about the moon?" I ask. He just shrugs. He wouldn't pick now, I know.

We feel like tumbling back into bed, having had no time since arriving last night to get beyond the twenty-hour trip, with storms buffeting the plane most of the way across the ocean. I felt like kissing the ground when we stepped out on the tarmac at Fiumicino. We crazily went into Rome to do a little shopping, then were really beyond thinking as we drove to Cortona in a hilarious rented Twingo, purple with mint green interior. We hit the *autostrada* in a bumper car and in a state of exhaustion. Still, the wet and vibrant landscape filled us with elation—that lit-from-within green and many trees still twirling colored leaves. When we left in August, it was sere and dry; now the freshness has reasserted itself. At dark we finally arrived. In town we picked up bread and a pan of veal *cannelloni*. The air felt charged and invigorating; we no longer wanted to collapse. Laura, the young woman who cleans, had turned up the radiators two days ago and the stone walls had time to lose their chill. She even had brought in wood, so on our first night here, we had a little feast by the fire, then wandered from room to room, checking and touching and greeting each object. And so to bed, until Marco aroused us this morning. "Laura said you arrived. I thought you'd want the doors right away." Always, always when we arrive there is something to haul from A to B. Ed helped him hoist the doors and held them steady while Marco wiggled the hinges onto the metal spurs.

The venerable mill at Sant'Angelo uses the purest methods, Marco tells us, cold-pressing each person's olives individually, rather than requiring small growers to double up with someone else. However, you must have at least a *quintale,* one hundred kilograms. Our trees, not yet recovered from thirty years of neglect, may not give us that bounty yet. Many trees have nothing at all.

The mill smells thickly oleaginous and the damp floor feels slippery, possibly oily. Rooms where grapes and olives are pressed have the odors of time, as surely as the cool stone smell of churches. The permeating ooze and trickle must move into the workers' pores. The man in charge tells us of several mills that press small batches. We never knew there were so many. All his directions involve turning right at the tallest pine or left beyond the hump or right behind the long pig barn.

Before we leave, he extols the virtues of the traditional methods and to prove his point dips two tablespoons into a vat of new oil and hands them to us to taste. It can't be poured onto the floor; there's nothing to do but swallow the whole thing. I can't but I do. First, a tiny taste and the oil is extraordinary, of a meltingly soft fragrance and essential, full olive taste. The whole spoon at once, however, is like taking medicine. *"Splendido,"* I gulp and look at Ed, who still hesitates, pretending to appreciate the greeny beauty. "What happens to that?" I ask, gesturing to troughs of pulp. Our host turns and Ed quickly slips his oil back in the vat, then tastes what's left on the spoon.

"Favoloso," Ed says to him. And it is. After the first cold pressing, the pulp is sent on to another mill and

pressed again for regular oils, then pressed last for lubricating oils. The dried-out remains, in a wonderful cycle of return, often are used to fertilize olive trees.

As we start to drive away, we see that the doors of San Michele Arcangelo, a church we've admired, are open today. The threshold is scattered with rice—*arborio,* I notice, the rice for risotto. A wedding has taken place and someone must be coming to take down the pine and cedar boughs. The church is almost a thousand years old. Just across the road from each other, the church and mill have served two of the basic needs—and the grain and the vine are not far away. The beamed and cross-beamed ceilings of these old churches often remind me of ship hulls. I've never mentioned this before but now I do. "The church structures reminded someone else of boats, too. 'Nave' comes from *'navis'* in Latin—ship," Ed tells me.

"And what does 'apse' come from then?" I ask, since the lovely rounded forms remind me of bread ovens standing alone in farmyards.

"I believe that root means a fastening together of things, just practical, no poetry there."

There is poetry in the rhythm of the three naves, the three apses, the classic basilica plan in miniature. The lines rhyme perfectly in their stony movement along such a small space. The only adornment is the scent of evergreens. As much as I love the great frescoed churches, it's these plain ones that touch me most deftly. They seem to be the shape and texture of the human spirit, transformed into stone and light.

Ed swings the car out onto what once was a Roman road. Later it led pilgrims on their way to the Holy Land.

San Michele was a place to rest and restore. I wonder if a mill stood here, too. Perhaps the pilgrims rubbed oil into their weary feet. We, however, are just searching for a mill that will transform our sacks of black olives into bottles of oil. Two of the mills already have closed. At the third, a woman in about six layers of sweaters comes down her steps and tells us we're too late, the olives should have been picked and now the moon is wrong. "Yes," we tell her, "we know." Her husband has closed his mill for the season. She points down the road. At a grand stone villa, we turn in. A discreet sign, IL MULINO, directs us to the rear but when we drive around, two workers are hosing off their equipment. Too late. They direct us to the large mill near town.

Whizzing along, I look at the winter gardens. Everyone's growing pale, stalky *cardi,* cardoons—called *gobbi* in the local dialect—and green-black *cavolo nero,* black cabbage, which grows not in a head but in upright plumes. Red and green radicchio star in every garden. Most have a few artichoke plants. Until winter, I never knew there were so many persimmon trees. With the lacquered orange fruit dangling in bare limbs, the trees look composed of quick brush strokes, like Japanese drawings of themselves.

At the mill, everyone is so busy that we're ignored. We walk around watching the process and aren't drawn to having our precious olives pressed here. It's all quite mechanized looking. Where are the big stone wheels? We can't really tell if they use heat, a process that supposedly damages the taste. We watch a customer come in, have his fruit weighed, then see it dumped into a large cart. Maybe the olives are all the same and mixing doesn't matter but somehow, this time, we would love to have the pleasure of oil from the land we've worked on. We exit quickly and drive to our last hope, a small mill near Castiglion Fiorentino. Outside the door, three huge stone wheels lean against the building. Just inside, wooden bins of olives are stacked, each one with a name on it. Yes, they can press ours. We are to come back tomorrow.

The afternoon warms and clears. Marco gives us the O.K. to begin. Moon or no, we start picking. It's fast. We empty our baskets into the laundry basket and, as that fills, pour the olives into the sack. Few have fallen though they yield easily to our fingers. A strong wind could cause a lot of damage unless one had spread nets under the trees. The shiny black olives are plump and firm. Curious about the raw drupe, I bite one and it tastes like an alum stick. How did anyone ever figure out how to cure them? The same people, no doubt, who first had the nerve to taste oysters. Ligurians used to cure them by hanging bags in the sea; inland people smoked them over the winter in their chimneys, something I'd like to try. We peel off jackets, then sweaters as we work, hanging them in the trees. The temperature has climbed to about fifty-five degrees and although our boots are wet, the air feels balmy. Off in the distance, we see the blue swath of Lake Trasimeno under an intense blue sky. By three, we have stripped every single olive off twelve trees. I've put my sweater on again. Days are short here in winter and already the sun is headed for the rim of the hill behind the house. By four, our red fingers are stiff and we quit, hauling the sack and basket down the terraces into the cantina.

Not for the first time in our history here, my body is jarred into awareness. Today: shoulders! Nothing would be nicer than a long soak in a bubble bath and a massage. I have left my body oil to warm on the radiator in anticipation. But with only twenty days here every minute counts. We force ourselves to go into town to stock up on food. My daughter and her boyfriend Jess arrive in three days. We're planning several major feasts. We drive in just as the stores are reopening after siesta. Strange—it's already dark as the town comes back to life. Swags of white lights strung across the narrow streets swing in the wind. The A & O market, where we shop, has a rather ratty artificial tree (the only tree in town) outside and big baskets of gift foods inside.

From our brief Christmas visit last year, we know that the focus of the season is twofold: food and the *presepio,* the crèche. We're ready to launch into one and are intrigued by the other. The bars display fancy candies and that lighter Italian parallel to our ubiquitous Christmas fruitcake, the *panettone,* in colorful boxes. A few shops have distinctly homemade wreaths. That's it for decoration, except for the crèches in all the churches and in many windows. *"Auguri, auguri,"* everyone says, best wishes. No one is rushing about. There seems to be no gift wrap, no hype, no frantic search.

The window of the *frutta e verdura* is steamed. Outside, where we're used to seeing the fruits of summer, we find baskets of walnuts, chestnuts, and fragrant clementines, those tiny tangerines without seeds. Maria Rita, inside in a big black sweater, is cracking almonds. *"Ah, benissimo!"* she greets us. *"Ben tornato!"* Where there were luscious tomatoes, she has piled stacks of *cardi,* which I've never tasted. "You boil it but first you must take off all the strings." She cracks a stalk and peels back the celerylike filaments. "Throw it in some lemon water quickly or it will turn black. Then boil. Now it's ready for the *parmigiano,* the butter."

"How much?"

"Enough, enough, signora. Then the oven." Soon she's telling us to make *bruschetta* on the grill in the fireplace and pile on it chopped black cabbage cooked with garlic and oil in a frying pan. We buy blood oranges and tiny green lentils from a jar, chestnuts, winter pears, winy little apples, and broccoli, which I've never seen in Italy before. "Lentils for the New Year," she tells us. "I always add mint." She piles in our bags all the ingredients for *ribollita,* the wintery soup.

At the butcher's, new sausages are in, looped along the front of the meat case. A man with a sausage-shaped nose himself elbows Ed and acts out saying the rosary, then points to the long links of fat sausages. It takes us a moment to make the connection, which he thinks is very funny. Quail and several birds that look as though they should be singing in a tree lie still in their feathers in the case. Color photos on the wall show the butcher's name written on the backsides of several enormous white cows, source of the Val di Chiana steak that Tuscany celebrates. There's Bruno with his hand possessively around the neck of a great beast. He motions for us to follow him. He opens the freezer room and we follow him in. A cow the size of an elephant hangs from ceiling hooks. Bruno slaps a flank affectionately. "The finest *bistecca* in the world. A hot grill, rosemary, and a little lemon at the table." He turns up both hands, a gesture that adds "What else is there in life?" Suddenly, the door slams shut and we are locked inside with this massive body encased in white fat.

"Oh, no!" I flash on the three of us caught as in the child's game of Freeze. I swing around toward the door but Bruno is laughing. He easily opens the door and we rush out. I don't want any steak.

*

We intended to cook but we have lingered. We deposit all the food in the car and walk back to Dardano, a favorite *trattoria,* for dinner. The son who has waited tables since we came here suddenly looks like a teenager. The whole family sits around a table in the kitchen. Only two other customers are here, local men bent over their bowls of *penne,* each eating as though he were alone. We order pasta with black truffles, a carafe of wine. Afterward we walk around in the quiet, quiet streets. A few boys play soccer in the empty piazza. Their shouts ring in the cold air. The outdoor tables are stored, the bar doors closed tight with everyone inside breathing smoke. No cars. A lone dog on a walk. Totally emptied of foreigners, except us, the town reveals its silences, the long nights when men play cards way past the nine o'clock bells, the deserted streets that look returned to their medieval origins. At the *duomo* wall, we look out over the lights of the valley. A few other people lean on the wall, too. When we're really freezing we walk back up the street and open the bar door to a burst of noise. The cocoa, steamed on the espresso machine, is thick as pudding. One day back and I'm falling in love with winter.

*

At first light, we are out on the terraces, even though heavy dew is on the olives. We intend to finish today, not leaving them time to mildew. Below us the valley surges with fog as thick as mascarpone. We are above it in clear, frosty air, utterly fresh and sharp to inhale, as if we're looking down from a plane: a disembodied feeling—this hillside is floating. Even the red roof of our neighbor Placido's house has disappeared. The lake gives this landscape some of its mystery. Large mists rise off the water and spread over the valley. Fog billows and rises. As we pick olives, wisps of clouds pass us. Soon the sun asserts itself and begins to burn off the fog, showing us first the white horse in Placido's pen, then his roof and the olive terraces below him. The lake stays hidden in a pearly swirl of clouds. We come to trees with nothing on them, then a laden tree. I take the lower branches. Ed leans the ladder into the center and reaches up. To our joy, Francesco Falco, our caretaker of the olives, joins us. He's the quintessential olive picker in his rough wool pants and tweed cap, basket strapped to his waist. He sets to work like the pro he is, picking more than we're able to. He's not as careful, just lets twigs and leaves fall in, whereas we've fastidiously removed any stray leaf after reading they add tannin to the taste of oil. Now and then he pulls out his machete from the back of his pants (how does he not get poked in the bottom?) and hacks off a sucker sprouting up. We must get the olives in, he tells us, a big freeze may be coming. We pause for a coffee but he keeps picking. All fall he has cut back the dead wood so that new growth is encouraged. By spring he will have hacked off everything except the most promising limbs and cleared around each tree. We ask about bush olives, more experimental techniques of pruning we've read about but he will hear nothing of those. The way to take care of olives is second nature, unquestionable. At seventy-five, he has the stamina of someone half his age. The same stamina, I suppose, that gave him the strength to walk home to Italy from Russia at the end of World War II. We identify him so totally with the land around Cortona that it's hard to imagine him as the young soldier stranded thousands of miles from home when the ugly war ended. He jokes constantly but today he has left his teeth at home and we have a hard time understanding him. Soon he heads for the lower terraces, an area still overgrown, because he has seen from the road that some of the olives there are bearing fruit.

With the olives from below, we do have a *quintale*. After siesta, which we've worked through, we hear Francesco and Beppe coming up the road on a tractor pulling a cart of olives. They've taken the sacks of their friend Gino and are on their way to the mill. They load Gino's olives into Beppe's Ape and help us load ours on, too. We follow them. It's almost dark and the temperature is dropping. Many California winters have dimmed my memory of real cold. It's a presence of its own. My toes are numb and the Twingo heater is sending out a forlorn stream of tepid air. "It's only about twenty-five degrees," Ed says.

He seems to radiate warmth. His Minnesota background reawakens anytime I complain that I'm cold.

"Feels like Bruno's freezer to me."

*

Our sacks are weighed, then the olives are poured into a bin, washed, then crushed by three stone wheels. Once mashed, they're routed to a machine that spreads them on a round hemp mat, stacks on another mat, spreads more until there is a five-foot stack of hemp circles with the crushed olives sandwiched between each. A weight presses out the oil, which oozes down the sides of the hemp into a tank. The oil then goes through a centrifuge to get all the water out. Our oil, poured into a demijohn, is green and cloudy. The yield, the mill owner tells us, was quite high. Our trees have given us 18.6 kilograms of oil from our *quintale*—about a liter for each fully bearing tree. No wonder oil is expensive. "What about the acid?" I ask. I've read that oil must have less than one percent of oleic acid to qualify as extra virgin.

"One percent!" He grinds his cigarette under his heel. *"Signori! Più basso, basso,"* he growls, lower, lower, insulted that his mill would tolerate inferior oil. "These hills are the best in Italy."

At home we pour a little into a bowl and dip in pieces of bread, as people all over Tuscany must be doing. Our oil! I've never tasted better. There's a hint of a watercress taste, faintly peppery but fresh as the stream watercress is pulled from. With this oil, I'll make every *bruschetta* known and some as yet unknown. Perhaps I'll even learn to eat my oranges with oil and salt as I've seen the priest do.

The sediment will settle in the big container over time but we like the murky, fruity oil, too. We fill several pretty bottles I've saved for this moment, then store the rest in the semidarkness of the cantina. Along the marble counter, we line up five bottles with those caps bartenders use to pour drinks. I've found those perfect for pouring slowly or dribbling oil. The little lid flaps down after you pour so the oil stays clean. We'll cook everything this holiday season in our oil. Our friends will have to visit and take bottles home with them; we have more than we can use and no one to give it to, since everyone here has their own, or at least a cousin who supplies them. When our trees yield more, we may sell the extra oil to the local consortium. I've bought the terrific *comune* oil in a gallon jug for about twenty dollars. I once lugged one home and it was worth the long flight with the cold jug balanced between my feet.

Our herbs still thrive, despite the cold. I cut a handful of sage and rosemary sprigs, quarter onions and potatoes, and arrange them around a pork roast and pop it in the oven, after a liberal sprinkling of our first season's oil baptizes the pan.

The next afternoon, we find an olive oil tasting in progress, the town's first *festa* for *olio extravergine del colle Cortonese,* the extra virgin oil of the Cortona hills. I remember my tablespoon at the *mulino,* but this time there's bread from the local bakery. Nine growers' oils are lined up along a table in the piazza, with pots of olive trees around for ambiance. "I couldn't have imagined this, could you?" Ed asks me as we try the fourth or fifth oil. I couldn't. The oils, like ours, are profoundly fresh with a vigorous element to the taste that makes me want to smack my lips. The shades of difference among the oils are subtle. I think I taste that hot wind of summer in one, the first rain of autumn in another, then the history of a Roman road, sunlight on leaves. They taste green and full of life.

FLOATING WORLD:
A WINTER SEASON

THERE IS SOMETHING AS INEVITABLE AS LABOR that takes over around Christmas. I feel impelled to the kitchen. I feel deep hungers for star-shaped cookies and tangerine ices and caramel cakes, things I never think of during the rest of the year. Even when I have vowed to keep it simple, I have found myself making the deadly Martha Washington Jetties my mother made every year on the cold back porch. You have to make them in the cold because the sinful cream, sugar, and pecan fondant balls are dipped by toothpick into chocolate and held up to set before being placed on the chilled wax-papered tray. The chocolate dip, of course, constantly turns hard and must be taken into the kitchen and heated. My mother made Jetties endlessly because her friends expected them. We professed to find them too rich but ate them until our teeth ached. I still have the cut-glass candy jar they spent their brief tenures in.

The other absolute was roasted pecans. Nuts roasted in butter and salt; the arteries tense even to read this—we ate them by the pound. I cannot get through a Christmas without them, although now I usually give most to friends and save only a small tin for the house. For guests, of course.

This year, no Jetties. But our almond crop must be used so roasted almonds seem inevitable. This weather demands the red soup pot. In preparation for Ashley and Jess's arrival, I'm making the big pot of *ribollita,* a soup for ending a day of fieldwork, or, as I think of it, for arriving from New York. Reboiled is the unappetizing translation and, naturally, it is, like so many peasant dishes, a soup of necessity: beans, vegetables, and hunks of bread.

Winter food makes me understand Tuscan cooking at a deeper level. French cooking, my first love, seems light years away: the evolution of a bourgeois tradition as opposed to the evolution of a peasant tradition. A local cookbook talks about *la cucina povera,* the poor kitchen, as the source of the now-abundant Tuscan cuisine. *Tortellone in brodo,* a Christmas tradition here, seems like a sophisticated concept. Three half moons of stuffed pasta steaming in a bowl of clear broth—but, really, what is more frugal than to combine a few leftover *tortellone* with extra broth? More than pasta, bread is the basic ingredient of the repertoire. Bread soups, bread salads, which seem rich and imaginative in California restaurants, were simply someone's good use of leftovers, possibly when there was little in the house except a little stock or oil to work with. The clearest example of the poor kitchen must be *acquacotta,* cooked water—probably a cousin of stone soup. This varies all over Tuscany but always involves invention around a base of water and bread. Fortunately, wild edibles always abound along the roadsides. A handful of mint, mushrooms, a little sweet burnet, or various greens might flavor cooked water. If an egg was handy, it was broken into the soup at the last moment. That Tuscan cooking has remained so simple is a long tribute to the abilities of those peasant women who cooked so well that no one, even now, wants to veer into new directions.

✳

Ashley and Jess arrive within an hour of each other, a miracle of scheduling since she is coming to Chiusi from the Rome train and he is coming into Camucia from Pisa and Florence after landing from London. We pick her up, then speed the forty minutes back and arrive just as he steps off the train.

The people one's children bring home are problematic. One came to visit when we were renting a house in the Mugello, north of Florence. He was deeply into Thomas Wolfe and sat in the backseat engrossed in *Look Homeward Angel.* We madly drove all over Tuscany to show them (both artists) the Piero della Francescas but he only turned pages and sighed now and then. Once he looked up and saw the round gold bales of hay in the lovely fields and said, "Cool, those look like Richard Serra sculptures." We never were sure anything else penetrated. A young woman Ashley brought over suffered from dire toothache except when shopping was mentioned. She miraculously recovered long enough to buy everything in sight—she had an excellent eye for design—then relapsed in her room, requiring meals on trays. Nothing was wrong with her appetite. When she returned to New York, she had to have extensive root canal work on three teeth, so her forays into the shops *were* remarkable mental triumphs over pain. Another never paid me for his round-trip New York–Rome ticket, which was charged to my AmEx because Ashley picked up their tickets. Naturally, we have been wondering about the person who will be spending a couple of weeks.

If I'd had a boy, I'd have wanted him to be like Jess. We both fall right away for Jess's humor, intellectual curiosity, and warmth. He arrives with a wicker hamper of smoked salmon, Stilton, oat biscuits, honeys, and jams. He spent his last two days in London buying beautifully wrapped gifts for everyone. Best of all, we don't seem like capital P parents to him but potential friends. Relieved that this will be effortless, I'm buoyed, too, by that expansion I feel when someone new is admitted into my life. My Iranian friend maintains that attractions among people are based on smell, which seems logical enough to me. Most of those most important to me I've liked instantaneously and have known I wanted a permanent friendship. (The times the connection has not lasted still sting.) Jess knows all the words to every rock song. Ashley is laughing. We're already singing in the car. What luck.

It's midday and too warm for *ribollita*. We stop in town and have sandwiches at a bar and Jess tells us about the wedding he was just in at Westminster Abbey. Ashley has had the longer trip and wants to fade. Ed and I take a walk, then, because the day is warm and the force of habit strong, we start to work in the garden. I pull weeds away from herbs and lift geraniums out of pots, shake off dirt from the roots and wrap them in newspaper to store over the winter. Ed mows the long grass and rakes. Everything is drenched, sweet, lush; even the weeds are beautiful. I decorate the shrine with boughs of spruce and its nuts, olive branches and a gold star over Mary's head. Ed tries to burn a pile of leaves we never were able to burn last summer because of the dryness. They're so wet now that they just smoke. When Ashley and Jess reappear, we drive to the nursery and buy a living tree and a big pot to plant it in. Small as it is, it dominates the living room. Since we have nothing for decoration except a string of white lights, we decide to go to Florence tomorrow and buy a few ornaments. I've brought over some candles shaped like stars and some distinctly non-Tuscan *farolitos,* a Santa Fe custom I've kept since spending a Christmas there once and loving the candles in paper bags outlining the adobe houses. These are glazed bags with cut-out stars. We line the front stone wall with a dozen of them and they look magical with their glowing stars. We fill the fireplace overhang with pinecones and branches of cypress Ed cut this afternoon. How easy everything seems and what a pleasure to recover the fun of Christmas. The bowls of *ribollita* and a fire act as knock-out drops. In the big armchairs, we're wrapped in mohair blankets, listening to Elvis singing blue, blue, blue Christmas on the CD.

*

At the outdoor market in Florence, we find papier-mâché balls and bells with decoupage angels. A wagon off to the side serves bowls of *trippa,* tripe, a special love of the Florentines. Business looks brisk. If I thought yesterday that I was falling in love with winter, today it's certain. Florence is redeemed and magnificent on a cold

December morning. As in all the towns, the decorations are sweet—lights strung across the narrow streets at short intervals, necklaces of light with dangling pendants. Obviously the women of this city have not heard of cruelty to wildlife; I never have seen so many long, lavish fur coats. We look in vain for fake fur. The men are dressed in fine wool overcoats and elegant scarves. Gilli, one of my favorite bars, is crowded with noisy voices and clinks of cups and constant rushes of steam from the espresso machine. In the middle of the street, Ed pauses and holds up his hands. "Listen!"

"What is it?" We all stop.

"Nothing! How could we not have noticed? No motorcycles. It must be too cold for them."

Ashley wants boots for Christmas. Obviously, this is the place. She finds black boots and brown suede ones. I see a black bag I really admire, don't need, and manage to resist. Just before everything closes, we dash over to San Marco, the serene monastery with Fra Angelico frescoes in the cells. Jess never has seen it and the twelve angel musicians seem good to look at during this season. Siesta catches up with us, so we settle into a long lunch at Antolino's, a righteous *trattoria* with a potbellied stove in the middle of the room. The menu lists pastas with hare and boar *ragù*, duck, polentas and risottos. The waiters rush by with platters of big roasts.

There's plenty of time for a long walk before the town reopens. Florence! The tourists are gone, or if they're here, the fine misty rain must keep them inside. We pass the apartment we rented five years ago, when I swore off Florence. In summer, wads of tourists clog the city as if it's a Renaissance theme park. Everyone seems to be eating. That year, a garbage strike persisted for over a week and I began to have thoughts of plague when I passed heaps of rot spilling out of bins. I was amazed that long July when waiters and shopkeepers remained as nice as they did, given what they had to put up with. Everywhere I stepped I was in the way. Humanity seemed ugly—the international young in torn T-shirts and backpacks lounging on steps, bewildered bus tourists dropping ice cream napkins in the street and asking, "How much is that in dollars?" Germans in too-short shorts letting their children terrorize restaurants. The English mother and daughter ordering *lasagne verde* and Coke, then complaining because the spinach pasta was *green*. My own reflection in the window, carrying home all my shoe purchases, the sundress not so flattering. Bad wonderland. Henry James in Florence referred to "one's detested fellow-pilgrim." Yes, indeed, and it's definitely time to leave when one's own reflection is included. Sad that our century has added no glory to Florence—only mobs and lead hanging in the air.

In early morning, though, we'd walk to Marino's for warm brioche, take them to the middle of the bridge and watch the silvery celadon light on the Arno. Most afternoons we sat in a café at Piazza Santo Spirito, where a sense of neighborhood still exists even in summer. The sun angling through the trees hit that grand undecorated sculptural facade of Brunelleschi's, with the boys playing ball beneath it. Somehow it must make a difference to grow up bouncing your ball against the wall of Santo Spirito. Perhaps many who come to Florence in summer are able to find moments and places like this, times when the city gives itself over by returning to itself.

Today, the stony streets take a shine from the mist. We walk right in the Brancacci chapel. No line; in fact, only a half dozen young priests in long black gowns, following an older priest as he points and lectures about the Masaccio frescoes. I haven't seen Adam and Eve leaving Eden since the vines over their genitals, painted during some fit of papal modesty, were removed and the frescoes cleaned and restored. Shocking to see them lifted out of the film of centuries of candle smoke: all these distinct faces and the chalky rose and saffron robes. Every face, isolated and examined, reveals character. "I wanted to see what made each one that one," Gertrude Stein said about her desire to write about many lives. Masaccio had a powerful sense of character and narrative and a sharp eye for placing the human in space. A neophyte kneels in a stream to be baptized. Through the transparent water we see his knees and feet. San Pietro flings the basin, showering his head and back with water. All the symbolism of earlier art is abandoned for the cold splash on the boy. Another pleasure is Masaccio's (and Masolino's and Lippi's, whose hands are apparent) attention to architecture, light, and shadow. Here's Florence as he saw, or idealized it, with the sun falling logically—not the sourceless light of his predecessors—on this cast of characters who surely walked the streets of this city.

We hurry to the six-nineteen train and miss it. As we wait, I mention the black bag I didn't buy and Ed decides it would be a terrific Christmas present, although we have said we only are buying things for the house. He and Jess literally *run* back to the shop, halfway across town from the train station. Ashley and I are uneasy when it's five minutes until departure but here they come, smiling and panting, waving the shopping bag just as the train is announced.

On Christmas Eve eve, we take off on a quest in Umbria. Ed thinks we must have one of his favorite reds for Christmas dinner, the Sagrantino, impossible to find this far from its origins. I am after the ultimate *panettone*. I called Donatella, an Italian friend who's a wonderful cook, and asked if we could make one together, thinking the homemade would be better than the commercial ones stacked in colorful boxes in every grocery and bar. "It takes twenty hours of rising," she says. "It must rise four times." I remember how many times I've killed the yeast when making simple bread. When her mother was small, she tells me, *panettone* was just ordinary bread with some nuts and dried fruits tucked into the dough. *La cucina povera* again. "It's really best to buy it." She gave me several brands and I picked out one for Francesco's family. As I was about to take another, a woman buying at the same time told me that the very best are made in Perugia. She wrote the name of a shop, Ceccarani, on a piece of paper. So we are off to Perugia.

Ceccarani's window display is a full crèche intricately executed in glazed bread dough. Dough must be a good medium; the figures have expressive faces, sheep look woolly, fronds on the palm trees are finely detailed. The nativity scene is surrounded by marzipan mushrooms and *panettoni* hollowed out on the side. Inside each—what else but a miniature crèche? Incredible!

Throngs of women fill the shop. I push to the back and select a *panettone* as tall as a top hat.

Deeper into Umbria, we come to Spello and walk all over the steeply terraced town. Coming down from Spello, we see the early moon hoisting itself over the hills. We keep losing it as we turn then face it again, the largest, whitest, spookiest moon I've ever seen. All the way to Montefalco, home of the Sagrantino, we dodge the moon. Two or three times we see it rise again, over a different hill. Jess has taken to calling Ed "Montefalco" for his black leather jacket and tendency to speed. He makes up Montefalco adventures as we take several wrong turns. In the piazza, the wine store is open but the proprietor is missing. We look around, look outside, come back—no sign of him. We take a walk around the piazza. The store stands wide open but still the owner is gone. Finally, we ask at the bar and the bartender points to a man playing cards. We buy our four bottles and head home, chasing the moon across Umbria.

On Christmas Eve, Ashley and I launch into cooking. Jess, a novice, is given tasks and entertains us with rock lyrics. Ed dedicates the morning to squeezing silicone around the windows. He runs into town to pick up tonight's first course, *crespelle,* from the fresh pasta shop. The delicate crêpes are filled with truffles and cream. Our menu after the *crespelle:* a warm salad of *porcini,* roasted red peppers, and field lettuces, grilled veal chops, the local cardoons with béchamel and toasted hazelnuts. For dessert, a family cake I know by heart and *castagnaccio,* the classic Tuscan chestnut flour cake. My neighbor says not to try it. Her grandmother used to make it when they were very poor. "All it takes is chestnut flour, olive oil, and water," she says, grimacing. "My grandmother said that they always had those. They flavored it with rose-mary and some pine nuts, fennel seeds, and raisins if they had some." I've never worked with chestnut flour, an ingredient I'd considered esoteric until I learned that it was a staple of *la cucina povera*. This recipe is decidedly weird. As my neighbor indicates, it must be one of those acquired tastes.

"But where are the sugar and eggs—can this really turn into a cake? And how much water to use? The rec-ipe only says to use enough for the batter to pour easily." My neighbor just shakes her head. I'm intrigued. This cake will send us back to the roots of Tuscan cooking. Ashley and Jess are not so sure they want to be trans-ported that far.

Before siesta, we walk over the Roman road into town for last-minute lettuces and bread. Where is our "angel"? In winter, he does not seem to come to the shrine. I watch for his slow approach, his eyes on the house, then his long pause while he places his flowers. Would he bring a twig of bright rose hips, a shriveled bunch of dried grapes, a spiny chestnut casing split to reveal three brown nuts? Perhaps he walks elsewhere in winter, or stays in his medieval apartment, feeding logs into the woodstove.

Cortona is hopping. Everyone carries at least one *panettone* and one basket of cellophane-wrapped gift foods. No shop plays that canned, generic Christmas mu-sic I find so dispiriting at home. People crowd the bars, stoking themselves with coffee and hot chocolate because the sharp *tramontana* has started to blow in from the north, bringing frigid air from the Alps and northern Apennines.

Peaceful eve, bountiful feast, dessert by the fire. We all hate the chestnut cake. Flat and gummy, it probably has the exact taste of a Christmas dessert during the last war, when chestnuts could be foraged in the forest. We trade it for a platter of walnuts, winter pears, and Gorgonzola, a dessert for the gods. Long before midnight mass, which we'd hoped to experience in one of the small churches, we fade.

*

Ed calls up from downstairs, "Look out the window." Snow fell in the night, just enough to dust the fronds of the palm tree and glaze the terraces with a sheen of white.

"Beautiful! Turn up the heat." My bare feet feel icy. I pull on a sweatshirt, jeans, and shoes and run downstairs. The front doors are wide open, the frosty light pouring in. Ed scrapes a snowball off the outdoor table. I jump aside and it lands in the hall. The sleeping beauties have not yet emerged. We take our coffee to the wall, brush it off, and watch the fog below us moving like an opalescent sea. Snow on Christmas!

Is this much happiness allowed? I secretly ask myself. Will the gods not come down and confiscate this health, abundance of cheer, these bright expectations? Is this the old scar, this rippling of want and fear? My father died on the eve of Christmas Eve when I was fourteen. The funeral day was rainy, so rainy that the coffin floated for a moment before it settled into the earth. My pink tulle Christmas dance dress hung on the back of my closet door. Or is this unrest just part of the great collective holiday blues all the newspapers focus on every year?

Many Christmases in my adult life have been exquisite, especially when my daughter was a child. A few have been lonely. One was very rocky. Either way, the season of joy comes with a primitive urge that runs deep into the psyche.

After breakfast, we build up the fire and open presents. We brought over a few and slowly have accumulated the usual pile around the tree. We hadn't intended to have so many but the day in Florence inspired us to pick out soaps, notebooks, sweaters, and a surprisingly huge quantity of chocolate. One of our gifts is a chestnut roasting pan, which we put to immediate use. We're gathering at four at Fenella and Peter's and one of our contributions will be roasted chestnuts in red wine. We cut a thin slit on each, shake them over the coals for less than ten minutes, then prepare to ruin our nails peeling them. Perhaps because they are fresh, the shells come right off, revealing the plump toasted nut. Everyone takes a job and we fly through the preparation of two *faraone,* guinea hens, and a rustic apple tart made by rolling a large round of pastry on a cookie sheet, piling the buttered and sugared fruit and toasted hazelnuts in the center, then flapping the pastry irregularly around it. Our cook, Willie Bell, would be proud of my variation on her cream gravy. To the *faraone* pan juices, I add béchamel and chopped roasted chestnuts. I want chestnuts in everything. Fenella is preparing a pork roast and polenta, Elizabeth will bring salad, and Max is in charge of another vegetable and dessert. We could fast before such a feast but we have a light lunch of wild mushroom lasagne. A Christmas walk is a long tradition, for Ashley and me at least. Ed and I haven't told them yet where we are going.

We drive to the end of a road near our house and get out. We discovered this walk purely by chance one day when we walked this road and spotted a path at the end of it. We kept walking and made a fantastic discovery. It was one of the great walks I've ever had and we decided then to come back at Christmas. Water is flowing where I've never seen it in summer. Sudden streams gush out of crevices and wash over the road. We come to a waterfall and several torrents. Soon we're in a chestnut and pine forest of huge ancient trees. We see a few patches of snow in the woods and more snow higher up in the distance. The air, deeply moist, smells of wet pine needles. We come to paving stones laid end to end. "Look, a path," Ashley says. "What is this? It's wider up ahead." Out here in nowhere, we're on a Roman road in incredibly good condition for long stretches. We never have reached the end but Beppe, who knows it from childhood, told us it goes to the top of Monte Sant'Egidio, twenty kilometers away. Instead of winding and skirting, Roman roads tend to go straight to the top. The chariots were light and the shortest distance between two points seemed to have governed their surveyors. I've read that some of their road-beds go down twelve feet. We're on the lookout for the distance markers but they have disappeared. Cortona lies below us, and below the town the valley and the horizon look polished and gleaming. We see mountains in the distance we've never seen, and the hilltowns of Sinalunga, Montepulciano, and Monte San Savino rise sharply like three ships sailing against the sky. The last knot of my unrest unravels. I start to hum "I saw three ships come sailing in on Christmas Day, on Christmas Day in the morning." A red fox leaps down onto the path ahead of us. He sweeps his plumy tail back and forth, regards us for a moment, then darts into the woods.

✳

The road to Fenella and Peter's noble farmhouse is rough enough in summer. Now we're holding on to pots and trays and trying not to empty them into one another's laps. The poor Twingo's axle! We ford several impromptu streams and almost get stuck in a washout of near-ditch proportions. When we arrive everyone is gathered by the gigantic fireplace, already into the red wine. This is one of the most magnificent houses in the local vernacular. The living room, formerly a granary, soars two stories high with rows of dark beams. The immense room is filled with a lifetime collection of antiques, rugs, and treasures. The space is too large to heat, however, so we settle into big sofas in the former kitchen, with its fireplace large enough for the original cooks to set their chairs inside it and tend their pots. Downstairs the thirty-foot-long table is laid with pine boughs and red candles. Ghosts of Christmases past join us in everyone's stories of other holidays. Fenella pours the hot polenta onto a cutting board. Ed carves the *faraone* while Peter slices the succulent roast. We pile our plates. Fenella has journeyed to Montepulciano for a stash of her favorite *vino nobile,* which travels around the table. "To absent friends," Fenella toasts. "To the polenta!" Ed rejoins. Our little expatriate band is merry, merry.

En route home, we stop in town for a coffee. We expect the streets to be deserted on Christmas night at nine o'clock, but *everyone* is out, every baby and grand-mother and everyone in between. Walking and talking, always talking. "Well, Jess, you're objective," I say. "You're new here so you must tell me if I'm under an illusion—or is this the most divine town on the planet."

Without a pause, he says, "I'd say so. Yes. Extra *primo* good."

The *passeggiata* activity is to stroll from church to church, viewing the scenes of Christ's birth. The reminder of birth is everywhere, is still the major focus of Christmas here. Pagan, I suppose I am, but I think what a glorious *metaphor* the birth is at year's end, the dark and dead end of the year. The one cry of the baby in the damp straw and death is denied. The baby in every scene has a nimbus of light around his head. The sun is crossing the celestial equator, bringing back the days I love. One foot over and we're on a swing toward light. That restless urge at this season, maybe it's the desire to find the light of one's own again. I've read that the body contains minerals in the exact proportions that the earth does; the percentages of zinc and potassium in the earth are the same amounts we have in our bodies. Could the body have an innate desire to imitate the earth's push toward rebirth?

All the Cortona churches display their *presepi,* nativity scenes. Some are elaborate reproductions of paintings in wax and wood models with elaborate architecture and costume; some are terra-cotta. One crib is made of ice cream sticks. At the middle school's exhibit of students' *presepi,* we're touched to see the children's less ornate versions. Most are traditional, with small dolls, twig trees, and hand-mirror ponds, but one astonishes us. Paolo

Alunni, aged perhaps ten, is a true heir of the Futurists and their love for the mechanical and its energy. His crèche—stable, people and animals—is constructed entirely of keys. The animal keys are horizontal and it's clear which are sheep, which are cows. The humans are upright except for the cunning little diary-sized key that is the baby Jesus. He's made the stable roof from a hinge. Eerie and effective—a stunning piece of art among all the earnest projects.

*

Every morning I look out the window at the valley filled with fog, pink tinted at dawn on clear days, a roiling gray when high clouds blow across from the north. These are seamless days of walks and books, of taking trips to Anghiari, Siena, Assisi, and nearby Lucignano, whose town walls describe a graceful ellipse. At night, we grill in the fireplace—*bruschetta* with melted *pecorino* and walnuts, slices of fresh *pecorino* with *prosciutto,* and sausages. *Scamorza,* more native to the Abruzzo but growing popular in Tuscany, is a hard rind cheese shaped like an 8. It melts to almost a fondue and we spread it on bread. I learn to use the hearth to warm plates and keep food hot, just as my imagined *nonna* must have done. Our favorite pasta becomes *pici con funghi e salsicce,* pencil-thick pasta with wild mushrooms and the grilled sausages. A seven-mile walk along the fire road cancels the effects of one evening of grilling.

On New Year's Eve, I am coming home from town with a carload of groceries. We're cooking the traditional lentils (tiny coin shapes are the symbol of prosperity) and *zampone,* sausage in the shape of a pig's foot. As I climb the road toward home, I pass the dome of Santa Maria Nuova below me. Fog completely surrounds the church and the dome floats above the clouds. Five intersecting rainbows dive and arch around the dome. I almost run off the road. At the curve, I stop and get out, wishing everyone were with me. This is staggering. If it were the Middle Ages, I'd claim a miracle. Another car stops and a man dressed in fancy hunting clothes jumps out. Probably he is one of the murderers of song birds but he, too, looks stunned. We both just stare. As the clouds shift, the rainbows disappear one by one but the dome still drifts, ready for any sign that might be about to happen. I wave to the hunter. *"Auguri,"* he calls.

*

Before Ashley and Jess go back to New York, where serious winter waits to kick in, and before we go back to San Francisco, where paper-white narcissi already are blooming in Golden Gate Park, we plant the Christmas tree. I expect the ground to be hard but it is not. Loamy and rich, it yields to the shovel. As Jess shovels dirt, the white skull of a hedgehog turns up with its perfectly articulated jaw and teeth still attached by a string of ligament. *Memento mori,* a useful thought as the end of one year folds into the new. The sturdy tree looks immediately at home on the lower terrace. As it grows it will tower over the road below. From the upstairs, we'll see its peak growing higher and higher each year. If the rains these first few years are plentiful, in fifty years it may be the giant tree of the hillside. Ashley, old by then, may remember planting it. Because she is flush with beauty, I can't imagine her old. She will come with her friends or family, all of whom will marvel. Or strangers who own the house may take its lower limbs for firewood. Surely Bramasole will still be here, with the olives we've planted thriving on the terraces.

WINTER KITCHEN NOTES

CIBO, FOOD, A BASIC WORD. I'M GATHERING A BAG of *cibo* to take back to California with me. I'm not sure exactly when my carry-on bag became a grocery bag in disguise. Besides olive oil (each of us carries back two liters), I take tubes of those pastes that are marvelous for quick hors d'oeuvres: white truffle, caper, olive, and garlic. They're very inexpensive here and easy to transport. I take boxes of *funghi porcini* bouillon cubes, which I can't get at home, and a pound or so of dried *porcini*. The bright boxes and foil bags of Perugina chocolates make handy gifts. I would like to take a wheel of *parmigiano* but my bag is not that accommodating. This time I'm stuffing in a truffle-flavored vinegar and a good *aceto balsamico*. I notice that Ed has added a bottle of *grappa* to the bag, as well as a jar of chestnut honey.

To the question "Are you carrying any food items?" on the customs form, I must answer yes. As long as products are sealed, no one seems to care. A friend who had special sausages from his hometown of Ferrara stuffed in his raincoat pockets was sniffed by airport beagles and stripped of his heirlooms.

The only kitchen item I usually bring with me *to* Italy is plastic wrap; the Italian kind always gets off to a bad start, leaving me untangling a two-inch strip. This time, however, I have brought one bag of Georgia pecans and a can of cane syrup, pecan pie being a necessary ingredient of Christmas. All the other ingredients of Christmas in Tuscany seem new. One pleasure of the cook is that now and then you learn all over again.

Winter food here recalls the hunter stepping in the door with his jacket pockets filled with birds, the farmer bringing in the olive harvest and beginning the cold-weather work of clearing and preparing the trees, trimming back vines for spring. Tuscan food of this season calls for massive appetites. For us, long walks build us up to the hefty dishes that we order in *trattorie:* pasta with wild boar *ragù, lepre,* hare, fried mushrooms, and polenta. The rich smells drifting from our kitchen are different in winter. The light summer fragrances of basil, lemon balm, and tomatoes are replaced by aromas of succulent pork roast glazed with honey, guinea hens roasting under a layer of *pancetta,* and *ribollita,* that heartiest of soups. Subtle and earthy, the fine shavings of Umbrian truffle over a bowl of pasta prick the senses. At breakfast, the perfumed melons of summer are forgotten and we use leftover bread for slabs of French toast spread with plum jam I made last summer from the delicate *coscia di monaca,* nun's thigh, variety that grows along the back of the house. The eggs always startle me; they're so *yellow.* The freshness does make a tremendous difference, so that a platter of eggs scrambled with a big dollop of mascarpone becomes a very special treat.

I didn't anticipate the extent of the excitement of

cooking in winter: The entire shopping list is changed by the cold season. In winter here, there are no asparagus from Peru, no grapes from Chile. What's available, primarily, is what grows, though citrus comes up from the south and Sicily. A mound of tiny orange clementines, bright as ornaments, shines in a blue bowl on the windowsill. Ed eats two or three at a time, tossing the peels into the fire, where they blacken and shrivel, sending out the pungent scent of their burning oil. Because the days are so short, the evening dinners are long, and long prepared for.

ANTIPASTI

❋

Winter Bruschette

Crostini, the *antipasti* that appear on every menu in Tuscany, and *bruschette* are both pieces of bread onto which various topping are piled or spread. The *crostini* are rounds of bread; the baguette-shaped loaves are sold at the *forno.* A typical platter of *crostini* includes several choices; *crostini di fegatini,* chicken liver spread, is the most popular. I often serve *crostini* with garlic paste and a grilled shrimp on each. *Bruschette* are made from regular bread, sliced, dipped quickly in olive oil, grilled or broiled, then rubbed with a clove of garlic. In summer, topped with chopped tomatoes and basil, it appears frequently as a first course or snack. Winter's robust *bruschette* are fun to prepare at the fireplace. When friends stop in, we open a hefty *vino nobile.*

Bruschette with Pecorino and Nuts

Prepare bruschette *as described above. For each* bruschetta, *slowly melt a slice of* pecorino *(or fontina) in a pan on hot coals or on the stove. When slightly melted, sprinkle chopped walnuts over the cheese. With a spatula, slide the cheese onto the grilled bread.*

Bruschette with Pecorino and Prosciutto

Prepare bruschette. *In an iron skillet over the coals or in a nonstick pan on the stove, slightly melt slices of* pecorino, *top with* prosciutto, *then another slice of* pecorino. *Flip over so that both sides melt and are crisp around the edges. Slide onto bread.*

Bruschette with Greens

Chop cavolo nero, *black cabbage (or Swiss chard). Season and sauté in olive oil with 2 cloves of minced garlic. Spread 1 or 2 tablespoons on each* bruschetta.

Bruschette con Pesto di Rucola

This variation on the standard pesto is equally good with pasta. Arugula is satisfying to grow. It sprouts quickly and the young peppery leaves are best. By the time the leaves are large, the taste usually turns bitter.

Prepare bruschette, *this time cutting the bread into small pieces. In a food processor or mortar, combine a bunch of arugula, salt and pepper, 2 cloves of garlic, and $1/4$ cup of pine nuts. Blend together, then slowly incorporate enough olive oil to make a thick paste. Add $1/2$ cup of grated* parmigiano. *Spread on grilled bread. Makes about 1-$1/2$ cups.*

Bruschette with Grilled Eggplant

I've often burned eggplant on the grill—by the time it's done it's black—so now I bake the whole eggplant in the oven for about 20 minutes, then slice it and, for taste, just finish it off on the grill.

Bake an eggplant on a piece of foil in a moderate oven until it is almost done. Slice and salt. Let rest on paper towels for a few minutes. Brush each slice lightly with olive oil, sprinkle with pepper, and grill. Chop 1/2 cup of fresh parsley, mix with some chopped fresh thyme and marjoram. Lightly brush the eggplant with oil again if it looks dry. Place a slice on a piece of prepared bruschetta, *sprinkle with some of the herb mixture and a little grated* pecorino *or* parmigiano. *Heat briefly in the broiler to melt cheese slightly.*

PRIMI PIATTI

✳

Wild Mushroom Lasagna

Dried lasagna in boxes leaves me cold—those wavy edges like tractor tires, the gummy pasta. Thin sheets of fresh pasta create a light, light lasagna. I watched a real pro with pasta in a local shop. Hers is thin as a bedsheet and supple. In summer, this recipe works well with vegetables instead of mushrooms: sliced zucchini, tomatoes, onions, and eggplant, seasoned with fresh herbs. Both recipes can be used as a filling for long, rolled *crespelle,* crêpes, as well.

Cut sheets of pasta to fit 6 layers in a large baking dish. (Some of the middle layers can be in more than 1 piece.) Prepare a béchamel sauce: Melt 4 tablespoons of butter. Stir in 4 table-

spoons of flour, and cook but do not brown. After 3 or 4 min-
utes, remove from heat and whisk in 2 cups of milk all at once.
Return to heat, stir and simmer until the sauce thickens. Mince
3 cloves of garlic and add it to the sauce, along with 1 tablespoon
of chopped thyme, salt and pepper. Grate 1-1/2 cups of
parmigiano. *In a large pan, heat 2 tablespoons of olive oil or*
butter and sauté 3 cups of sliced fresh mushrooms—preferably
porcini *or* portobello. *If you don't have wild mushrooms, use a*
mixture of button mushrooms and dried porcini *that have been*
revived by soaking them for 30 minutes in stock, water, wine, or
cognac.

Assembly: Cook 1 sheet of pasta until it is barely done,
remove it from the boiling water, and let it briefly drain on a
cloth towel spread on the counter. Place the semidry pasta sheet
in the lightly oiled baking dish and cover it with a layer of
béchamel sauce, a layer of sautéed mushrooms, and a sprinkling
of the cheese. Continue cooking the next pasta sheet as you
prepare each layer. Add a spoonful or two of the pasta water to
the sauce if you've used too much on the first layers. Tuscan
cooks usually use some of the pasta water in their sauces. Top the
dish with buttered bread crumbs and more parmigiano. *Bake,*
uncovered, at 350° for 30 minutes. Serves 8.

❊

Ribollita

A thick, soul-stirring soup with white beans, the ubiquitous bread, and vegetables. As the translation "reboiled"
indicates, this is a soup that is easily made using leftovers,
probably from a big Sunday dinner. The classic recipe
calls for hunks of bread to be added to the pot at the end.
Tuscans pour oil into each bowl at the table. The soup,

with a salad, is a complete meal—unless you've been out plowing. Almost any vegetable can be used. If I say "zuppa" to Maria Rita, she piles in everything I'll need, plus handfuls of fresh parsley, basil, and garlic. I take her advice to include the heel of the *parmigiano*. Once cooked, the softened heel is the cook's treat.

Prepare a pound of white beans by washing them well. Cover with water in a stock pot and bring them to a boil. Take them off the heat and let them sit in the water for a couple of hours. Add more water to cover, add seasonings, and simmer until barely done. They should be watched because they tend to become mushy soon after they're done. Clean and cut into medium dice: 2 onions, 6 carrots, 4 ribs of celery, a bunch of curly cabbage or chard, 4 or 5 cloves of garlic, and 5 large tomatoes (or a box of chopped tomatoes in winter). Mince a bunch of parsley. Sauté the onions and carrots in olive oil. After a few minutes, add the celery, then the chard and the garlic, adding more oil as needed. Cook 10 minutes, then add the tomatoes, a heel of parmigiano, *and the beans. Add enough stock (vegetable, chicken, or meat) to cover. Bring to a boil, then simmer 1 hour to blend flavors. Add the cubes of bread. Allow to rest for several hours. Add the parsley, reheat, and serve with grated* parmigiano *on top and olive oil to pass around the table. Leftover pasta, green beans, peas,* pancetta, *and potatoes all can be added to the pot the next day. At least 15 servings, depending on the amount of stock used.*

❋

Pici with Quick Tomato-Cream Sauce

Hearty sauces of hare and boar adhere especially well to the long, thick strands of this local pasta, which is almost as thick as a pencil. I use this sauce on *fusilli* and *pappardelle* or any broad pasta. This is a favorite.

Cook 4 or 5 slices of pancetta, *drain on paper towels, then crumble and set aside. Chop 2 medium onions and 2 or 3 cloves of garlic and sauté in olive oil for 5 minutes. Chop and add 1 large red pepper and 4 or 5 tomatoes. Season and cook 5 minutes more. Season with chopped thyme, oregano, and basil. Stir in* $1/2$ *cup of light cream and* $3/4$ *cup of puréed tomatoes. Add a spoonful or so of the pasta water to the sauce. Stir the* pancetta *into the sauce at the last minute to retain crispness. Cook and drain enough pasta for 4. Mix the pasta with half the sauce; serve the rest of the sauce over the pasta. Pass the* parmigiano! *Serves 4.*

SECONDI

❉

Quail, Slowly Braised with Juniper Berries and Pancetta

My father was a hunter and our cook, Willie Bell, often was lost in a cloud of tiny feathers as she plucked a mound of quail. The drooping little heads all fell in the same direction. I wouldn't eat them, even after she smothered them with cream and pepper in the huge covered frying pan on the outdoor fireplace. With more equanimity, I've met them in a new guise. The balsamic vinegar should come from Modena. Those that are labeled *Aceto Balsamico Tradizionale di Modena* and are marked *API MO* are the real thing, aged for at least twelve years. Some of the ancient balsamics are so fine that they're sipped like liqueur. I think Willie Bell would approve of these quail.

Flour and quickly brown 12 quail (2 per person) in hot olive oil. Arrange the quail in a heavy casserole with a tight-fitting lid and pour in ¹/₄ cup of balsamic vinegar. Cover quail with strips of pancetta and 2 minced shallots. Sprinkle with sprigs of thyme, crushed peppercorns, and juniper berries. Braise in a slow oven (275°) for 3 hours. Turn the quail over after about an hour and a half. Moisten with a little red wine or more balsamic vinegar if they look dry. They are excellent served with polenta. Serves 6.

❋

Roast Chickens Stuffed with Polenta

In Georgia when I was growing up, the Christmas turkey always was stuffed with a cornmeal dressing. This adaptation of my mother's recipe uses Italian ingredients.

Soak 2 cups of polenta in 2 cups of cold water for 10 minutes, then add it to 2 cups of boiling water in a stock pot. Bring to a boil, then lower the heat and cook, stirring constantly, for 10 minutes. Stir in 1 cup of butter. Remove from the heat and beat in 2 eggs. Add 2 cups of fresh croutons, 2 chopped onions, 3 ribs of chopped celery, and season generously with salt, pepper, sage, thyme, and marjoram. Stuff 2 chickens (or 1 turkey) loosely, tie the legs together, and scatter sprigs of thyme over the birds. Roast on oiled racks in a large pan. 25 minutes a pound at 350° is a rough estimate for the perfectly roasted bird—but start testing sooner. Leftover stuffing can be baked separately in a buttered dish. Serves 8.

✳

Faraone (Guinea Hens) with Fennel

Delicate and flavorful, guinea hens are always available at the butcher. For Christmas, we roasted two and presented them on a large platter, surrounded by grilled local sausages and a wreath of herbs. The bones made a rich stock for soup the next day. Oven-roasted potatoes with rosemary and garlic are a natural companion.

I'm afraid the faraone must first be approached with tweezers to remove remaining pin feathers. Wash and dry 2 birds well. Simplest preparation is best—the flavor of the bird is emphasized. Lay rosemary branches on an oiled roasting pan and place the birds on top. Rub with a mixture of chopped rosemary, basil, and thyme, then lard with strips of pancetta. Remove the tough outer portions of 2 fennel bulbs. Cut in half-inch crescents, drizzle with olive oil, and scatter them around the birds, along with a couple of quartered onions. Roast at 350° at 20 minutes per pound. These birds are leaner than chickens; be careful not to overcook. For a rich sauce, add béchamel sauce and roasted chestnuts to the pan juices. Serves 4.

✳

Rabbit with Tomatoes and Balsamic Vinegar

Coniglio, rabbit, is a staple of the Tuscan diet. At the Saturday market, a farm woman usually has three or four fluffy bunnies looking up at you from an old Alitalia flight bag. In the butcher's case, they're more remote, clean and lean, ruddy pink, sometimes with a bit of fur left on the tail to prove it's not cat. Unappetizing as this note is, the rabbit, simmered in thick tomato sauce with herbs, is delightful. Just call it *coniglio* for the children's sake.

Have the rabbit cut into pieces. Flour them and quickly brown in olive oil. Arrange in a baking dish and cover with the following tomato-balsamic sauce. Sauté 1 large chopped onion and 3 or 4 cloves of minced garlic until translucent. Chop 4 or 5 tomatoes and add them to the pan. Season with 1/2 teaspoon of turmeric, rosemary, salt, pepper, and toasted fennel seeds. Stir in 4 tablespoons of balsamic vinegar and simmer until sauce is thick and reduced. Roast the rabbit, uncovered, for about 40 minutes in a 350° oven. Midway, baste with 2 to 3 tablespoons of additional balsamic vinegar. Serves 4.

❋

Polenta with Sausage and Fontina

In winter, the local fresh pasta shop sells polenta with chopped walnuts, a simple but interesting accompaniment to roasts or chicken. The polenta and sausages, with a grand salad, is a robust meal in itself.

Prepare classic polenta (page 158). Pour half of the polenta into an oiled baking dish. Thinly slice or grate 1-1/2 cups of Fontina and spread over the layer of polenta. Season with salt and pepper. Pour on the rest of the polenta. Slice 6 sautéed Italian sausages over the top and pour on the pan juices. Bake for 15 minutes at 300°. Serves 6.

❋

Honey-Glazed Pork Tenderloin with Fennel

The tenderest, leanest pork is the tenderloin. One tenderloin serves two hungry people and the fennel pairs well with the pork. Wild fennel grows all over our land.

Whether its local popularity first came from its aphrodisiacal powers or its curative uses for eye problems, I don't know. I like its feathery foliage and its mythic connections. Prometheus is said to have brought the first fire to humans inside the thick, hollow stalk.

Brush 2 tenderloins lightly with honey. In a mortar or food processor, crush 1 tablespoon of fennel seeds. Add them to 1 tablespoon of finely chopped rosemary, salt, pepper, and 2 cloves of minced garlic. Spread this mixture on the pork. Place in a shallow, oiled pan. Roast in the oven at 400° until the pork is faintly pink in the middle, about 30 minutes. Meanwhile, cut 2 fennel bulbs in ¹/₄-inch slices. Toss out the tough root end. Steam for about 10 minutes, until cooked but not soft. Purée until smooth, then add ¹/₄ cup of white wine, ¹/₂ cup of grated parmigiano, and ¹/₂ cup of mascarpone (or sour cream). Place tenderloins into a buttered dish and pour sauce over; top with buttered bread crumbs. Cook at 350° for about 10 minutes. Garnish tenderloins with fennel leaves, if available, or with wands of fresh rosemary. Serves 4.

CONTORNI

❋

Chestnuts in Red Wine

Even though I'm living near a chestnut forest, chestnuts still seem luxurious. We roast a few every night to enjoy with a glass of *amaro, grappa,* or a last coffee. Just a short gash or x in the shell before they're put in the pan and they open easily while still hot. Many cookbooks advise roasting chestnuts for up to an hour! In the fireplace, they're ready quickly—15 minutes at the most, depending on how hot the coals are. Jiggle the pan often and remove them at the first sign of charring. Chestnuts taste good with all the flavorful winter meats, especially with guinea hens.

Roast and peel 30 or 40 chestnuts. Simmer the chesnuts in just enough red wine to cover for half an hour, long enough for the two flavors to intertwine. Pour off most of the wine. Serves 6.

❋

Garlic Flan

Excellent with any roast.

Separate the cloves from a large head of garlic. Without peeling, place the cloves in boiling water for 5 minutes. Cool, and squeeze out the garlic. Mince and crush the cloves with a fork, then stir into 2 cups of cream. Bring cream and garlic just to a simmer in a saucepan. Add a little ground nutmeg, salt, and pepper. Remove from the flame and beat in 4 egg yolks. Pour into 6 individual molds, well-oiled, or into a shallow baking pan. Bake in a bains-marie at 350° for 20 minutes or until set. Cool for 10 minutes before unmolding.

❋

Cardoons

As long as your arm, prickly, and pale green, cardoons are trouble but worth it. This vegetable was new to me. I learned to strip the tough, stringy exterior from the stalks—the stalks are somewhat like celery—and quickly place the cardoon pieces in water and lemon juice because they otherwise turn dark in a hurry. At first I steamed them but they never seemed to get done. I found that boiling them is best, just to the point of fork tenderness. They have a taste and texture similar to heart of artichoke—not surprising since they come from the same family.

After stripping a large bunch of cardoons and bathing them in acidulated water, cut in two-inch pieces and boil until just done. Drain and arrange in a well-buttered baking dish. Season with salt and pepper and lightly cover with a béchamel sauce (see recipe on page 270), dots of butter, and a sprinkling of parmigiano. *Bake at 350° for 20 minutes.*

❋

Warm Porcini (or Portobello) Salad with Roasted Red and Yellow Peppers

Serve this colorful composed salad as a first or main course.

Grill 2 large mushrooms or sauté them topside down in olive oil (this prevents them from losing their juices). Slice and drizzle lightly with vinaigrette. Grill 2 peppers, one red and one green, and let them cool in a bag, then slide off the charred skin. Slice and drizzle with the vinaigrette. Separate a Bermuda (red) onion into rings. Toast ¼ cup of pine nuts. Toss greens— radicchio, arugula, and other lettuces of varying textures and colors—with vinaigrette and arrange on each plate. Arrange the warm peppers, rings of onion, and mushroom slices over the greens and top with pine nuts. Serves 6.

DOLCI

✳

Winter Pears in Vino Nobile

Steeped pears are pretty to serve. Their taste seems heightened when served along with some Gorgonzola, toasted bread, and walnuts roasted with butter and salt.

Peel 6 firm pears and stand them upright in a saucepan. Leave stems on, if they still have them. Squeeze lemon juice over each. Pour 1 cup of red wine over them and sprinkle ¹/4 cup of sugar over the tops. Add ¹/4 cup of currants, a vanilla bean, and a few cloves to the wine. Cover and simmer for 20 minutes (or longer, depending on the size and ripeness of the pears); don't allow them to become soft. Midway, turn pears on their sides and baste several times with the wine sauce. Transfer to serving dishes, pour the currants and some of the wine over each, and garnish with thin strips of lemon peel. Serves 6.

✳

Rustic Apple Bread Pudding

I'm surprised that the gnarly apples I find at the Saturday market have intense flavor. Even our long-neglected apple trees bravely put forth their scrawny crop. Too tiny to slice, they at least make a respectable apple butter. For this husky dessert, cut the apples in chunky slices.

Peel, core, and cut 4 or 5 crisp baking apples in large slices. Squeeze lemon juice over them, then dust with nutmeg. Toast 1 cup of sliced almonds. Remove any hard crust from a loaf of leftover bread (fresh bread would be too soft for this recipe). Cut the bread into slices and lay some of them on the bottom of a buttered rectangular pan, 9 by 12 inches or so. In a sauté pan, melt 6 tablespoons of butter and 6 tablespoons of sugar. Add ³/₄ cup of the toasted almonds, 2 tablespoons of lemon juice and ¹/₄ cup of cider or water. Toss the apple chunks in this. Layer the apple mixture and bread in the pan, ending with a layer of bread. Beat together 6 tablespoons of softened butter and 4 tablespoons of sugar. Beat in 4 eggs, then 1-¹/₄ cups of milk and ³/₄ cup of light cream. Pour evenly over the bread. Sprinkle the top with a little sugar, nutmeg, and the remaining toasted almonds. Bake at 350° for an hour. Allow to rest for 15 or 20 minutes. Serve with sweetened mascarpone or whipped cream. Serves 8.

❋

Tangerine Sorbet

If I'd grown up here, I'm sure the fragrance of citrus would be indelibly associated with Christmas. The holiday decorations in Assisi are big lemon boughs on all the stores. Against the pale stones, the fruit glows like lighted ornaments and the scent of lemons infuses the cold air. Outside the groceries all over Cortona, baskets of clementines brighten the streets. Bars are squeezing that most opulent of juices, the dark blood orange. The first taste, tart as grapefruit, quickly turns to a deep aftertaste of sweetness. This sorbet, which works wonders as a pause in a winter dinner, can be made with other juices. Equally good as a light dessert, the sorbet is delectable served with thin chocolate butter cookies.

Make a sugar syrup from 1 cup of water and 1 cup of sugar by bringing them to a boil, then simmering for about 5 minutes. Stir in 1-¹/₄ cups of fresh tangerine juice, 1 cup of water, 1 tablespoon of lemon juice, plus the zest of the tangerines you've used. Chill thoroughly in the fridge—until cold to the touch.

Process in an ice cream machine, according to manufacturer's instructions. Serves 6.

✱

Lemon Cake

A family import, this Southern cake is one I've made a hundred times. Thin slices seem at home here with summer strawberries and cherries or winter pears—or simply with a small glass of one of the many fantastic Italian dessert wines, such as Banfi's B.

Cream together 1 cup of sweet butter and 2 cups of sugar. Beat in 3 eggs, one at a time. The mixture should be light. Mix together 3 cups of flour, 1 teaspoon of baking powder, ¹/4 teaspoon of salt, and incorporate this with the butter mixture alternately with 1 cup buttermilk. (In Italy, I use one cup of cream since buttermilk is not available.) Begin and end with the flour mixture. Add 3 tablespoons of lemon juice and the grated zest of the lemon. Bake in a nonstick tube pan at 300° for 50 minutes. Test for doneness with a toothpick. The cake can be glazed with ¹/4 cup of soft butter into which 1-¹/2 cups of powdered sugar and 3 tablespoons of lemon juice have been beaten. Decorate with tiny curls of lemon rind.

ROSE WALK

IN THE TEN HOURS UPRIGHT IN MY AISLE SEAT, headed toward Paris, I read with intense concentration a history of experimental French poetry, the flight magazine, even the emergency instruction card. So many crises happened at work before I left San Francisco at the end of May that I wanted to be loaded onto the plane on a stretcher, wrapped in white, put in the front aisle of the plane with curtains around me, the flight attendant looking in now and then with a cup of warm milk—or a sapphire gin martini. I left a week before Ed finished his classes, fled, really, on the first plane smoking on the runway the day after graduation.

After a short wait at Charles de Gaulle, I caught an Alitalia flight. The pilot wasted no time in heading straight up. An Italian driver, I guess, is an Italian driver; suddenly I felt a surge of energy. I wondered if he was trying to pass someone. Soon he aimed down, almost straight down, toward the Pisa airport. No one seemed alarmed, so I practiced breathing evenly and holding up the plane by the armrests.

I'm staying overnight. If we had been late, the prospect of changing trains in Florence at night sounded exhausting. I check into a hotel and find I'm ready to walk. It's *passeggiata* hour. Hoards of people mingling, visiting, strolling, running errands. The tower still leans, tourists still take photos of themselves leaning to one side or the other in front of it. The pastel and ocher houses still curve along the river like an aquarelle of themselves. Women with shopping bags crowd into the fragrant bread store. Splendid to arrive alone in a foreign country and feel the assault of difference. Here they are all along, busy with living; they don't talk or look like me. The rhythm of their day is entirely different; I am thoroughly foreign. I have dinner at an outdoor restaurant on a piazza. Ravioli, roast chicken, green beans, salad, a half carafe of local red. Then my elation ebbs and a total, delicious tiredness rushes over me. After a soaking bath with all the hotel's bubble bath, I sleep for ten hours.

The first morning train takes me through fields of red poppies in bloom, olive groves, and by now familiar stony villages. Haystacks, nuns in white four abreast, bed linens flung out the window, sheepfold, oleander, Italy! I stare out the window the whole way. As we approach Florence, I worry about banging my new small computer against something while juggling my bag. Most of my summer clothes are at the house so I can travel lightly. Even so, I feel like a pack animal with my handbag, computer, and carry-on bag hanging on me. But it's fun to get off at the Florence station, which always brings me the fresh memory of my first trip to Italy almost twenty-five years ago, the exotic, smoky sound of the loudspeaker announcing the arrival from Rome on *binario undici* and the departure for Milano on *binario uno,* the oily train smells and everyone going somewhere.

Fortunately, the train is almost empty and I easily stow my bags. Midway home (*home,* I've said to myself), a cart comes through with sandwiches and drinks. The train doesn't stop at Camucia so I get off at Terontola, about ten miles away, and call a taxi.

Fifteen minutes later a taxi pulls up. As soon as I get in, a second taxi pulls alongside us and the driver starts to shout and gesture. I assumed the taxi I got in was the one I called but no, he just happened along. He does not want to give up the fare. I tell him I called a taxi but he starts to take off. The other driver bangs on the door shouting louder, he was having lunch, he drove here especially for the *Americana,* he has to earn his bread, too. Spit gathers in the corners of his lips and I'm afraid he's about to foam at the mouth. "Stop, please, I should go with him. I'm very sorry!" He growls, slams on brakes, jerks my bag out. I get in the other taxi. They face off to each other, both talking at once, jowls and fists shaking, then abruptly come to terms and start shaking hands, smiling. The deserted driver comes around to me, smiles, and wishes me a good trip.

When I arrive, my sister, nephew, and friends of theirs have been at the house for a couple of weeks. My sister has had all the pots planted with white and coral geraniums. The green smell of freshly cut grass tells me Beppe must have mown the lawn this morning. Despite my severe pruning in December, the roses we planted last summer are as tall as I am. They're profuse with bloom— apricot, white, pink, yellow. Hundreds of butterflies flitter among the lavender. The house has vases of gold lilies and daisies and wildflowers. It's clean and full of life. My sister even has a pot of basil going outside the kitchen door.

They are on a day trip to Florence when I arrive so I have the afternoon to pull the duffel out from under the bed and air out my summer clothes. Since five others are here and settled, I will be sleeping in my study for a few days. I make up the narrow bed with yellow sheets, set up the computer on my travertine desk, open the windows, and I'm here.

Late, I find my boots and walk the terraces. Beppe and Francesco have cut the weeds. Again, I've lost the battle of the wildflowers. In their zeal to clear, they have stopped for nothing, not even the wild (what I know as Cherokee) roses. Poppies, wild carnations, some fluffy white flower, and the host of yellow blooming weeds survive only along the terrace edges. The big news is the olives. In March, they planted thirty in the gaps on the terraces, bringing us up to a hundred and fifty trees. Already they're flowering. We ordered larger trees this year than the ten Ed planted last year; at the rate olives grow, we want to be around to collect a little oil. Beppe and Francesco staked each new tree and stuffed a nest of weeds between the stake and the trunk to prevent chaffing. Ed knew to dig a big hole for each tree but he didn't know to dig an enormous, deep one; Beppe explained that the new trees need a big *polmone,* a lung. Around each, they've dug to a circumference of about four feet. They also planted two more cherries, to go with the ones Ed planted last spring.

For a week, we cook, run around to Arezzo and Perugia, walk, buy scarves and sheets at the Camucia market, and catch up on family news. Ed arrives in time for a farewell dinner with liberal pourings of several Brunellos my nephew bought in Montalcino, then they pack, pack, pack (so much to buy here) and are gone.

They've had a warm May; now it begins to rain. The run-rampant roses bend and sway in the wind. We run out with shovels and stake them, getting soaked. Ed digs while I clip off the dead blooms, cut back some of the stalky branches, and give them fertilizer, though I'm afraid it will promote even more of the Jack and the Beanstalk mode. I cut an armful of white ones that bloom in ready-made bouquets. Inside, we iron our clothes, rearrange what has been shifted as many people made themselves comfortable to their own tastes. Everything quickly falls into place. Eons ago, it seems, I arrived in June to find ladders, workmen, pipes, wires, rubble, and dust everywhere. Now we just begin living.

A pot of minestrone for the rainy nights. A walk over the Roman road into town for cheese, arugula, coffee. Maria Rita's cherries are the best ever; we eat a kilo every twenty-four hours. All the stump and stone removal and clearing has paid off. Cleaning up the land is easier now. Not as many rocks fly up when the weed machine splits through the weeds. How many stones have we picked up? Enough to build a house? Fireflies flickering on the terraces at night, cuckoos (don't they say *whoocoo* instead?) in the soft blue dawns. A timid bird that sings "Sweet, sweet." Hoopoes all dressed up in their exotic plumage with nothing more to do than peck in the dirt. Long days with birdsongs instead of the sound of the telephone.

We plant more roses. In this area of Tuscany, they bloom spectacularly. Almost every garden spills and flourishes with them. We select a Paul Neyron, with ruffled hot-pink petals like a tutu and an astonishing lemony-rose scent. I must have two of the soft pink ones the size of tennis balls called Donna Marella Agnelli. Their perfume carries me back to the memory of being hugged to the bosom of Delia, one of my grandmother's friends, who wore immense hats and was a kleptomaniac no one ever accused because it would embarrass her husband to death. When he noticed a new object around the house, he would stop into the store he figured it came from and say, "My wife completely forgot to pay for this—just walked right out with it in her hand and remembered last night. How much do I owe you?" Perhaps her powdery rose perfume was stolen.

"Don't plant any Peace roses," a friend and connoisseur of roses advised. "They're such a cliché." But not only are they dazzling, the vanilla cream, peach, and rosy blush colors repeat the colors of the house. They belong in this garden. I plant several. Last year's gold-orange roses open to flagrant size, the rash colors contributing to their beautiful vulgarity. Now we have a line of roses all along the walk up to the house, with lavender planted between each one. I'm coming to believe in aromatherapy. As I walk to the house through waves of scent, it's impossible not to inhale deeply and feel an infusion of happiness.

At the steps up to the front terrace, the old iron pergola remains at the top and bottom, with jasmine we planted two years ago twining around them and down the iron railings of the steps. Now we decide on another long row of roses on the other side of the walk and a pergola at the opposite end of that walk. This restores the

impression of the original rose pergola that existed when
we first saw the house, but now we want the open feeling
to the wide walk instead of reconstructing the continuous
pergola. Two roses we choose—one milky pink, one a
velvet red—are Queen Elizabeth and Abe Lincoln (pronounced Eh-bay Lin-cónay at the nursery). Nice to think
of those two forces side by side. My favorites start as one
color and open to another. *Gioia,* Joy, is pearly as a bud
and full blown turns straw yellow, with some petals still
veined and edged with pink. We plant more of the apri-
cot-dawn roses, one that's traffic-light yellow, a
Pompidou, and one named for Pope John XXIII. So
many important people just blooming in our garden. I
don't resist a decadent, smoked lilac one that looks as if it
belongs in the hand of someone in a coffin.

We visit a *fabbro,* blacksmith, just over the river in
Camucia. His two boys gather near as we talk to their
father, their chance to see weird foreigners up close. One
boy, about twelve, has icy, eerie green eyes. He's lithe
and tan. I can't help but stare back at him. All he needs is
a goatskin and a crude flute. The *fabbro* also has green eyes
but of a more direct color. By now, I've visited the work-
shops of five or six *fabbri.* The craft must attract particularly intense men. This shop is open on one side so it
doesn't have the sooty air of most. He shows us his well
covers and manhole grids, practical items. I think of the
brooding *fabbro* we first met, now dead from stomach
cancer, him wandering in his own world in his blackened
shop, fingering the serpentine torch holder and the
archaic animal-headed staffs. Our gate still leans open; he
died before he repaired it and we've grown used to its
rust and bends. The green-eyed *fabbro* shows us his garden

and nice house. Perhaps his faun son will follow him in the craft.

Some things are so easy. We'll simply dig holes, fix the iron poles, then fill the holes with cement. We choose a pink climbing rose ("What's its name?" "No name, signora, it's just a rose. *Bella, non*?") for either side.

I've had several gardens but never have planted roses. When I was a child, my father landscaped around the cotton mill he managed for my grandfather. With a single-mindedness I can only wonder at, he planted a thousand roses, all the same kind. *L'étoile de Holland,* a vital heart's blood red rose, is the flower of my father. To put it mildly, he was a difficult man and to complicate that, he died at forty-seven. Until he died, our house always was filled with his roses, large vases, crystal bowls, single silver bud vases on every available surface. They never wilted because he had someone cut a fresh armful every day during seasons of bloom. I can see him at noon coming in the back door in his beige linen suit, somehow not rumpled from the heat. He carries, like a baby in his arms, a cone of newspaper around a mass of red, red buds. "Would you look at these?" He hands them to Willie Bell, who already is waiting with scissors and vases. He twirls his Panama hat on the tip of his finger. "Just tell me, who needs to go to heaven?"

In my gardens I have planted herbs, Iceland poppies, fushsias, pansies, sweet William. Now I am in love with roses. We have enough grass now that I can walk out in the dew barefooted every morning and cut a rose and a bunch of lavender for my desk. Memory cuts and comes again: At the mill, my father kept a single rose on his desk. I realize I have planted only one red one. As the morning sun hits, the double fragrance intensifies.

*

Now that so much work is finished, we taste the future. A time is coming when we will just garden, maintain (astonishingly, some of the windows inside already need touching up), refine. We have a list of pleasurable projects such as stone walkways, a fresco on the kitchen wall, antique hunting trips to the Marche region, an outdoor bread oven. And a list of less glorious projects: figuring out the septic system, which sends out a frightening turnip smell when lots of people are using the house; cleaning and repointing the stone walls of the cantina; rebuilding sections of stone walls that have collapsed on several terraces; retiling the butterfly bathroom. These would have seemed major once and now just seem like things on a list. Still, days are near when we will work with an Italian tutor, take the wildflower book on long walks, travel to the Veneto, Sardinia and Apulia, even take a boat from Brindisi or Venice to Greece. To embark from Venice, where the first touch of the East is felt!

That time is not yet, however; the last big project looms.

SEMPRE PIETRA (ALWAYS STONE)

PRIMO BIANCHI CHUGS UP THE DRIVEWAY IN HIS Ape loaded with bags of cement. He jumps out to direct a large white truck full of sand, steel I-beams, and bricks as it backs up the narrow driveway, scraping its mirror on the pine trees and pulling off one limb of a spruce with a loud crack. Primo was our choice for remodeling three years ago but was unable to work then because of a stomach operation. He looks the same—like an escapee from Santa's workshop. We go over the project. The yard-thick living room wall will be opened to connect with the *contadina* kitchen, which will get a new floor, new plaster, new wiring. He nods. *"Cinque giorni, signori,"* five days. This crude room, totally untouched, serves as a storage room for garden furniture over the winter and as the last bastion for scorpions. Because of earthquake standards, the opening will be only about five feet, not as wide as we wanted. But there will be doors opening to the outside, and the rooms, at last, will be joined.

We tell him about Benito's men running out of the house when they opened the wall between the new kitchen and the dining room. I'm reassured when he laughs. Will they start tomorrow? "No, tomorrow is Tuesday, not a good day for starting work. Work started on Tuesday never ends—an old superstition, not that I believe it but my men do." We agree. We definitely want the project to end.

On evil Tuesday, we take all the furniture and books out of the living room, remove everything from the walls and fireplace. We mark the center of the wall and try to visualize the expanded room. It's the imagination that carries us through the stress of these projects. Soon we will be happy! The rooms will look as though they've always been one! We'll have lawn chairs on that end of the front terrace and can listen to Brahms or Bird wafting out of the *contadina* kitchen door. Soon it will not be called that anymore; it will be the living room.

Intercapedine is a word I know only in Italian. My dictionary translates it as "gap, cavity." It's a big word in the lingo of restoring humid stone houses. The *intercapedine* is a brick wall constructed part of the way up a humid wall. A gap *due dita,* two fingers, wide is left between the two so that moisture is stopped by the brick barrier. The *contadina* kitchen has such a wall on the far end of the house. It looks deeper than is usual. Impatient, Ed and I decide to take down some of it, to see if possibly the *intercapedine* could be moved farther back toward the wall, thus enlarging the small room. As the bricks fall, we are stunned to find that there *is* no end wall of the house on the first floor; it was built directly *into, onto* the solid stone of the hillside. Behind the *intercapedine* we find Monte Sant'Egidio! Craggy, huge rock! "Well, now we know why this room had a moisture problem." Ed is pulling out fig and sumac roots. Along the edge of the floor, he uncovers the rubble-filled remains of a moisture canal that must have functioned once.

"Great wine cellar," is all I can think of to say. Not knowing what else to do, we take a few photos. This discovery definitely doesn't conform to the transcendent dream of a hundred angels.

Auspicious Wednesday arrives and with it, at seven-thirty, Primo Bianchi with two *muratori,* masons, and a worker to haul stone. They arrive without any machinery at all. Each man carries a bucket of tools. They unload scaffolding, sawhorses, called *capretti,* little goats, and T-shaped metal ceiling supports called *cristi* (named for the cross Jesus was crucified on). When they see the natural stone wall we uncovered, they stand, hands on hips, and utter a collective *"Madonna mia."* They're incredulous that we took the wall down, especially that I was involved. Immediately, they go to work—first spreading heavy protective plastic on the floor—opening the wall between this room and the living room. Next, they remove a line of stones along what will be the top of the door. We hear the familiar *chink, chink* sound of chisel on stone, the oldest building song there is. Soon, the I-beam goes in. They pack in cement and bricks to hold it in place. Until the cement dries there's nothing more they can do on the door so they begin to take up the ugly tile floor with long crowbars.

They talk and laugh as fast as they work. Because Primo is a little hard of hearing, they've all learned to converse in a near shout. Even when he's not around, they continue. They're thoroughly neat, cleaning up as they go: no buried telephone this time. Franco, who has glistening black, almost animal eyes, is the strongest. Although he's slight, he has that wiry strength that seems to come more from will than from muscle. I watch him lift a square stone that served as a bottom step for the back stairway. When I marvel, he shows off a bit and hoists it to his shoulder. Even Emilio, whose job it is to haul, actually seems to enjoy what he's doing. He looks perpetually amused. Hot as it is, he wears a wool cap pulled down so far that his hair all around sticks out in a ruff. He looks to be around sixty-five, a little old for a *manovale,* manual laborer. I wonder if he was a *muratore* before he lost two fingers. As they lift out the hideous tile and a layer of concrete, they find a stone floor underneath. Then Franco lifts some of these stones and discovers a second layer of stone floor. *"Pietra, sempre pietra,"* he says, stone, always stone.

True. Stone houses, terrace walls, city walls, streets. Plant any rose and you hit four or five big ones. All the Etruscan sarcophagi with likenesses of the dead carved on top in realistic, living poses must have come out of the most natural transference into death they could imagine. After lifetimes of dealing with stone, why not, in death, turn into it?

The next day, they open the same cavity along the top of the door on the living room side. They call us in. Primo pokes the end of a major beam with his chisel. *"È completamente marcia, questa trava."* He pokes the exposed part. *"Dura, qua."* It's completely rotten inside the wall, although the exposed part is sound. *"Pericoloso!"* The heavy beam could have sheared, bringing down part of the floor above. They support the beam with a *cristo* while Primo takes a measurement and goes off to buy a new chestnut beam. By noon the I-beam on that side is in. They take no breaks, go off for lunch for one hour, and are back at work until five.

By the third full day of work they've accomplished an amazing amount. This morning the old beam comes down as easily as pulling a loose tooth. With long boards held up by *cristi* on either side of the beam, they secure the brick ceiling, knock out stones, wiggle the beam a bit, and lower it to the floor. The new one slides right in. What fabulously simple construction. They wedge rocks around it, pack in cement, then pack more cement into the small space between the beam and the ceiling. Meanwhile, two men shovel and dig the floor. Ed, working in the yard just outside the door, hears *"Dio maiale!"* a strange curse meaning God-pig. He looks in and sees underneath the enormous stone Emilio is propping up with his bar a third layer of stone. The first two layers were of smooth, big stones, burdensome to lug out; this layer is rough—suitcase-sized boulders, some jagged and deep in the ground. From the kitchen, I hear alarming groans as they upend them and roll them up a plank and dump them out the door. I'm afraid they're going to strike water soon. Emilio carts the small stones and dirt to the driveway, where a mountain of rubble is growing. We will keep the giant ones. One has elongated glyphic markings. Etruscan? I look at the alphabet in a book but can't correlate these markings with anything. Perhaps they are a farmer's diagram of planting or prehistoric doodling. Ed hoses off the stone and we look at it sideways. The carving then makes perfect sense. The Christian IHS topped by a cross, with another crude cross off to the side. A gravestone? An early altar? The stone has a flat top and I ask them to drag it aside; we can use it for a small outdoor table. Emilio shows no interest. *"Vecchio,"* old, he says. But he insists there always will be a use for such stones. All afternoon, they dig. I hear them muttering *"Etruschi, Etruschi,"* Etruscans, Etruscans. Under the third layer they come to the stone of the mountain. By now they've uncorked a bottle of wine and take gulps now and then.

"Come Sisyphus," like Sisyphus, I try to joke.

"Esattamente," Emilio replies. In the third layer, they're uncovering lintels and *una soglia,* a threshold in *pietra serena,* the great building stone of the area. Evidently, an earlier house's stones were used in building this house. These they line up along the wall, exclaiming at the fineness of the stone.

✳

Out on one of the terraces, we have a stack of *cotto* for the floor, saved when the new bathroom was built and the upstairs patio was replaced. We hope to salvage enough of them to use in the new room. Ed and I pull the good ones, chip off mortar, wash them in a wheelbarrow, and scrub them with wire brushes. We have a hundred and eighty of them, a few of which are too pitted but may be useful as half bricks. The men are still hauling stones. The floor level is down about two feet now. The white truck maneuvers up the driveway again to deliver long, flat tiles about ten by twenty-five inches, with air channels through them. Regular bricks are laid in ten lines on the dug-out, leveled floor, now mostly bedrock, with some mountain rock locally referred to as *piscia,* piss, for its characteristic dribble of water in crevices. The bricks form drainage channels. Long tiles are cemented over them. They mix cement as though it were pasta dough—they dump sand into a big mound on the ground, then make a hole and start stirring in cement and water, kneading it with a shovel. On top of the tiles, they spread *membrane,* something that looks like tar paper, and a grid of thick iron wire reinforcement. On that, a layer of cement. A day's work, I'd say.

We're spared the whining churn of a cement mixer. We laugh to remember Alfiero's mixer in the summer of the great wall. One day he mixed cement, worked awhile, then ran off to another job. When he came back, we saw him beating the mixer with his fists; he forgot the cement, which by afternoon was solid. We laugh now at the other foibles of past workers; these are princes.

Plaster cracks, like the ones in my dining room in San Francisco after the earthquake, have appeared on the second and third floors above where the door is being opened. Some large chunks have fallen. *Could* the whole house simply collapse into a heap? By day, I'm excited by the project. I dream each night the oldest anxiety dreams—I must take the exam, I have no blue book, I don't know what the course is. I have missed the train in a foreign country and it is night. Ed dreams that a busload of students drives up to the house with manuscripts to be critiqued before tomorrow. In the morning, slightly awake at six, I burn the toast twice.

The wall is almost open. They've inserted a third steel beam over the opening, made the brick supporting column on one side, and have worked on the new double-thick brick wall that will separate us from the mountain. Primo looks over the bricks we've cleaned. As he lifts one, a large scorpion scuttles out and he smacks it with his hammer, laughing when I wince.

Later, reading in my study, I see a tiny scorpion crawling up the pale yellow wall. Usually, I trap them in a glass and escort them outside; this one I just let crawl along the wall. From here, the stone tapping of three masons takes on a strange, almost Eastern rhythm. It's hot, so hot I want to run from the sun, as from a rainstorm. I'm reading about Mussolini. He collected wedding rings from the women of Italy to finance his Ethiopian war, only he never melted them down. Years later, when he was caught trying to escape, he still had a sack of gold rings. In one photo, he has popping eyes, distorted hairless skull, set jaw. He looks demented or like Casper the ghost. The *chink, chink* sounds like a gamelan. In the last photo, he's hanging upside down. The caption says a woman kicked him in the face. I'm sleepy and imagining the men in an Indonesian dance with Il Duce downstairs.

❋

The mountain of stone on either side of the door grows daunting. We must get a start on moving it. Stanislao, our Polish worker, comes at dawn. At six, Francesco Falco's son Giorgio arrives with his new plow, ready to ply the olive terraces, and Francesco follows shortly on foot. As usual, he has his cutting tool, a combination machete and sickle, stuffed into his pants in back. He prepares to help Giorgio by clearing stones from the path of the tractor, holding aside branches, and smoothing out the ground. But our pitchfork is wrong. "Look at this." He holds it out, prongs up, and it quickly turns over, prongs down. He hammers the metal until it separates from the handle, turns the handle, then reattaches it. He then holds out the pitchfork, which does not flip over. We've used the pitchfork a hundred times without noticing but, of course, he's right.

"The old Italians know everything,' " Stanislao says.

Wheelbarrow after wheelbarrow, we haul stone to a pile out on one of the olive terraces. I lift only the small and medium stones; Ed and Stanislao wrestle with the giants. Low-impact aerobics video, eat your heart out. Drink eight glasses of water a day? No problem, I'm parched. At home, in my burgundy leotard, I lift and lift, and one and two, and lift . . . but this is work versus workout. Bend and stretch—easy when I'm clearing a hillside. Whatever, I'm worn out by this labor and I also like it tremendously. After three hours, we've moved about one fourth of the stones. *Madonna serpente!* Don't try to calculate how many more hours we're in for—and all the really huge stones are in the other pile. Dirt and sweat run down my arms. The men are bare-chested, smelly. My damp hair is clotted with dust. Ed's leg is bleeding. I hear Francesco above us on a terrace talking to the olive trees. Giorgio's tractor tilts amazingly on one of the narrow terraces but he is too skilled to come tumbling down the mountain. I think of the long, melting bath I will take. Stanislao begins to whistle "Misty." One stone they can't budge is shaped like the enormous head of a Roman horse. I take the chisel and start to work on eyes and mane. The sun wheels in great struts across the valley. Primo hasn't seen us at hard labor. He's shouting at his men about it. He has worked on many restorations. The foreign *padrone,* he says, only stands and watches. He poses with his hands on his hips, a curled lip. As for a woman working like this, he raises his arms to heaven. Late in the afternoon, I hear Stanislao curse, *"Madonna sassi,"* Madonna-stones, but then he goes back to whistling his theme song, "It's cherry pink and apple blossom white when you're in love . . ." The men come down and we drink beer on the wall. Look at what we've done. This is really fun!

✳

The white truck is back, delivering sand for plaster—plaster, they are nearing the end—and hauling away a mound of rubble. The three workers shout about the World Cup soccer matches taking place in the United States, about ravioli with butter and sage, about how long it takes to drive to Arezzo. Thirty minutes. You're crazy, twenty.

Claudio, the electrician, arrives to reroute the plait of dangling wires that somehow provides electricity for that section of the house. He has brought his son Roberto, fourteen, who has continuous, glorious eyebrows and almond-shaped Byzantine eyes that follow you. He is interested in languages, his father explains, but since he must have a practical trade, he is trying to train him this summer. The boy leans indolently against the wall, ready to hand tools to his father. When his father goes out to the truck for supplies, he grabs the English newspaper that protects the floor from paint and studies it.

Canals for wire must be dug in the stone walls before the plastering. The plumber must move the radiator we had installed when the central heating went in. I've changed my mind about the location. So much action. If they hadn't had days of excavating those levels of stone floor, the primary work would be finished. The Poles, who were in Italy working the tobacco fields, now have gone home. Only Stanislao stayed. Who will move all those great stones? Before the masons leave, they show us a neatly woven swirl of grass and twig they found in the wall, a *nido di topo,* so much nicer in Italian than rat's nest.

They're slinging the base for the plaster, literally slinging so it sticks to the wall, then smoothing it out. Primo brought old *cotto* for the floor from his supply. Between his and ours, we must have enough. Since the floor is last, surely we're nearing the end. I'm ready for the fun part; it's hard to think of the furniture when the room looks like a gray solitary confinement space. Finally, we're treated to the first machine noise of the project. The electrician's son, with some uncertainty, attacks the walls with a drill, making channels for the new wiring. The electrician himself left, after receiving a shock when he touched one of the frayed wires. These *must* be among the sorriest wires he's ever come across.

The plumber who installed the new bath and the central heating sends out two of his assistants to move the radiator pipes they disconnected last week. They, too, are extremely young. I remember that students not on an academic track finish school at fifteen. Both are plump and silent but with ear-to-ear grins. I hope they know what they're doing. Everyone talks at once, most of them shouting.

Maybe all will come together quickly now. At the end of each day, Ed and I drag in yard chairs and sit in the new room, trying to imagine that soon we will sit there with coffee, perhaps on a blue linen loveseat with an old mirror hanging above it, music playing, discussing our next project . . . .

✳

Because the undercoat for the plaster has to dry, Emilio is working alone, scratching off the old plaster in the back stairwell, carting off fuming loads of it to the rubble mountain.

The electrician can't finish until the plaster is on. I can see the boon of the invention of wallboard. Plastering is an arduous business. Still, it's fun to see the process, which hardly has changed since the Egyptians slathered the tombs. The plumber's boys didn't cut off the water line as far back as they should have and we have to call them to come back. To escape, we drive over to Passignano and have an eggplant pizza by the lake. The five-day estimate! I'm longing for days of *dolce far niente,* sweet to do nothing, because in seven weeks, I must go back. I hear the first cicada, the shrill yammering that alerts us that deep summer is here. "Sounds like a duck on speed," Ed says.

Saturday, and a scorcher. Stanislao brings Zeno, who recently arrived from Poland. They dispense with shirts right away. They're used to heat; both are laying pipes for methane during the week. In less than three hours, they've hauled away a ton of stone. We've separated the flat ones for paths and for large squares of stone around each of the four doors along the front to prevent tracking in. They set to work after lunch digging, laying a sand base, chipping and fitting stone, filling in the cracks with dirt. They easily pull up the puny semicircles we laid out last year from stones we found on the land. The stones from the floor they're choosing are as big as pillows.

I'm weeding when I brush my arms against a patch of nettles. Those plants are fierce. They "sting" immediately, the hairy leaves letting out an irritating acid on contact. Odd that the tiny ones are good in risotto. I run in the house and scrub down with a skin disinfectant but my arms feel alive, as though hot electric worms are crawling on me. After lunch, I decide to bathe, put on my pink linen dress, and sit on the patio until the shops open. Enough work. I find a breeze there and pleasantly waste the afternoon looking at a cookbook and watching a lizard, who appears to be watching a parade of ants. It's a magnificent little creature in sparkling green and black with deft and intricate feet, palpitating throat, and an inquisitive head that jerks. I would like for it to crawl on my book so I could see more, but my every move sends it scuttling. It keeps coming back to look over the ants. What the ants watch, I don't know.

In town, I buy a white cotton dress, navy linen pants and shirt, some expensive body cream, pink nail polish, a bottle of great wine. When I get back, Ed is showering inside. The Poles have slung the hose over a tree limb and opened the nozzle to spray. I glimpse them stripping down for a rinse-off before changing their clothes. The four doorways are now protected by well-fitted entrances of stone.

*

Franco begins the smooth final coat of plaster. The owner of the plumbing company, Santi Cannoni, arrives in blue shorts to inspect the work his boys have done. We have known him since his company installed our central heating—but only fully dressed. He looks as though he simply forgot his pants. His hairless, moon-white legs so far below his pressed shirt, distinguished tanned face, and gray coifed hair keep drawing my eye. That he has on black silky socks and loafers contributes to his obscene look of undress. Since his boys moved the radiator, the one in the next room has begun to leak.

Francesco and Beppe pull up in the Ape with their weed machines, ready to massacre wild roses and weeds. Beppe speaks clearly and we understand him better, mainly because Francesco still refuses to wear his teeth. Since he loves to talk, he gets mad when Beppe interprets for him. Naturally, when Beppe sees that we don't understand, he explains. Francesco starts calling Beppe *maestro,* teacher, with heavy sarcasm. They argue about whether Ed's blades need to be sharpened or turned over. They argue about whether the stakes in the grape stones should be iron or wood. Behind Beppe's back, Francesco shakes his head at us, eyes turned to heaven: Can you believe this old coot? Behind Francesco's back, Beppe does the same.

A load of sand arrives for the floor but Primo says his old bricks are not the same size as ours and that he must locate another fifty before the floor can be laid.

Piano, piano, the watchword of restoration, slowly, slowly.

More plastering. The mixture looks like gray gelato. Franco says he has a tiny old house and it's all he wants; these big houses, always something wrong. He patches the walls upstairs that cracked when the living room stones were removed, and I ask him to break the plaster and look at what holds up the doors Benito reopened. He finds the original long stones. No sign of the steel I-beams he was supposed to install. Franco says not to worry, stone is just as good on a regular-sized door.

The walls look dry to me but not to them. Another day off. We're anxious to get in there, scrub down the walls, stain the beams, scrape and paint the brick ceiling. We're ready, past ready, to move in. Four chairs have gone to the upholsterer with yards of blue and white checked linen my sister sent for two, and a blue and yellow striped cotton I found in Anghiari for the others. We have ordered the blue loveseat and two other comfortable chairs. The CD player has been in a pile of boxes and books, the chairs and bookcase stuffed into other rooms. Will this go on forever?

During the Renaissance, it was a custom to open Vergil at random and place a finger on a line that would foretell the future or answer a burning question. In the South, we used to do this with the Bible. People always have had ways to grasp for revelation: The Etruscans' haruspication, reading omens from sacrificed animals' livers, is no stranger than the Greeks' finding significance in the flight patterns of birds and the droppings of animals. I open Vergil and put my finger down on "The years take all, one's wits included." Not very encouraging.

✳

Tuscany is a xeric land in summer but this year it is deeply green. From the patio the terraces seem to ripple down the hill. No use moving today. Under the barbed sun, I'm reading about saints, admiring especially Giuliana Falconieri, who asked, when dying, to have the host placed on her breast. It dissolved into her heart and disappeared. A pheasant is pecking away at my plot of lettuces. I read on about Colomba, who ate only hosts, then vomited them into a basket, which she stored under her bed. I'm enchanted with Veronica, who chewed five orange seeds in memory of Christ's five wounds. Ed brings up enormous sandwiches and iced tea with a little peach juice in it. I'm progressively more fascinated with the women saints, their politics of denial. Perhaps it's a corrective for the voluptuousness of Italian life. There's always a mystery within a sudden attraction to a subject. Why is one suddenly lugging home four books on hurricanes or all the operas of Mozart? Later, much later sometimes, the reason for the quest emerges. What will I come to realize from these quirky women?

Primo arrives with still more old bricks and Fabio starts cleaning them. He's working in spite of toothache and shows us the rotting lower left area of his mouth. I bite my lip to keep from looking startled. He's having four pulled next week, all at once.

Primo's tools for laying out the floor are some string and a long level. His skill is sure and quick; he knows instinctively where to tap, what fits where. After all the stone is hauled out, the floors between the two rooms are almost even; he builds in a slight rise, barely noticeable, in the doorway. They begin tamping down and leveling. Fabio cuts through bricks with a high wheezing machine that sends up a cloud of red dust. His arms are brick-colored up to his elbows. Laying brick looks fun. Soon the floor is down, matched to the interlocking L pattern of the adjoining room.

Houseguests arrive, despite the plastic-covered piles of

lamps, baskets, books in the hallways, the living room furniture scattered around the house. Simone, a colleague of Ed's, is celebrating her Ph.D. with a trip to Greece, and Barbara, a former student, who is just finishing a two-year stint in Poland with the Peace Corps, is en route to Africa. I suppose Italy always has been a crossroads. Pilgrims to the Holy Land skirted Lake Trasimeno in the Middle Ages. Latter pilgrims of all sorts traverse Italy; our house is a good spot to rest for a few days. Madeline, an Italian friend, and her husband, John, from San Francisco are coming for lunch.

We're running back and forth between guests and decisions that need to be made. The workers are finishing today! The well-timed lunch is a double celebration. We've ordered *crespelle* from Vittorio, who makes fresh pasta in town. His crêpes are air. Though we are only six, we've ordered a dozen each of the *tartufo* (truffle), the pesto, and, our favorite, *piselli e prosciutto* (peas and cured ham). Before that, *caprese* (tomato, mozzarella, and basil salad dribbled with oil) and a platter of olives, cheeses, breads, and slices of various local salami. We're able to make the salad from the arugula in our garden. The wine we bought at Trerose, a chardonnay called Salterio, may be the best white I've tried in Italy. Many chardonnays, especially California ones, are too oaky and syrupy for my taste. This one has a peach-tinged, flinty taste with just a faint hint of oak.

The long table under the trees is set with yellow checked linen and a basket of sun-colored broom. We offer wine to the workmen but no, they're pressing into the final hours. They've spread cement over the floor to fill in the narrow cracks between bricks. To clean up, they wash down the floor, then sprinkle sawdust and sweep. They build two columns against the outside of the house for the stone sink we discovered in the dirt. It has rested these two years in the old kitchen. Primo calls to Ed to help move the monstrous stone. Two men "walk" it across the front terrace and up the three steps into the shady area where we are having lunch. Our guest, John, jumps up to help. Five men lift. *"Novanta chili, forse cento,"* Primo says. The sink weighs around two hundred pounds. After that, they load their *cristi,* their tools, and that's it—the room is finished. Primo stays to make a few repairs. He takes a bucket of cement and patches minor cracks in the stone wall, then goes upstairs to secure a few loose floor tiles.

Doesn't everything reduce in the end to a poetic image—one that encapsulates an entire experience in one stroke?

Not only this project but the whole major restoration that has stretched over three years is ending today. We're entertaining friends in the sun-dappled bower, just as I envisioned. I go into the kitchen and begin arranging a selection of local cheeses on grape leaves. I'm flushed and excited in my white linen dress with short sleeves that stand out like little wings. Above me, Primo is scraping the floor. I look up. He has removed two tiles and there is a hole in the ceiling. Just as I look back at my cheese platter, Primo accidentally kicks over his bucket and cement pours onto my head! My hair, my dress, the cheese, my arms, the floor! I look up and see his startled face peering down like a cherub in a fresco.

The humor is not entirely lost on me. I walk out to the table, dribbling cement. After dropped jaws and

stunned looks, everyone laughs. Primo runs out, hitting
the heel of his hand to his forehead.

The guests clear up while I shower. With Primo,
they're all sitting along the sun-warmed wall when I
come down. Ed is asking about Fabio's dental surgery.
He only missed two days of work and will get new teeth
in a month. Now Primo *will* join us in a toast. The guests
are toasting an amusing day and the end of the project. Ed
and I, having been literally doused in this restoration,
raise our glasses, too. Primo just enjoys himself. He
launches into a history of his own teeth and shows us big
gaps in his mouth. Five years ago he had such a toothache—he holds his head and leans over moaning—that he
pulled out his own tooth with the pliers. *"Via, via,"* he
shouts, motioning the tooth out of his jaw. *Via* somehow
sounds more emphatic than "go."

✳

I don't want him to go. He has been such a charmer and
so careful as a *muratore.* The work is impeccable as well as
miraculously reasonable. Yes, I do want him to go! This
project was estimated to last five working days; this is day
number twenty-one. No way, of course, to predict three
levels of stone floor and a rotten beam. He'll be back next
summer—he will retile the butterfly bathroom and re-
point the stones in the cantina. He hoists his wheelbarrow into the Ape. Those are small projects, *cinque giorni,
signori,* five days . . . .

RELICS OF SUMMER

THE FONTS IN ALL THE CHURCHES ARE DRY. I RUN my fingers through the dusty scallops of marble: not a drop for my hot forehead. The Tuscan July heat is invasive to the body but not to the stone churches that hold on to the dampness of winter, releasing a gray coolness slowly throughout the summer. I have a feeling, walking into one, then another, that I walk into palpable silence. A lid seems to descend on our voices, or a large damp hand. In the vast church of San Biago below Montepulciano, there is an airy quiet as you enter. Right under the dome, you can stand in one spot and speak or clap your hands and far up against the inner cup of the dome an eerie echo sends the sound rapidly back. The quality of the sound is not like the hello across a lake but a sharp, repeated return. Your voice flattened, otherworldly. It is hard to think a mocking angel isn't hovering against the frescoes, though more likely a pigeon rests there.

Since I have been spending summers in Cortona, the major shock and joy is how at home I feel. But not just at home, *returned* to that primal first awareness of home. I feel at home because dusty trucks park at intersections and sell watermelons. The same thump to test for ripeness. The boy holds up a rusty iron scale with discs of different sizes for counterweight. His arm muscle jumps up like Popeye's and the breeze brings me a whiff of his scent of dry grasses, onions, and dirt. In big storms, lightning drives a jagged stake into the ground and hailstones bounce in the yard, bringing back the smell of ozone to me from Georgia days when I'd gather a bowlful the size of Ping-Pong balls and put them in the freezer.

Sunday is cemetery day here, and though our small-town Southern plots are austere compared to these lavish displays of flowers on almost every grave, we, too, made Sunday pilgrimages to Evergreen with glads or zinnias. I sat in the backseat, balancing the cool teal vase between my knees while my mother complained that Hazel never turned her hand to pick one stem and it was *her* own mother lying there, not just a mother-in-law. Gathered around Anselmo Arnaldo, 1904–1982, perhaps these families are saying, as mine did, Thank God the old goat's lying here rather than still driving us crazy.

Sweltering nights, the air comes close to body temp, and shifting constellations of fireflies compete with stars. Mosquito nights, grabbing at air, the mosquito caught in my hair. Long days when I can taste the sun. I move through this foreign house I've acquired as though my real ancestors left their presences in these rooms. As though this were the place I always came home to.

Living near a small town again certainly is part of it. And living again with nature. (A student of mine from Los Angeles visited. When I walked him out to the end of the point for the wide-angle view of lake, chestnut forests, Apennines, olive groves, and valleys, he was unprepared. He stood silently, the first time I'd known he could, and finally said, "It's, uh, like nature.") Right, nature: Clouds swarm in from over the lake and thunder cracks along my backbone, booms like waves boom far out at sea. I write in my notebook: "The dishwasher was struck. We heard the sizzle. But isn't it good, the gigantic storm, the flood of terror they felt beside fires in the cave? The thunder shakes me like a kitten the big cat has picked up by the neck. I ricochet home, heat lightning; I'm lying on the ground four thousand miles from here, letting rain soak through me."

Rain flays the grapes. Nature: What's ripe, will the driveway wash away, when to dig potatoes, how much water is in the irrigation well? Early life reconnects. I go out to get wood; a black scorpion scuttles over my hand and suddenly I remember the furry tarantulas in the shower at Lakemont, the shriek when my barefooted mother stepped on one and felt it crunch, then squash up soft as a banana between her toes.

Is it the spill of free days? I dream my mother rinses my tangle of hair with a bowl of rainwater.

Sweet time, exaggerated days, getting up at dawn because when the midsummer sun tops the crests across the valley, the first rays hit me in the face like they strike some rock at Stonehenge on the solstice. To be fully awake when the sky turns rose-streaked coral and scarves of fog drift across the valley and the wild canaries sing. In Georgia, my father and I used to get up to walk the beach at sunrise. At home in San Francisco what wakes me is the alarm at seven, or the car pool horn blowing for the child downstairs, or the recycle truck with its crashing cascade of glass. I love the city and never have felt really at home there.

I was drawn to the surface of Italy for its perched towns, the food, language, and art. I was pulled also to its sense of lived life, the coexistence of times that somehow gives an aura of timelessness—I toast the Etruscan wall above us with my coffee every morning—all the big abstracts that act out in everything from the aggression on the *autostrada* to the afternoon stroll through the piazza. I cast my lot here for a few short months a year because my curiosity for the layered culture of the country is inexhaustible. But the umbilical that is totally unexpected and elides logic reaches to me through the church.

To my surprise I have bought a ceramic Mary with a small cup for home use of holy water. As a fallen-away Methodist, then a fallen-away Episcopalian, I suppose my holy water is a sham. However, I have taken it from the spring I discovered near the house, the artesian spring where clear water rises in a declivity of white stone. This looks like holy water to me. It must have been the house's original source. Or it's older than the house—medieval, Roman, Etruscan. Though some interior juggling is going on, I do not expect to emerge as Catholic, or even as a believer. I am essentially pagan by birth. Southern populism was boiled into my blood early; the idea of a pope with the last word gives me hives. "Idolatrous," our minister called the worship of Mary and the saints. "Mackerel snapper," my classmates teased Andy Evans, the lone Catholic in our school. Briefly, in college, I was drawn to the romance of the Mass, especially the three A.M. fishermen's Mass in St. Louis's Cathedral in New Orleans. I lost interest in the whole show when my good friend, a New Orleans Catholic, told me in complete seriousness that mortal sin began if you kissed longer than ten seconds. A ten-second French kiss was O.K., but a dry twenty-second kiss would land you in trouble. Though I still like rituals, even empty ones, what magnetizes me here feels more radical.

Now I love the quick Mass in tiny upper Cortona churches, where the same sounds have provided a still point for the residents for almost eight hundred years. When a black Labrador wandered in, the priest interrupted his holy spiel to shout, "For the love of God, somebody get that dog out of here." If I stop in on a weekday morning, I sit there alone, enjoying the country Baroque. I think: *Here I am.* I love the parade of relics through the streets, with gold-robed priests travelling along in a billow of incense, their way prepared by children in white, scattering the streets with petals of broom, rose, daisy. In the noon heat, I almost hallucinate. What's in the gold box held aloft with banners—a splinter from the cradle? Never mind we thought Jesus was born in a lowly manger; this is the splinter of the true cradle. Or am I confused? It's a splinter of the true cross. It is on its way through the streets, brought out into the air one day a year. And suddenly I think, What did that hymn mean, *cleft for me,* rising years ago, perpendicular from the white board church in Georgia?

❋

In my South, there were signs on trees that said "Repent." Halfway up a skinny pine, up beyond the tin trough that caught the resin, hung a warning, "Jesus is coming." Here, when I turn on the car radio, a lulling voice implores Mary to intercede for us in purgatory. In a nearby town, one church has as its relic a phial of Holy Milk. As my student would say, that's from, like, Mary.

On the terrace at noon, I'm tanning my legs as I read about early martyrs and medieval saints. I'm drawn to the martyred San Lorenzo, who was put on a grill for his troublesome faith and seared until he reportedly said, "Turn me over, I'm done on this side," and thereby became the favorite saint of chefs. The virginal young women martyrs all were raped, stabbed, tortured or locked away because of their devotion to Christ. Sometimes the hand of God reached down and swept one away, like Ursula, who did not wish to marry the barbarian Conan. With her ten thousand virgins (all avoiding men?) loaded into boats, she was lifted miraculously by God and sailed across the unfriendly skies, then deposited in Rome, where they all bathed in lime-scented water and formed a sacred order. Stunning, the prevalence of the miracle. In the Middle Ages, some of the venerated women found the foreskin of Jesus materialized in their mouths. I don't know if there exists a relic of that. (Would it look like a chewed rubber band? A dried wad of bubble gum?) The foreskin stops me for a good ten minutes and I stare out at the bees swarming the *tigl* trees, trying to imagine that event happening, and not just once. The moment of recognition, what she said what the reaction was—a boggling speculation. Somehow, I'd never heard of these kinkier saints in America although someone once sent me a box of new books each one about a saint's life. When I called the bookstore they told me my benefactor wished to remain anonymous. Now I read on and find that some had "holy an-

orexia" and lived on the wafer alone. If a saint's bones
were dug up, a flowery fragrance filled the town. After
Saint Francis preached to the birds, they flew up into the
shape of a cross then separated into the four directions.
The saints would eat the pus and lice of the poor to show
their humility; in turn, the faithful liked to drink the
bathwater of a holy person. If, after a death, a saint's heart
was cut out, perhaps an image of the Holy Family carved
in a ruby would be found inside. *Oh,* I realize, *here's where
they put their awe. I understand that.*

I understand because this everyday wildness and wonder come back so naturally from the miracle-hungry
South. They almost seem like memories somehow, the
vertebrae of the Virgin, the toenail of San Marco. My
favorite, the breath of San Giuseppe, foster father of
Christ. I imagine an opaque green glass bottle with a
ground stopper, the swift exhaling of air as it opened. At
home when I was small, our seamstress kept her jar of
gallstones on the windowsill above her Singer. Marking
my hem, her mouth full of pins, she'd say, "Lord, I don't
want to go through nothing like that again. Now you
turn round. Those things won't even dissolve in gaso-
line." Her talisman against sickness. Emblems and omens.

Santa Dorotea immured in her cell for two years,
against a high-walled pit in the dank cathedral. Commu-
nion through a grate and a diet of bread and gruel. I
hated visiting Miss Tibby, who treated the corns on my
mother's little toes, shaving yellow curls of skin off with a
vegetable peeler, then rubbing her feet with thick lotion
that smelled like crank case oil and Ovaltine. The bare
bulb lit not only my mother's foot on a cushion but also a

coffin where Miss Tibby slept at night so there would be no surprises later.

In high school my friends and I parked a block away and secretly peered in the windows of the Holy Rollers, who spoke in tongues, sometimes screaming with a frightening ecstatic look on their faces and falling to the floor writhing and jerking. We were profane, smothering our laughter at the surely sexual fervor and the contorted postures. Later we'd sit in the car, Jeff smoking, and watch them file out of the peeling church, looking as normal as anyone. In Naples, the phial of San Gennaro's congealed blood liquifies once a year. There's also a crucifix that used to grow one long hair of Jesus that would have to be barbered once a year. That one seems particularly close to Southern sensibilities.

In the United States, I think there is no *sanctioned* place to put such fixated strangeness so it just jumps out when it has to. Driving through the South recently, I stopped near Metter, Georgia, for a barbecue sandwich. After the sweet salty pork and iced tea, I was directed out back to the bathroom by the owner; pork-bellied, sweating over his pit, he merely nodded toward the rear. No sign at all that as I opened the screen door I would encounter two molting ostriches. How they came to be in that remote town in South Georgia and what iconographical necessity led the family to gaze on and house these dusty creatures is a philosophical gift I've been given to ponder in nights of insomnia.

Growing up in the God-fearing, faith-healing, end-of-the-world-is-at-hand South gave me many chances to visit snake collections beside gas stations when my parents stopped to fill up; to drive past roadside religious ceremonies in which snakes were ecstatically "handled"; to see shabby wonders-of-the-world exhibits—reliquaries of sorts—in the towns bordering the swamps. I know a box of black cat's bones makes a powerful conjure. And that a bracelet of dimes can ward it off. I was used to cages of baby alligators crawling on the back of the mother of all, a fourteen-foot beauty who opened her jaws wide enough that I could have stood in them. The sagging chicken-wire fences couldn't save you if those sleeping logs rose up and decided to take off after you—alligators can run seventy miles an hour. Albino deer covered with ticks that leapt on my hand when I petted their mossy noses, a stuffed painter (panther) with green marbles for eyes, a thirty-foot tapeworm in a jar. The owner explains that it was taken from the throat of his seventeen-year-old niece when the doctor lured it out of her stomach with a clove of garlic on a toothpick. They waited until it showed its head, lured it out further, then grabbed, chopped off its head with a straight razor while hauling the thing out of Darleen's stomach like a rope out of the river.

Wonders. Miracles. In cities, we're less and less capable of the imagination for the super real, ground down as we are by reality. In rural areas, close to the stars and groves, we're still willing to give it a whirl. So I recover the cobra, too, so much more impressive with his flattened head than rattlesnakes, whose skins paper the office of the owner of the Eighth Wonder of the World, where we have stopped for gas at the Georgia border. We are close to Jasper, Florida, where my mother and father were married in the middle of the night. I am amazed, despite my mother's warning that the owners are carnival people and it is not worth seeing and I have exactly ten minutes or they will go on to White Springs without me. The slight thrill at the possibility of being left behind on this curve of road lined with moss-draped oaks, the silverbullet trailer set up on concrete blocks, a woman glimpsed inside, washing her hair over a tin bowl and the radio blaring "I'm So Lonesome I Could Cry." I knew then and still know that the man with the phosphorescent glow-in-the-dark torch tattooed on his back and the fullblown roses tattooed on his biceps believed his wonders were real. I follow him to the bamboo hut, where the cobra from darkest Calcutta rises to the song made by blowing on a comb covered with cellophane. The cobra mesmerizes the mangy dog thumping his tail in the doorway. The peacock gives a powerful he-haw, shakes himself into full regalia, the blues in his fan of feathers more intense than my own or my mother's eyes, and, as everyone knows, we have the purest sky-blue eyes. The peacock's eyes look exactly like the snake's. The owner's wife comes out of the trailer with a boa constrictor casually draped around her neck. She checks on another snake, to whom she has fed a large rat without even cutting it up. The rat is simply disappearing, like a fist into a sweater sleeve. I buy a Nehi and an oatmeal cookie sandwich, run out to the Oldsmobile vibrating in the heat. My father scratches off; gravel spumes behind us. "What have you got?" My mother turns around.

"Just a cold drink and this." I hold up the large cookie.

"Those things have lard in the middle. That's not icing—that's pure-T lard with enough powdered sugar to make your teeth crack."

I don't believe her but when I break open the cookie, it is crawling with maggots. I quickly throw it out the window.

"What did you see in that awful gyp joint?"

"Nothing," I answer.

Growing up, I absorbed the Southern obsession with place, and place can seem to me somehow an extension of the self. If I am made of red clay and black river water and white sand and moss, that seems natural to me.

However, living as a grown woman in San Francisco, I never have that belonging sensation. The white city with its clean light on the water, the pure, heart-stopping coast, and the Marin hills with the soft contours of sleeping giants under blankets of green—I am the awed tourist, delighted to have made this brief escape, which is my adult life. My house is just one of thousands; my life could be just another story in the naked city. My eye looks with insouciance at the scissors point of the Transamerica pyramid and jagged skyline I can see from my dining room window. Everyone seems to have cracked the door two inches to see who's there. I see you through my two inches; you see me through yours. We are monumentally self-reliant.

❋

I never tire of going into Italian churches. The vaulted arches and triptychs, yes. But each one also has its characteristic blue dust smell, the smell of time. The codified Annunciations, Nativities, and Crucifixions dominate all churches. At the core, these all struggle with the mystery of the two elementals—birth and death. We are frangible. In the side altars, the high arches, the glass manuscript cases in the crypts, the shadowed curves of the apse, these archetypal concerns and the dreamland of religious fervor lock horns with the painterly subject matter in individualized ways. I'm drawn to a bizarre painting that practically leaps off the wall. In a dark, high panel close to the ceiling in San Gimignano, there's Eve rising boldly out of supine Adam's open side. Not the *whoosh* of instantaneous creation I've imagined from reading Genesis, when she appeared as easily as "Let there be Light." This is graphic, someone's passion to be *present* at the miracle. As graphic as the wondrous cobra of Calcutta spiraling up in the humid air of South Georgia before my very eyes. Adam is meat. The vision grabs the viewer like the glow-in-the-dark torch. Now hear this, loud and clear. In Orvieto's Duomo, Signorelli's humans, just restored to their flesh on Judgment Day, stand grandly and luxuriously beside the grinning skeletons they were just moments before. Parts of the body still glow with the aura of the bare bone, a gauzy white light emanating from the firm, new flesh in its glory. A strange turn—we're used to thinking of the decay of the flesh; here's the dream of rejuvenation. Flitting around in the same arena of that cathedral are depictions of hell, green-headed devils with snaky genitals. The damned are twisted, poked, jabbed, while one voluptuous blonde (no doubt what *her* sins were) flies away on the back of a devil with stunted, unaerodynamic wings. Clearly we are in someone's head, midnight imaginings of the descent, the fall, the upward turn. The paintings can be sublime but there is a comic book aspect to much church painting, a wordless progression of blunt narrative very close to those of fire-and-brimstone fundamentalists who still hold forth in the

South. If there was more than one word, Repent, hanging on those Southern pines, it was bound to be Doomsday.

Wandering around in churches, I see over and over San Sebastiano pierced with arrows, martyred Agata holding out her breasts on a plate like two over-easy eggs, Sant'Agnes kneeling piously while a lovely youth stabs her in the neck. Almost every church has its locked relic box like a miniature mausoleum, and what does this mean? Thorn from the crown. Finger digits of San Lorenzo. The talismans that say to the viewers, "Hold on; like these, have faith." Standing in the dim crypt in a country church where a handful of dust has been venerated for several hundred years, I see that even today, toward the end of the century, the case is remembered with fresh carnations. I uncover my second realization: *This is where they put their memories and wants.* Besides functioning as vast cultural repositories, these churches map intimate human needs. How familial they begin to seem (and how far away from the historical church, the bloody history of the Papacy): the coarse robe of St. Francis, another phial of Mary's, this one filled with tears. I see them like the locket I had, with a curl of light brown hair, no one remembered whose, the box of rose petals on the closet shelf behind the blue Milk of Magnesia bottle and the letters tied with frayed ribbon, the translucent white rock from Half Moon Bay. *Never forget.* As I wax the floor tiles and wring out the mop, I can think of Santa Zita of Lucca, saint of housekeeping, as was Willie Bell Smith in my family's house. Basketmaker, beggar, funeral director, dysentery sufferer, notary, speleologist— everyone has a paradigm. *I once was lost but now I'm found.*

The medieval notion that the world reflects the mind of God has tilted in my mind. Instead, the church I perceive is a relief map of the *human* mind. A thoroughly secular interpretation: that *we* have created the church out of our longing, memory, out of craving, and out of the folds of our private wonders.

If I have a sore throat from drinking orange juice when I know I'm allergic to it, the saint is there in his monumental church at Montepulciano, that town whose syllables sound like plucked strings on the cello. San Biago is a transubstantiated metaphor and a handful of dust in a wrought box. Its small keyhole reminds us of what we most want to be reminded of, *you are not out there alone.* San Biago focuses my thoughts and throws me beyond the scratchy rawness of my own throat. *Pray for me, Biago, you are taking me farther than I go.* When the TV is out of whack and the buttons won't improve the picture, nor will slapping the side soundly, Santa Chiara is out here somewhere in saintland. *Chiara,* clear. She was clairvoyant and from there is only a skip and jump to *receiver,* to patron saint of telecommunications. So practical for such a transcendent girl. A statue of her on top of the TV won't hurt a thing. Next year on July 31, the wedding ring of Mary will be displayed in the Duomo in Perugia. The history says it was "piously stolen"—isn't that an oxymoron—from a church in Chiusi. Without a shred of literal belief, I, for one, will be there.

❋

At the top of the stairs, I touch the spring water in my ceramic Mary with my fingertip and make a circle on my forehead. When I was baptized, the Methodist minister dipped a rose in a silver bowl of water and sprinkled my hair. I always wished I'd been baptized standing knee deep in the muddy Alapaha, held under until the last moment of breath then raised to the singing congregation. My spring water in Mary's cup is not transformed to wash away my sins or those of the world. She always seems like *Mary,* the name of my favorite aunt, rather than Santa Maria. Mary simply became a friend, friend of mothers who suffered their children's pain, friend of children who watched their mothers suffer. She's hanging over almost every cash register, bank teller, shot giver, bread baker in this town, and I've grown used to her presence. The English writer Tim Parks says that without her ubiquitous image to remind you that all will go on as before, "you might imagine that what was happening to you here and now was unique and desperately important . . . I find myself wondering if the Madonna doesn't have some quality in common with the moon." Yes. My unblessed water soothes. I pause at the top of the stairs and repeat the lovely word *acqua.* Years ago, the baby learned to say *acqua* on the lake shore at Princeton, under a canopy of trees blooming madly with pink pompons. *Acqua, acqua,* she shouted, scooping up water and letting it rain on her head. *Acqua* sounds closer to the sparkle and fall, closer to wetness and discovery. Her voice still reverberates but now I touch my little finger as I remember. The gold signet ring, a family treasure, slipped off in the grass that day and was not to be found. *Water of life. Intimacy of memory.*

Intimacy. The feeling of touching the earth as Eve touched it, when nothing separated her.

In paintings, the hilltop town rests in the palm of

Mary's hand or under the shelter of her blue cloak. I can walk every street of my Georgia town in my mind. I know the forks in the pecan trees, the glut of water in the culverts, the hog pear in the alley. Often the Tuscan perched villages seem like large castles—extended homes with streets narrow as corridors, and the *piazze,* like public receptions rooms, teeming with visitors. The village churches have an attitude of privacy; the pressed linen and lace altar cloths and scarlet dahlias in a jar could be in family chapels; the individual houses, just suites in the big house. I expand, as when my grandparents' house, my aunt's, my friends', the walls of home were as familiar to me as the lines in my own palm. I like the twisted streets up to the convent where I may leave a bit of lace to be mended on a Catherine wheel, spin it in to the invisible nun, whose sisters have tatted in this great arm of the castle for four hundred years. I do not glimpse even the half moons of her nails or the shadow of her habit. Outside two women who must have known each other all their lives sit in old wooden chairs between their doorways and knit. The stony street slopes abruptly down to the town wall. Beyond that stretches the broad valley floor. Here comes a miniature Fiat up this ridiculously steep street no car should climb. Crazy. My father would drive through swollen streams that flooded sudden dips in the dirt roads. I was thrilled. While he laughed and blew the horn, water rose around the car windows. Or was the water really that high?

We can return to live in these great houses, unbar the gates, simply turn an immense iron key in the lock and push open the door.

SOLLEONE

SOLLEONE. HOW USEFUL THE -ONE SUFFIX IN ITAL-
ian; the noun expands. *Porta,* door, becomes *portone,* and
there's no doubt which is the main door. *Torre* becomes
torreone, the name of our part of Cortona, where a great
tower must have stood once. *Minestrone,* then, always is a
big soup. Days of high summer: *Solleone*—big sun. Dog
days we called them in the South. Our cook told me the
name was because it was so hot that dogs went mad and
bit people and I would be bitten if I didn't mind her.
Eventually, I was disappointed to find the name only
meant that Sirius, the dog star, was rising and setting with
the sun. The science teacher said Sirius was twice the size
of the sun and I thought, secretly, that somehow the heat
was augmented by that fact. Here, the expanded sun fills
the sky, as in the archetypal child's drawing of house,
tree, and sun. The cicadas are in the know—they provide
the perfect accompaniment to this heating up. By dawn
they're hitting their horizon note of high screech. How a
finger-sized insect can make such a racket only by vibrating its thorax, I don't know. As they tune up to their
highest pitch, it sounds as though someone is shaking

tambourines made from the small bones of the ear. By noon, they've switched to sitars, that most irritating of instruments. Only the wind quiets them; perhaps they must hang on to a limb and can't clutch and vibrate at the same time. But the wind seldom blows, except for the evil appearance now and then of the *scirocco,* which gusts but doesn't cool, while the sun roars. If I were a cat, I would arch my back. This hot wind brings particles of dust from the African deserts and deposits them in your throat. I hang out the clothes and they're dry in minutes. The papers in my study fly around like released white doves, then settle in the four corners of the room. The *tigli* are dropping a few dry leaves and the flowers suddenly seem leached of color, although we have had enough rain this summer that we have been able to water faithfully every day. The hose pulls water directly from the old well and they must feel blasted at the end of the hot day by the rush of icy water. Perhaps this has exhausted them. The pear tree on the front terrace has the look of a woman two weeks overdue. We should have thinned the fruit. Branches are breaking under the weight of golden pears just turning ruddy. I can't decide whether to read metaphysics or to cook. The ultimate nature of being or cold garlic soup. They are not so far apart after all. Or if they are, it doesn't matter; it's too hot to think about it.

The hotter the day, the earlier I walk. Eight, seven, six o'clock, and even then I rub my face with number thirty sunblock. The coolest walks start at Torreone. A downhill road leads to Le Celle, a twelfth-century monastery where Saint Francis's minute cell still opens onto a seasonal torrential stream. Many of the first Franciscan monks who lived as hermits on Monte Sant'Egidio started Le Celle in 1211. The architecture, a stacked stone honeycomb up against the hillside, recalls their caves. When I walk there, peace and solitude are palpable. In early summer, the rush of water down the steep canyon makes its own music and sometimes, above that, I hear singing. By now the stream is almost dry. Their vegetable garden looks like a model. One of the Capuchin friars who lives there now trudges uphill barefooted toward town. He's wearing his scratchy brown robe and strange pointed white hat (hence cappuccino), using two sticks to pull himself along. With his white beard and fierce brown eyes, he looks like an apparition from the Middle Ages. When I pass him he smiles and says, *"Buon giorno, signora. Bene qua,"* nice here, indicating the landscape with a rotation of his beard. He glides by, Father Time on cross-country skis.

But I take the slightly uphill road this morning, passing a few new houses, then a kennel, where dogs go into an uproar until I am about five feet beyond their pen; the road is then just a white track through pine and chestnut forests, no cars, no people. The shoulders look as though someone scattered one of those cans of native wildflowers seeds and they all took root, then flourished. I climb a hill to look at an abandoned house so old that it still has a thick slate roof. Brambles surround the doors and windows. I glimpse dark rooms with stone walls. In front, I look down on a 180-degree view of Cortona in profile and on the entire length of the Val di Chiana, a yellow and green patchwork of sunflower and vegetable fields. The upstairs must have a low ceiling, right for a crude bed made of chestnut limbs, a white goose-down quilt.

The terrace should go there—in front of the lilac bushes. A pink rose still blooms its heart out without any care at all. Whose was it? The wife of a silent woodcutter who smoked his pipe and drank *grappa* in the winter evenings when the *tramontagna* shook the windows on the back of the house? Perhaps she growled at him for sticking her so far in the country. No, she was content with her work embroidering the linens for the *contessa*.

The house is small—but who would stay inside when there's a broad terrace overlooking the world? The waiting house: all potential. To see one and start dreaming is to imagine being extant in another version. Someone eventually will buy it and perhaps will run all over Tuscany looking for old slate to restore the roof authentically. Or the new owner might rip off the roof and put on flat new tiles. Whatever the predilections, the owner will respond to the aerie's isolation, that and the magnetic pull of the panorama, a place to linger and soothe the restless beast every day.

At the end of the road, a path through the woods leads to our favorite Roman road. I suppose it was laid by slaves. When I first heard about the Roman road near our house, I assumed it was unique. Not long after that I saw a rather thick book on the many Roman roads of this area. Walking alone, I try to think of chariots tearing down the hill, though the only thing I'm likely to meet is a *cinghiale,* a wild boar, roaming around. One stream still has a trickle of water. Maybe a Roman messenger verging on heat stroke paused here and cooled his feet, as I do, when running south with news of how Hadrian' wall was coming along. There have been more recen visitors; on the grassy bank, I see a condom and a wad of tissue.

When I walk into town, I see a shriveled, pasty man who, clearly, is dying. He has been propped in the doorway with the sun fully on him, his last chance for revival. He spreads out his fingers on his chest, warming everything he can. He has enormous hands. Yesterday I received a shock so hard my thumb went numb for half an hour. I was trying to pull the cord that turns on the overhead light in my study from the inside of the radiator, where it somehow had fallen. The clicker I had hold of split, leaving me with my thumb on the hot wires, my other hand on the metal radiator. I screamed and jumped back. That mindless, animal feeling of shock—I wonder if the man in the doorway feels that way in the sun. His life force siphoning off, the great solar energy coming at him, filling him up. His wife sits beside him and appears to be waiting. She's not mending or pinching back her flowers. She's his guard for his trip to the underworld. Perhaps she'll dry his dead body, then anoint his bones with olive oil and wine. Or maybe the heat is getting to me, too, and he's just recovering from an appendectomy.

*

We must go to Arezzo, about half an hour away, to pay our insurance for next year. They seem to expect us to turn up rather than send a check. We park in the broiling train station lot. The station's full-sun digital thermometer-clock says it is 36°(103°F). After our pleasant interview with Signor Donati, an ice cream, a stop for Ed to buy a shirt at his favorite store, Sugar, and one for me to buy hand towels at my favorite shop, Busatti, we come back to the car and find the big 40 (111°) flashing over the car. The door handles appear to be on fire. The heat inside slams into us. We air out the car and finally get in. My eyelids and earrings are hot. Ed touches the steering wheel with his thumbs and index fingers. My hair seems to be steaming. Stores are closing; it's the hottest part of the hottest day of the year. At home, I lower myself into a cool bath, wet washcloth over my face, and just lie there until my body takes on the temperature of the water.

Siesta becomes a ritual. We pull in the shutters, leaving the windows open. All over the house, ladders of light fall across the floor. If I am mad enough to take a walk after one-thirty, no one is out, not even a dog. The word *torpor* comes to mind. All shops close during the sacred three hours. If you need something for bee sting or allergy, too bad. Siesta is prime time for TV in Italy. It's prime time for sex, too. Maybe this accounts for the Mediterranean temperament versus the northern: children conceived in the light and children conceived in the dark. Ovid has a poem about siesta, written before the first millennium turned. He's lying relaxed in sultry summer, one shutter closed, the other ajar, "the half-light shy girls need," he wrote, "to hide their hesitation." He goes on to grab the dress, which didn't hide much. Well, everything is always new under the sun. Then, as now, a quick wash in the bidet and back to work.

What a marvelous concept. For three hours in the middle of the day, you are invited to your own interests and desires. In the good part of the day, too, not just the evening after an eight- or nine-hour day slogging away.

Inside the high-roomed, shuttered house, it's completely silent. Even the cicadas have quit. Peaceful,

dreamy afternoon. Partly for the pleasure of my feet sliding on soothing *cotto* floors, I walk from room to room.
The classic look—I've seen it eleven times before and
now I see it again in the new living room: dark beams,
white brick ceiling, white walls, waxy brick floors. To
my eye, the rugged textures and the strong color contrasts
of the typical Tuscan house create the most welcoming
rooms of any architectural style I know. Fresh and serene
in summer, they look secure and cozy in winter. Tropical
houses with bamboo ceilings and shuttered walls that
open to catch every breeze, and the adobe houses of the
Southwest, with their banquettes and fireplaces that are
rounded like the curves of the human body, impart the
same connected sense: *I could live here.* The architecture
seems natural, as if these houses grew out of the land and
were easily shaped by the human hand. In Italian, a coat
of paint or wax is a *mano,* a hand of that substance. Before
the plastering started, I noticed Fabio's initials scratched
in a patch of wet cement. The Poles, I remembered,
wrote POLONIA at the base of the stone wall. I wonder
if archaeologists find many reminders of the anonymous
hands behind enduring work. On the wall of the prehistoric Pech Merle cave in France, I was stunned to see
handprints, like ones children make in kindergarten,
above the spotted horses. The actual "signature" of the
preliterate artist outlined in blood, soot, ashes! When
the great tombs of Egypt were opened, the footprints of
the last person out before the entrances were sealed remained in the sand: the last work finished, a day's work
over.

A butterfly, trapped inside, bats and bats the shutter

but does not find the way out. As I fall asleep, the fan drones, a shimmering head looking left and right.

✳

I love the heat. I love the excessive insistence. Something in me says yes. Maybe it's only that I grew up in the South, but it feels like a basic yes, devolving back to those old fossil heads of the first people who came into being under a big sun.

The landscape appears cool although it's cooking. The terraces aren't bleached this year, as they sometimes are. Our view to the Apennines is green and forested. In someone's swimming pool at the bottom of the valley, I see a little stick figure jump in.

Since we're up high, nights cool off to a lovely softness. In late afternoon, heaps and piles of clouds cross over, their shadows roving across the green hills. Tonight the Perseids shower, it's San Lorenzo's night of the shooting stars—cause for a celebratory dinner. We've seen them before and we know the gasps, our quick pointing a second too late, the bright cascade of a meteor, so momentary, so long expired. The garlic soup, chosen over Boethius, is chilling in the fridge. Lemon and Basil Chicken, an accidental discovery, and a terracotta dish of Gratin Dauphinois, an old Julia Child potato favorite I've made for years, are ready to cook. I have enough ripe pears to peel and slice and improvise a mascarpone custard for them to bake into. I scrub the bird droppings off the yellow table, spread the cloth I made over the winter from leftover fabric I used for the wicker on my Palo Alto patio fifteen years ago. I spent days on the double welting around the cushion for the chaise longue. I could walk out of that dining room door right now, fluff those cushions, tell the dog "Down," walk into the yard filled with kumquat and loquat, mock orange and olive. Or could I? Everything stays. What chance, when I bought that yellow-flowered bolt at Calico Corners, to think it would end up on a table in Italy, with me in a new life.

Like fanning through a deck of cards, my mind flashes on the thousand chances, trivial to profound, that converged to re-create this place. Any arbitrary turning along the way and I would be elsewhere; I would be different. Where did the expression "a place in the sun" first come from? My rational thought processes cling always to the idea of free will, random event; my blood, however, streams easily along a current of fate. I'm here because I climbed out the window at night when I was four.

✳

All the summer fruits of the great Mediterranean sun have ripened. Beginning with cherries when I arrive, the summer progresses to yellow peaches. Along the Roman road up Sant'Egidio, we pick handfuls of the most divine fruit of all, the minute wild strawberries that dangle like jewels under their jagged leaves. Then come the white peaches with pale and fragrant flesh. Gelato made of these makes you want to dance. Then the plums, all the varieties—the small round gold, the dusky purple-blue, and the pale green ones larger than golf balls. Grapes start to arrive from farther south. A few ruddy apples, then the first pears ripen. The small green ones couldn't be ripe but they are, then the globular speckled yellows. In August, the figs just start to plump up, not reaching their peak until September. But, finally, the blackberries, that heart-of-summer fruit, are ripe.

Days before I go home, at the end of August, I can take out my colander and pick enough for breakfast. Every morning the birds are wild for them but can't manage to eat quite all. Picking blackberries—a back-to-basics pleasure—passing over the ones still touched with a hint of red and those that squish to the touch, pulling off only the perfectly ripe ones until my fingers are rosy. The taste of sun-warmed berries brings me the memory of filling my jar with them in an abandoned cemetery. As a child, I sat down on a heaped mound of dirt, unconsciously eating luscious berries from a plant whose roots intertwined with old bones.

Bees burrow in the pears. Where they've fallen, thrushes feast. Who knows how the wants of our ancestors act out in us? The mellow scents somehow remind me of my mean Grandmother Davis. My father privately called her The Snake. She was blind, with Greek-statue eyes, but I always believed she could see. Her charming husband had lost all the land she inherited from her parents, who owned a big corner of South Georgia. On Sunday rides, she'd always want Mother to drive her by the property she'd lost. She couldn't see when we got there but she could smell peanut and cotton crops in the humid air. "All this," she'd mutter, "all *this.*" I'd look up from my book. The brown earth on either side of the car spread flat to the horizon. From there, who could believe the world is round? I first thought of her when we had the terraces plowed and the upturned earth was ready for planting. Fertile earth, rich as chocolate cake. Big Mama,

I thought, biscuit-face, old snake, just look at this dirt, all *this*.

The heat breaks with a fast rain, a pelting determined rain that soaks the ground then quits—gone, finished. The green landscape smears across the windows. The sun bounces back out but robbed of its terror now. Here, the edge of autumn. What is it? The smell of leaves drying. A sudden shift in the air, a slightly amber cast to the light, then a blue haze hanging over the valley at evening. I would love to see the leaves turn, pick up the hazelnuts and almonds, feel the first frost and build a little olive wood fire to take the chill off the morning. My summer clothes go in the duffle under the bed. I make a few wreathes of grape vine and twine them with sage, thyme, and oregano, herbs I can use in December. The fennel flowers I've been drying on a screen go in a painted tin I found in the house. Perhaps the *nonna* I've grown fond of kept hers here, too.

The man with his coat over his shoulders stops in front of the shrine with his handful of dried yarrow. He brushes out the shrine with the side of his hand. All fall, when I am busy with students, he will walk the white road, perhaps wearing an old knitted sweater, later a scarf around his neck. The man is walking away. I see him stop in the road and look back at the house. I wonder, for the thousandth time, what he is thinking. He sees me at the window, adjusts his coat over his shoulders, and turns toward home.

Scattered books go back to their proper shelves: my house in order. One final blackberry cobbler and I'm gone. A lizard darts in, panics, flees out the door. The thought of the future spins through me. What magnet out there is pulling now? I stack pressed sheets on the *armadio* shelves. Clearing my desk, I find a list: copper polish, string, call Donatella, plant sunflowers, double hollyhocks. The sun hits the Etruscan wall, turning the locust trees to lace. Two white butterflies are mating in midair. I walk from window to window, taking in the view.

Conversion Charts

LIQUID MEASURES

U.S. MEASURE	FLUID OUNCES	IMPERIAL MEASURES	MILLILETRES
1 teaspoon	$1/6$	1 teaspoon	5
2 teaspoons	$1/4$	1 dessertspoon	10
1 tablespoon	$1/2$	1 tablespoon	15
2 tablespoons	1	2 tablespoons	30
$1/4$ cup	2	4 tablespoons	56
$1/2$ cup	$2^2/3$		80
$2/3$ cup	5	$1/4$ pint/1 gill	140
$3/4$ cup	6		170
1 cup/$1/2$ pint	8		225
$1^1/4$ cups	10	$1/2$ pint	280
$1^1/2$ cups	12		420
2 cups/1 pint	16	generous $3/4$ pint	450
$2^1/2$ cups	20	1 pint	560
3 cups/$1^1/2$ pints	24		675
$3^1/2$ cups	27		750
$3^3/4$ cups	30	$1^1/2$ pints	840
4 cups/2 pints	32		900
$4^1/2$ cups	36		1000/1 litre
5 cups	40	2 pints/1 quart	1120
6 cups/3 pints	48	scant $2^1/2$ pints	1350
7 cups	56	$2^3/4$ pints	1600
8 cups	64	$3^1/4$ pints	1800
9 cups	72	$3^1/2$ pints	2000/2 litres
10 cups/5 pints	80	4 pints	2250

SOLID MEASURES

U.S. AND IMPERIAL	METRIC EQUIVALENT
1 oz	25 grams
1 1/2 oz	40
2 oz	50
3 oz	60
3 1/2 oz	100
4 oz/1/4 lb	110
5 oz	150
6 oz	175
7 oz	200
8 oz/1/2 lb	225
9 oz	250
10 oz	275
12 oz/3/4 lb	350
16 oz/1 lb	450
1 1/4 lb	575
1 1/2 lb	675
1 3/4 lb	800
2 lb	900
2 1/4 lb	1000/1 kilo
3 lb	1 kg 350g
4 lb	1 kg 800g
4 1/2 lb	2 kilos
5 lb	2 kg 250g
6 lb	2 kg 750g

OVEN TEMPERATURE EQUIVALENTS

FAHRENHEIT	CELSIUS	GAS MARK	HEAT OF OVEN
225°	110°	$1/4$	Very cool
250°	120°	$1/2$	Very cool
275°	140°	1	Cool
300°	150°	2	Cool
325°	160°	3	Moderate
350°	180°	4	Moderate
375°	190°	5	Moderately hot
400°	200°	6	Moderately hot
425°	220°	7	Hot
450°	230°	8	Hot
475°	240°	9	Very Hot